E/2004/75/Rev.1
ST/ESA/291

Department of Economic and Social Affairs

AF835536

World Economic and Social Survey 2004

Trends and Policies in the World Economy

United Nations
New York, 2004

DESA

The Department of Economic and Social Affairs of the United Nations Secretariat is a vital interface between global policies in the economic, social and environmental spheres and national action. The Department works in three main interlinked areas: (i) it compiles, generates and analyses a wide range of economic, social and environmental data and information on which States Members of the United Nations draw to review common problems and to take stock of policy options; (ii) it facilitates the negotiations of Member States in many intergovernmental bodies on joint courses of action to address ongoing or emerging global challenges; and (iii) it advises interested Governments on the ways and means of translating policy frameworks developed in United Nations conferences and summits into programmes at the country level and, through technical assistance, helps build national capacities.

Note

Symbols of United Nations documents are composed of capital letters combined with figures.

E/2004/75/Rev.1
ST/ESA/291
ISBN 92-1-109145-4

United Nations publication
Sales No. E.04.II.C.1
Copyright © United Nations, 2004.
All rights reserved
Printed by the United Nations
Publishing Section
New York

Preface

Like its predecessors, the ***World Economic and Social Survey 2004*** examines recent developments in and prospects for the world economy and addresses their implications for the developing countries in the struggle against poverty.

In 2004, the world economy continued the recovery that had begun in 2003, and the indications are that this progress will be sustained into 2005. Nevertheless, there are a number of immediate dangers, most notably higher oil prices and the large trade imbalances and fiscal deficits of some of the world's major economies. These threats call for international policy responses that will maintain the momentum of the world economy and reverse the development setbacks experienced by many developing countries in recent years.

Economic progress in the world's two most populous countries—China and India—is likely to enable the world as a whole to achieve the overarching Millennium Development Goal of reducing poverty by half by 2015. At the same time, based on current trends, many of the poorest countries are expected to fall well short. Yet even if these countries were to improve their policies and their management of development efforts, they would still need increased support, in the form of development assistance, debt relief and trading opportunities—to which the developed countries committed themselves in the Monterrey Consensus of the International Conference on Financing for Development.

Next year, a high-level plenary meeting of the United Nations General Assembly will review progress towards the Millennium Development Goals. I hope the international community will make this more than a simple stocktaking exercise, and will strive for a breakthrough that puts countries solidly on track to escape the poverty trap and reach the Goals. Such an outcome is possible—if *all* countries shoulder their responsibilities. With that hope in mind, I commend the information and analysis contained in this ***Survey*** to a wide global audience.

KOFI A. ANNAN
Secretary-General

Executive Summary*

Global economic conditions

After a mediocre performance for some three years, world economic growth began to improve in 2003 and continued to do so in early 2004: gross world product (GWP) grew by to 2.7 per cent in 2003, compared with 1.8 per cent in 2003, and is expected to grow by 3 3/4 per cent in 2004. Moreover, this improved economic strength is being widely shared among countries: most economies gained momentum as 2003 progressed and are expected to accelerate further in 2004. An important dimension of this diversification is characterized by the fact that prospects for continued global economic growth have been strengthened by the emergence of additional poles of growth, mostly in Asia, which reduces the vulnerability associated with the previous dependence of the world economy on the United States of America as the dominant driving force behind the recovery. At the same time, the strength in the global economy remains largely cyclical, reflecting a catch-up from the below-potential growth in many economies over the past few years. Reflecting the cyclical nature of the recovery, growth is expected to moderate in 2005, with the accelerating phase of the expansion ending in the second half of 2004 as stimulatory macroeconomic policies are phased out and the slack in production capacity is reduced. Notwithstanding this solid global growth, aggregate world output is below potential by one important benchmark, namely, employment: unemployment rates remain higher than the lows of the past few years in the majority of countries, and high unemployment and underemployment persist in many developing countries.

Macroeconomic policies have played a crucial role in stimulating the global recovery, but the present challenge is to transform the cyclical upturn into sustained long-run growth that generates additional employment. This requires striking a balance between accommodating, to the maximum extent possible, strong growth and at the same time managing the potential risks for the escalation of inflation. There have already been concerns about overheating in some countries and sectors, as manifested in the surge in the prices of many commodities, notably oil, the rapid credit expansion in some countries and rising inflation rates in some economies. If fears of overheating cause policy stimuli to be removed too soon, there is a risk that the economic recovery will be stifled; if action is delayed, there is the danger that inflation may accelerate and the likelihood that reducing it in the future will involve greater costs than preventing it before it occurs. The measured approach to tightening monetary policy being adopted in some countries reflects this need for caution.

However, macroeconomic policies alone are unlikely to be sufficient to resolve all the problems giving rise to unemployment. Additional actions, which will vary from country to country, are necessary to accelerate growth and development beyond the cyclical recovery. The need for measures to accelerate development should not be overlooked because of complacency about immediate prospects; to the contrary, the current strong upturn presents an opportunity to set in motion policies and actions that may not yield an immediate return and may even involve some short-term costs, but will be of benefit over the longer term.

International trade and financial flows both reflected, and contributed to, the global economic recovery in 2003. The international economic environment is expected to remain generally favourable and, with the exception of the mixed effects of higher oil prices across countries, is proving particularly beneficial for many developing economies. Growth

* For some years, the World Economic and Social Survey has comprised two main parts and a statistical annex. The first part has examined recent developments and immediate prospects for the world economy, while the second part has focused on a topic of a longer-term nature. This pattern has been maintained in this 2004 edition except that the second part (which addresses international migration) is being published as a separate volume. The present Executive Summary correspondingly relates only to the review of the global economy.

in the volume of world trade more than doubled to almost 6 per cent in 2003, with the developing countries accounting for most of the increase. The depreciation of the United States dollar meant that the growth of trade was even higher in nominal terms and the same factor was partially responsible for the increases in the international prices of many commodities during the year. The most notable of these was the surge in the price of oil, which continued into 2004. The short-term outlook for international trade remains positive, with a further increase in the growth of the volume of trade expected in 2004.

There was also an increase in net financial flows to developing countries in 2003. Official development assistance (ODA) rose to a record level in both real and nominal terms, but this was to a large extent because of special factors and, although increasing from 0.23 to 0.25 per cent, ODA still falls far short of the target of 0.7 per cent of the gross national income (GNI) of the developed countries. For those countries that have access to international capital markets, private capital flows increased in 2003 to a level not seen since the Asian financial crisis in 1997, despite a decline in inflows of foreign direct investment. The cost of external financing was also relatively low.

Despite the encouraging prospects in international commodity and financial markets, both the prices of commodities and the conditions in capital markets are highly volatile and can rapidly become a negative factor. At the present time, the possibility of either a tightening of monetary policy or a market-driven correction in the United States poses risks of this nature for developing countries that are heavily dependent on international capital flows or have substantial amounts of dollar-denominated debt.

From the perspective of developing countries, developments in international trade and financial policy in 2003 were less encouraging than the trends in the corresponding markets. The Fifth Ministerial Conference of the World Trade Organization, held in Cancún, Mexico, in September 2003, had failed to advance the trade negotiations launched in Doha in 2001 and no progress was made until the breakthrough on a framework for negotiation at the end of July 2004. The intervening hiatus meant that irreplaceable development opportunities were lost. However, while negotiations at the global level failed, second-best regional and bilateral solutions continued to burgeon. Among multilateral trading arrangements, the World Trade Organization Agreement on Textiles and Clothing is scheduled to expire on 31 December 2004, with potentially widespread consequences for many developing countries. In the financial arena, there was further progress in the implementation of the Heavily Indebted Poor Countries (HIPC) Initiative in 2003 but the Initiative is also due to expire at the end of 2004, even though all eligible countries are unlikely to be able to benefit from the programme by then. In addition to the outstanding need to enhance the debt relief provided to qualifying countries, there is a need to extend the deadline for qualification.

Regional performance

Despite the improvement in the economic performance and outlook for most countries, differences in economic strength across regions and economies have persisted. The economy of the United States expanded apace in 2003 and early 2004 and remained a key locomotive for the world economy. However, the country's large fiscal and trade deficits continue to be major concerns, not only for the United States economy itself but also for the rest of the world because of the downside risks those deficits pose.

The recovery in Japan was stronger than expected. Although it continues to face a number of structural challenges, the Japanese economy seems more likely to be able to sustain its recent higher growth than on previous occasions in the past decade, when an end to its stagnation and deflation appeared imminent.

Economic activity in most of Western Europe was largely anaemic in 2003 but there are signs of a gradual recovery in 2004. In addition to its own long-standing structural challenges, the region now has the task of integrating the new members into the European Union. Success in this venture has implications beyond the region itself.

The economies in transition were the most rapidly growing of the three major groups of countries in 2003, continuing to recover from the setbacks they had suffered in the 1990s. Most of these economies are forecast to sustain their rapid growth in 2004 and 2005, although the dependency on oil prices of some of the countries belonging to the Commonwealth of Independent States, particularly the Russian Federation, is a weakness with consequences for the region as a whole.

Developing countries are, once again and as they should, growing faster than the developed countries in 2004, with more of them than in any year since 2000 expected to achieve an increase in their per capita income. The two most populous of these countries, China and India, are emerging as engines of growth, most particularly for Asia and developing countries but also for the world economy as a whole. These countries' extended periods of rapid growth are good not only for the countries themselves and the large number of poor within them, but also—because of the sizeable stimulus their high growth provides—for other countries. Many developing countries have benefited from China's growing appetite for energy and raw materials and from the resulting higher prices of oil and other commodities. However, the rapid growth of these two economies may also require substantial structural adjustments for other developing countries, some of which may be costly. In addition, their economic performance will have far broader international implications than before, as reflected in the international concern about the possibility of a "hard landing" as a result of overheating in some sectors and areas in China.

Other developing countries in Eastern and Southern Asia maintained or strengthened their economic performance in 2003 and early 2004. Their dynamism in international trade complements the role of China and provides a stimulus not only for the region, but for the world economy as a whole.

In contrast, the situation in Western Asia remained mixed in 2003 and early 2004: higher oil prices brought an unexpected windfall of oil revenue but, for the poorer, oil-importing countries within the region, higher oil prices have created difficulties. Meanwhile, the security situation and other uncertainties in Iraq and the ongoing conflict between Israel and Palestine continue to cast a shadow over economic activity in the region, with the result that it is the only developing region where growth in 2004 is expected to be less—and substantially so—than in 2003.

Many African economies were among those that benefited from increased non-oil commodity prices in 2003 and early 2004 but less so from developments in financial markets where the depreciation of the dollar is likely to have had a net negative effect (since many commodity prices are dollar-based, whereas most of the region's imports are non-dollar-based). Growth in Africa improved marginally in 2003 and, with improved domestic policies and governance and a more favourable international economic environment in several respects, is expected to improve further in 2004. Nevertheless, the improvement will remain far short of the quantum leap that is necessary to extricate the continent from its "poverty trap".

After its setback in 2002, the Latin American and Caribbean region performed better than expected in 2003, achieving positive, albeit modest, growth. With increases in the demand for and the prices of commodities and with improved conditions for developing-country borrowers in international financial markets, a further improvement in growth is expected in 2004.

Downside risks

The positive short-term outlook for the world economy in mid-2004 is tempered by a number of downside risks. The least tangible of these risks are the geopolitical uncertainties and broader apprehensions about terrorism. Although these threats appeared to diminish in 2003 and early 2004, they have become a permanent feature of the global economic environment, with a dampening effect on consumer and business confidence and hence on the overall vitality of the world economy.

A new threat to world economic growth to emerge in 2003 was the surge in oil prices, driven mainly by stronger-than-expected global oil demand, geopolitical tensions in Western Asia and herd behaviour in the oil futures market. Higher oil prices brought sizable income gains to oil-exporting countries, but imposed a burden on oil-importing developing countries. Higher prices for their exports alleviated the situation in many of the latter cases, but are unlikely to continue to do so if oil prices fail to decline. More generally, however, there is fear that global economic growth may be slowed substantially if oil prices remain at or above the levels reached in mid-2004 for an extended period of time.

As the other major downside risk to the world economy and one of less recent vintage, the large twin deficits of the United States remained a potentially destabilizing factor for the world economy in 2003 and early 2004. During the economic slowdown, the increase in fiscal expenditure in the United States served a counter-cyclical purpose. However, the resulting fiscal deficit is not expected to dissipate in a correspondingly counter-cyclical manner during the recovery and, over the medium term, is likely to have negative effects for growth in the United States. Of broader concern, the likely effects of the deficit on global financial markets will also have adverse repercussions for developing countries that rely on private capital inflows to augment their domestic savings.

For the longer term, the focus of policy makers throughout the world must be on the fight against poverty and the attainment of the Millennium Development Goals and other outcomes of the global conferences,. At present, action falls short of what is required. To reinforce the actions already being taken by the majority of developing countries themselves, developed countries should expedite the implementation of their international development commitments of recent years. There is a need, above all, to make further progress in the areas of aid, trade and debt relief. The aim must be to ensure that decisive action is taken on the consensus that already exists in each of these areas and to identify the possibilities for taking such action further.

José Antonio Ocampo
Under-Secretary-General
for Economic and Social Affairs
July 2004

Contents

Annex

Boxes

Figures

Tables

Explanatory Notes

The following symbols have been used in the tables throughout the report:

.. **Two dots** indicate that data are not available or are not separately reported.

– **A dash** indicates that the amount is nil or negligible.

- **A hyphen (-)** indicates that the item is not applicable.

- **A minus sign (-)** indicates deficit or decrease, except as indicated.

. **A full stop (.)** is used to indicate decimals.

/ **A slash (/)** between years indicates a crop year or financial year, for example, 1990/91.

- **Use of a hyphen (-)** between years, for example, 1990-1991, signifies the full period involved, including the beginning and end years.

Reference to "dollars" ($) indicates United States dollars, unless otherwise stated.

Reference to "tons" indicates metric tons, unless otherwise stated.

Annual rates of growth or change, unless otherwise stated, refer to annual compound rates.

In most cases, the growth rate forecasts for 2004 and 2005 are rounded to the nearest quarter of a percentage point.

Details and percentages in tables do not necessarily add to totals, because of rounding.

The following abbreviations have been used:

ACP	African, Caribbean and Pacific (Group of States)
AGOA	African Growth and Opportunity Act (United States)
AIDS	acquired immunodeficiency syndrome
APEC	Asia-Pacific Economic Cooperation
ASEAN	Association of Southeast Asian Nations
BCBS	Basel Committee on Banking Supervision
BIS	Bank for International Settlements
bpd	barrels per day
bps	basis points
CAC	collective action clause
CAFTA	Central American Free Trade Agreement
CAP	Common Agricultural Policy (EU)
CARICOM	Caribbean Community
CCFF	Compensatory and Contingency Financing Facility (IMF)
CCL	Contingent Credit Line (IMF)
CFA	Communauté financière africaine
CFF	Compensatory Financing Facility (IMF)
CIS	Commonwealth of Independent States
COMTRADE	United Nations External Trade Statistics Database
CPI	consumer price index
DAC	Development Assistance Committee (of OECD)
DDO	deferred drawdown option (World Bank)
EAP	Enhanced Access Policy (IMF)
EBRD	European Bank for Reconstruction and Development
ECA	Economic Commission for Africa
ECB	European Central Bank
ECE	Economic Commission for Europe
ECLAC	Economic Commission for Latin America and the Caribbean
EFF	Extended Fund Facility (IMF)
EMBI+	Emerging Markets Bond Index Plus
EMEAP	Executives' Meeting of East Asia-Pacific Central Banks Group
EPAs	Economic Partnership Agreements (EU)
ESAF	Enhanced Structural Adjustment Facility (IMF)
EU	European Union
EURIBOR	Euro Interbank Offered Rate
Eurostat	Statistical Office of the European Communities
FAO	Food and Agriculture Organization of the United Nations
FASB	Financial Accounting Standards Board (United States)
FATF	Financial Action Task Force on Money Laundering
FDI	foreign direct investment
f.o.b.	free on board
FSF	Financial Stability Forum
FTAs	free trade agreements
FTAA	Free Trade Area of the Americas
GATT	General Agreement on Tariffs and Trade
GDP	gross domestic product
GNI	gross national income
GNP	gross national product

GSP	Generalized System of Preferences
GWP	gross world product
HICP	Harmonized Index of Consumer Prices
HIPC	heavily indebted poor countries
HIV	human immunodeficiency virus
IADB	Inter-American Development Bank
IASB	International Accounting Standards Board
IBRD	International Bank for Reconstruction and Development
ICP	International Comparison Programme
ICT	information and communication technologies
IDA	International Development Association
IEA	International Energy Agency
IFAC	International Federation of Accountants
IFAD	International Fund for Agricultural Development
IFC	International Finance Corporation
ILO	International Labour Organization
IMF	International Monetary Fund
INTRASTAT	system of data collection for intra-EU trade
IOSCO	International Organizations of Securities Commissions
IT	information technology
KCBT	Kansas City Board of Trade
LIBOR	London Interbank Offered Rate
LICUS	Trust Fund for Low Income Countries Under Stress (World Bank)
LME	London Metal Exchange
mbd	millions of barrels per day
MCA	Millennium Challenge Account (US)
MCC	Millennium Challenge Corporation (US)
MERCOSUR	Mercado Común del Sur (Southern Common Market)
MFN	most favoured nation
NAMA	non-agricultural market access
NBER	National Bureau of Economic Research (Cambridge, Massachusetts)
NEPAD	New Partnership for Africa's Development
NPL	non-performing loan
NTR	normal trade relations
ODA	official development assistance
OECD	Organisation for Economic Cooperation and Development
OPEC	Organization of the Petroleum Exporting Countries
pb	per barrel
PCF	Post-Conflict Fund (World Bank)
PPP	purchasing power parity
PRGF	Poverty Reduction and Growth Facility (IMF)
Project LINK	international collaborative research group for econometric modelling, coordinated jointly by the Economic Monitoring and Assessment Unit of the United Nations Secretariat, and the University of Toronto
PRSP	Poverty Reduction Strategy Paper (IMF and World Bank)
RTA	regional trade agreement
SACU	South African Customs Union
SAF	Structural Adjustment Facility (IMF)
SAFTA	South Asian Free Trade Area
SARS	severe acute respiratory syndrome
S&D	special and differential treatment
SDRs	special drawing rights (IMF)
SFF	Supplementary Financing Facility (IMF)
SITC	Standard International Trade Classification
SRF	Supplemental Reserve Facility (IMF)
STF	Systemic Transformation Facility (IMF)
TIM	Trade Integration Mechanism (IMF)
TRIPs	trade-related intellectual property rights
UNCTAD	United Nations Conference on Trade and Development
UNDAFs	United Nations Development Assistance Frameworks
UN/DESA	Department of Economic and Social Affairs of the United Nations Secretariat
VAT	value-added tax

The designations employed and the presentation of the material in this publication do not imply the expression of any opinion whatsoever on the part of the United Nations Secretariat concerning the legal status of any country, territory, city or area or of its authorities, or concerning the delimitation of its frontiers or boundaries.

The term "country" as used in the text of this report also refers, as appropriate, to territories or areas.

For analytical purposes, the following country groupings and subgroupings have been used:[a]

Developed economies (developed market economies):

Europe, excluding the European transition economies
Canada and the United States of America
Japan, Australia and New Zealand.

Major developed economies (the Group of Seven):

Canada, France, Germany, Italy, Japan, United Kingdom of Great Britain and Northern Ireland, United States of America.

European Union:[b]

Austria, Belgium, Denmark, Finland, France, Germany, Greece, Ireland, Italy, Luxembourg, Netherlands, Portugal, Spain, Sweden, United Kingdom of Great Britain and Northern Ireland.

Economies in transition:

Central and Eastern European transition economies (CEETEs, sometimes contracted to "Eastern Europe"):

Albania, Bulgaria, Czech Republic, Hungary, Poland, Romania, Slovakia and successor States of the Socialist Federal Republic of Yugoslavia, namely, Bosnia and Herzegovina, Croatia, Serbia and Montenegro, Slovenia, the former Yugoslav Republic of Macedonia.

Baltic States

Estonia, Latvia and Lithuania.

Commonwealth of Independent States (CIS)

Armenia, Azerbaijan, Belarus, Georgia, Kazakhstan, Kyrgyzstan, Republic of Moldova, Russian Federation, Tajikistan, Turkmenistan, Ukraine, Uzbekistan.

Developing economies:

Africa

Asia and the Pacific (excluding Japan, Australia, New Zealand and the member States of CIS in Asia)

Latin America and the Caribbean.

Subgroupings of Asia and the Pacific:

Western Asia:

Bahrain, Cyprus, Iran (Islamic Republic of), Iraq, Israel, Jordan, Kuwait, Lebanon, Oman, Qatar, Saudi Arabia, Syrian Arab Republic, Turkey, United Arab Emirates, Yemen.

Eastern and Southern Asia:

All other developing economies in Asia and the Pacific (including China, unless listed separately). This group has in some cases been subdivided into:

China

South Asia: Bangladesh, India, Nepal, Pakistan, Sri Lanka
East Asia: all other developing economies in Asia and the Pacific.

Subgrouping of Africa:

Sub-Saharan Africa, excluding Nigeria and South Africa (commonly contracted to "sub-Saharan Africa"):

All of Africa except Algeria, Egypt, Libyan Arab Jamahiriya, Morocco, Nigeria, South Africa, Tunisia.

For particular analyses, developing countries have been subdivided into the following groups:

Net-creditor countries:

Brunei Darussalam, Kuwait, Libyan Arab Jamahiriya, Oman, Qatar, Saudi Arabia, Singapore, Taiwan Province of China, United Arab Emirates.

Net-debtor countries:

All other developing countries.

Fuel-exporting countries:

Algeria, Angola, Bahrain, Bolivia, Brunei Darussalam, Cameroon, Colombia, Congo, Ecuador, Egypt, Gabon, Indonesia, Iran (Islamic Republic of), Iraq, Kuwait, Libyan Arab Jamahiriya, Mexico, Nigeria, Oman, Qatar, Saudi Arabia, Syrian Arab Republic, Trinidad and Tobago, United Arab Emirates, Venezuela, Viet Nam.

Fuel-importing countries:

All other developing countries.

Least developed countries:

Afghanistan, Angola, Bangladesh, Benin, Bhutan, Burkina Faso, Burundi, Cambodia, Cape Verde, Central African Republic, Chad, Comoros, Democratic Republic of the Congo (formerly Zaire), Djibouti, Equatorial Guinea, Eritrea, Ethiopia, Gambia, Guinea, Guinea-Bissau, Haiti, Kiribati, Lao People's Democratic Republic, Lesotho, Liberia, Madagascar, Malawi, Maldives, Mali, Mauritania, Mozambique, Myanmar, Nepal, Niger, Rwanda, Samoa, Sao Tome and Principe, Senegal, Sierra Leone, Solomon Islands, Somalia, Sudan, Timor-Leste, Togo, Tuvalu, Uganda, United Republic of Tanzania, Vanuatu, Yemen, Zambia.

The designation of country groups in the text and the tables is intended solely for statistical or analytical convenience and does not necessarily express a judgement about the stage reached by a particular country or area in the development process.

a Names and composition of geographical areas follow those of "Standard country or area codes for statistical use" (ST/ESA/STAT/SER.M/49/Rev.3), with one exception, namely, Western Asia, which in the *Survey* includes the Islamic Republic of Iran (owing to the large role of the petroleum sector in its economy) and excludes the transition economies of the region. Also, "Eastern Europe", as used in this *Survey*, is a contraction of "Central and Eastern Europe"; thus the composition of the region designated by the term differs from that of the strictly geographical grouping.

b Reflects membership of the European Union up to 30 April 2004. Ten additional countries joined the Union on 1 May 2004.

State of the World Economy

Chapter I
The World Economy in 2004

Summary

Prospects for growth of the world economy, after a sub-par performance for about three consecutive years, have improved conspicuously in 2004. The strength of the world economy remains, however, largely cyclical in nature, and the accelerating phase of the expansion in most economies is expected to end gradually in the second half of 2004. The key challenge for policy makers worldwide is therefore how to transform the strong cyclical upturn into sustained robust long-run growth.

The improvement in the economic outlook has been almost universal across countries but differences in economic vigour among regions and countries remain. The economy of the United States of America is expanding apace, with the latest indication of a long-awaited revival in employment providing one more vital support for continued growth. The recovery in Japan has been stronger and more tenacious than expected by most analysts, increasing the probability that the economy will be able to extricate itself from its decade-long stagnation and deflation. Developing economies in Asia have been further strengthening their performance, with the dynamism of their international trade generating growing synergies for the region and enhancing its role as a locomotive for global growth. However, emerging signs of overheating in some sectors and areas in China—the primary driver of growth for the region—have raised concerns. A noticeable increase both in the demand for and in the prices of commodities has contributed to growth in more and more economies in Latin America and Africa, but continued improvements in economic policy remain crucial if these regions are to attain the higher, sustainable rates of growth necessary to achieve meaningful development progress. Meanwhile, most economies in transition, which fared relatively well in the past global downturn, seem likely to increase growth further in the global upturn. By contrast, economic activity in most Western European economies has been largely anaemic, although there are signs of a gradual improvement. In Western Asia, economic prospects for many economies are still vulnerable to political instability and geopolitical tensions with such factors also remaining the main sources of uncertainty for the global economy as a whole.

In the past two years, macroeconomic policies have been crucial for stimulating the global recovery, but the present challenge is for policies to simultaneously sustain robust growth and maintain stable inflation.

Notwithstanding solid global growth, aggregate world output remains below potential, as indicated by widespread weak employment growth: unemployment rates remain higher than the lows of the past few years in the majority of countries, while high unemployment and underemployment persist in many developing countries. Nevertheless, there have been growing concerns about emerging signs of overheating in some countries and sectors, as implied by the surge in the prices of many commodities, the rapid credit expansion in some countries and rising inflation rates in many economies. Under such circumstances, macroeconomic policies in many economies have to strike a balance between accommodating, to the maximum extent, strong growth and at the same time managing the potential risks for an escalation of inflation.

Macroeconomic policies alone may not be sufficient to resolve all the problems giving rise to unemployment and inflation. Policies to reduce the prevailing macroeconomic imbalances are equally important for sustaining strong growth beyond the cyclical recovery. The implementation of such reforms is opportune when economic growth is accelerating, as at present; the positive economic outlook should not allow the urgency of reform to be overlooked.

Along with the global recovery, there have been changes occurring in the global geo-economic pattern with China and, to a lesser degree, India and a few other large emerging economies becoming more important as driving forces for world economic growth. The emergence as engines of global growth of the two most populous developing economies, together accounting for the majority of the world's poor, has potentially profound implications for the rest of the world: it has reduced, and will continue to reduce, poverty in the world and narrow international income gaps; it can also generate impetus for the growth of many other developing countries; and it may also require substantial structural adjustments on the part of other economies, some of which may be costly.

Although the world economic situation is improving, there are important downside risks. The increased price of oil, if it persists or rises further, is likely to slow the world economy and have particularly adverse effects on poorer oil-importing developing countries. Secondly, the prevailing large international imbalances, reflected primarily in the widening current-account and fiscal deficits of the United States, are not expected to narrow soon. To ensure more balanced global growth and, more importantly, to ensure the robust growth necessary to achieve the Millennium Development Goals in the majority of developing countries, policy makers worldwide should expedite the implementation of their international development commitments of recent years.

Sustaining robust growth

As projected,[1] the momentum gathered by the world economic recovery in the second half of 2003 has strengthened further in 2004 and has broadened to include a growing number of economies and sectors. Gross world product (GWP) is forecast to grow by 3.7 per cent in 2004, moderating to 3.4 per cent in 2005 (see table I.1).

The world economy is strengthening in 2004

For many economies, the recovery was initially driven by policy stimuli and/or external demand, but has gradually developed broad strength based on domestic demand.[2] Business profits and business investment have been recovering strongly, particularly in some major developed economies, but also in a number of developing countries. Meanwhile, rates of capacity utilization have also been rising steadily in a growing number of countries. Most equity prices, while below their previous "irrationally exuberant" peaks, have recuperated to a large degree. In contrast, the recovery of employment has been slow worldwide.

The international economic environment has also become more favourable. World trade grew by about 6 per cent in 2003, more than twice as fast as in the previous year, and prices for most commodities also rose, in some cases substantially. There were no major new trade restrictions, although progress in the Doha negotiations was negligible. The cost of borrowing on international capital markets fell and financial flows to developing countries and economies in transition increased, most notably because of a resurgence in bank lending (to its highest level since the Asian financial crisis in 1997). Official development assistance (ODA) rose to the highest level ever recorded, but total net official flows declined, mostly because of repayments of International Monetary Fund (IMF) loans.

The United States continues to lead global growth ...

The **United States of America** continues to lead global economic growth. After an exceptionally strong rebound in the second half of 2003, growth remains robust in 2004. Business investment in equipment and software is accelerating, supported by a solid improvement in corporate profits and historically low interest rates. Consumer spending continues to grow robustly. More importantly, exports, which were sluggish for the past few years, have revived. On the supply side, labour productivity has risen at an exceptionally strong rate and continues to improve. The recovery of employment has been slow, as gains in productivity from technological innovations and other structural changes may have delayed hiring. However, there was an improvement in the second quarter of 2004 and the employment situation is expected to improve over the course of 2004. The deteriorating fiscal position, the widening external deficit and the weakening of the dollar vis-à-vis other major currencies are among the major concerns.

... while Western Europe remains weak, although recovery is expected

Economic activity in **Western Europe**, with the exception of the **United Kingdom of Great Britain and Northern Ireland**, has been sluggish to date but a continuation of the gradual recovery is expected. The weak growth so far has been primarily supported by net exports, along with an increase in inventories and some recovery in fixed investment; consumer spending has been dragging. Industrial production rose significantly in late 2003, although it weakened slightly at the beginning of 2004, with most of the strength being in the intermediate, energy and capital goods sectors. The service sector was much weaker. Survey results indicate that, after a sharp improvement in industrial confidence over the past several months, there have been some signs of relapse lately, reflecting wavering views about future business conditions. The gradual rebound will continue to rely on an expansion of exports and investment spending. Consumption is expected to pick up, but not to such an extent as to play a major role in generating growth. The slow improvement in labour-market conditions, coupled with the uncertainties stemming from the out-

Table I.1
Growth of world output and trade, 1995-2005

Annual percentage change											
	1995	1996	1997	1998	1999	2000	2001	2002	2003[a]	2004[b]	2005[b]
World output[c]	2.8	4.0	3.7	2.4	3.2	4.0	1.3	1.8	2.7	3¾	3½
of which											
Developed economies	2.4	2.9	3.3	2.6	3.1	3.5	1.0	1.3	2.1	3¼	2¾
North America	2.5	3.6	4.5	4.2	4.6	3.8	0.6	2.3	3.0	4½	3½
Western Europe	2.4	1.7	2.5	2.8	2.9	3.5	1.6	1.1	0.8	2	2¼
Asia and Oceania[d]	2.1	3.4	2.1	-0.6	0.4	2.7	0.6	0.0	2.5	3	2
Economies in Transition	-0.2	0.2	2.5	-0.5	3.6	6.5	4.4	4.0	5.7	5¾	5½
Central and Eastern Europe	6.1	4.4	3.4	2.9	2.1	3.9	2.7	2.7	3.6	4	4¼
Baltic States	2.9	4.2	8.1	5.8	0.0	5.6	6.9	6.3	7.5	6½	7
Commonwealth of Independent States	-5.2	-3.7	1.4	-4.0	5.4	9.3	5.9	5.1	7.6	7¼	6½
Developing economies	4.7	5.8	5.4	2.0	3.6	5.8	2.3	3.4	4.4	5¼	5¼
Africa	3.1	5.3	3.4	3.0	3.0	3.3	3.1	2.9	3.3	4	4¾
Eastern and Southern Asia	8.2	7.4	6.2	1.3	6.3	7.2	4.0	5.7	6.1	7	6¼
Western Asia	4.1	4.9	3.9	2.6	-0.2	5.6	-0.5	3.1	4.6	2¾	3
Latin America and the Caribbean	0.5	3.9	5.3	2.4	1.1	4.4	0.4	-0.3	1.5	4	4½
World trade	8.6	5.5	9.2	3.3	5.2	11.5	-0.9	2.5	5.8	7¼	7½
Memorandum item											
World output growth with PPP-based weights[e]	3.5	4.0	4.2	2.6	3.6	4.7	2.3	2.9	3.7	4½	4¼

Source:
Department of Economic and Social Affairs of the United Nations Secretariat (UN/DESA).

a Partly estimated.
b Forecast, based in part on Project LINK, an international collaborative research group for econometric modelling, coordinated jointly by the Economic Monitoring and Assessment Unit of the United Nations Secretariat, and the University of Toronto.
c Calculated as a weighted average of individual country growth rates of gross domestic product (GDP), where weights are based on GDP in 2000 prices and exchange rates.
d Japan, Australia and New Zealand.
e Employing an alternative scheme for weighting national growth rates of GDP, based on purchasing power parity (PPP) conversions of national currency GDP into international dollars (see introduction to annex: statistical tables).

look for reforms regarding pensions, health care and the labour market, could cause consumers to raise savings rates, dampening consumption. Despite the appreciation of the euro, which negatively affects European exports to those countries whose exchange rates have moved with the United States dollar, the strength of world activity is expected to be sufficient to generate a significant acceleration in exports.

Japan's turnaround is stronger than expected ...

Japan is expected to grow by about 3 per cent in 2004. The resurgence has been driven mainly by exports, particularly from other Asian economies. The external demand-led recovery has gradually been feeding through to the domestic sector, with an increasing number of companies showing positive domestic earnings. Business capital spending is growing at a brisk pace as corporate profits grow strongly, and the latest surveys show that the improvement in corporate investment conditions is broadly based. For economic growth to become more self-sustained, the strength of the business sector needs to be transferred to the household sector through increases in wages and employment. Meanwhile, elimination of deflation requires action to be taken with regard to a number of structural problems, such as the decreasing but still large volume of non-performing loans, the fragile financial positions of both the public and the private sectors, and the need for corporate restructuring.

... and Canada is recovering, but growth in Australia and New Zealand is expected to moderate

In respect of other developed economies, the substantial appreciation of their currencies vis-à-vis the United States dollar has had an adverse impact on Australia, Canada and New Zealand, making monetary conditions in these economies more restrictive than indicated by their domestic interest rates. After a slowdown in 2003, gross domestic product (GDP) growth in Canada is expected to recover in 2004, supported by low interest rates and a recovery in exports. In Australia, consumption, residential construction and business investment are all growing robustly. Meanwhile, net exports have also started to show some improvement. Some moderation in GDP growth is expected in late 2004, as the rise in household debt, housing prices and the external deficit all seem to be unsustainable. In New Zealand, after growth averaging 3.7 per cent annually for the past five years, the strength of the economy is expected to moderate in 2004-2005, especially if housing prices reverse and net immigration slows.

An acceleration in growth is expected in Africa in 2004-2005

GDP growth in **Africa** is expected to accelerate in 2004-2005 as many countries achieve an increase in agricultural and industrial output. Higher consumer spending, increasing investment, including more foreign direct investment (FDI) in several countries, and expanded, though cautious, government expenditure in a growing number of countries are expected to support rising domestic demand. Meanwhile, a more auspicious external environment, including higher prices of commodities and increased demand for Africa's exports, should improve the prospects of a large number of countries in the region. However, the current boom from oil and non-oil commodity exports, as well as exports of manufactured goods to the European Union (EU) and the United States under improved market access agreements, will begin to taper off in 2005. The short-term outlook for Africa is favourable in the absence of any major supply-side shocks to domestic output such as adverse weather conditions that would disrupt agricultural output or, for fuel-importing countries, a prolongation of the surge in the price of oil.

Trade has again powered the strong growth in East Asia, with China acting as an engine

Economic growth is accelerating in **East Asia**, fuelled by the region's traditional source of dynamism—international trade. A recovery in the second half of 2003 was initiated by strengthening demand from the United States and an upturn in global information and communication technologies (ICT) product markets. While the impetus from powerful growth in China continues to increase, a better-than-anticipated recovery in Japan has added new strength to the region's growth, engendering a rapid expansion of intraregional trade. Meanwhile, supported by expansionary policies, rebounding equity prices and increased confidence, private consumption and business investment have strengthened further, with a broad-based recovery in both the service and manufacturing sectors. Moreover, imports in a growing number of Asian economies have recently begun to outpace exports, suggesting an increasing contribution to the recovery in the rest of the world. At the same time, the improvement in labour markets has been relatively weak. Inflation remains subdued in the region, and the small number of economies that experienced deflation in the past have either reversed it or improved the situation. The surge in the prices of commodities and the policy interventions in foreign exchange markets seem to have increased inflationary pressure in some economies, presaging a gradual removal of policy stimuli.

Growth in South Asia is expected to become more balanced, ...

After a rebound in 2003, growth in **South Asia** is expected to solidify further in 2004, with more balance across countries and sectors. The external sector of the region has been strong: while the extraordinary surge in Pakistan's exports in 2003 has moderated as the one-off effects of increased textile quotas wane, India's exports and imports are both increasing sharply, with exports being driven by ICT-related products and services. The appreciation of local currencies in the region against the United States dollar does not seem to have led to any significant dampening effects on the region's exports so far, but it has joined with the rebound in domestic demand to raise the demand for imports. That international tourism to the region has also been improving is especially important for the economies of Nepal and Sri Lanka. Meanwhile, a recovery in the agricultural sector (with the exception of Sri Lanka) has contributed to higher incomes in the region.

... whereas the outlook for Western Asia is critically subject to geopolitical uncertainties

The economic prospects for **Western Asia** are still heavily conditioned by geopolitical developments in the region, particularly the situation in Iraq and relations between Israel and Palestine. Since mid-2003, the economic improvement in Iraq has been dilatory, with oil production and exports increasing gradually; however, insecurity and a plethora of other difficulties and uncertainties remain and the attainment of economic and political normalcy in the country is likely to require both a longer time and more resources than anticipated. Meanwhile, the conflict between Israel and Palestine has escalated. The only propitious sign for the region, specifically for the oil-exporting economies, is the higher dollar price of petroleum, a benefit itself discounted by the depreciation of the United States dollar. GDP growth for the region as a whole in 2004 is expected to decelerate to 2.8 per cent, accelerating slightly in 2005.

Latin America and the Caribbean is benefiting from higher commodity prices and easier monetary conditions

The short-term economic outlook for **Latin America and the Caribbean** continues to improve. After a recession in 2001-2002, the momentum of recovery in the second half of 2003 has carried over into 2004. The global cyclical upturn has led to more favourable external conditions for the region. Stronger demand from North America, Japan and China and the substantial rise in the prices of commodities have boosted the growth of exports from the region. At the same time, the depreciation of the United States dollar, along with more flexible exchange-rate regimes, has allowed most countries to ease monetary policy: interest rates in many economies are now at multi-year lows. Meanwhile, investor confidence continues to improve, as reflected by the rebound in asset prices and the narrowing of sovereign debt spreads. For the first time in decades, the region has registered a current-account surplus. All these improvements suggest continued, but relatively modest, growth in 2004-2005. The region, however, faces downside risks, including susceptibility to the vicissitudes of commodity prices and to a tightening of monetary policy in the United States, potential difficulties in servicing its external debt and political tensions in some countries.

After acceleration in 2003, the outlook for the economies of the **Commonwealth of Independent States (CIS)** remains robust for 2004-2005. The economic vigour of the region is bolstered by a confluence of improved domestic fundamentals; higher production, exports and prices of petroleum and gas; and increased foreign investment. Improved consumer and investor confidence, due largely to increased political stability and progress in policy reforms, also continues to support growth. Household consumption has been recovering strongly, boosted by increases in real wages and pensions. Investment has also accelerated, although it is still concentrated in the energy sector. The Russian Federation continues to be the engine of growth for the region, supported by the rapid expansion of other large economies. If the prices of petroleum weaken, however, growth may moderate in 2004 from the rate of over 7 per cent in 2003. The diversification of economic growth away from the present heavy reliance on oil and gas will require steady progress in other sectors. Striking a balance between macroeconomic stability and implementing reforms to achieve longer-term growth remains the major challenge.

The CIS economies continue to fare well, with the Russian Federation leading robust growth in the region

The economic prospects for **Central and Eastern Europe** continue to improve. Growth in the region accelerated in 2003, mostly owing to the improved performance of the Polish economy, with the momentum of growth shifting to the countries of South-eastern Europe. Further acceleration is expected in 2004 as external demand increases. Stronger growth in South-eastern Europe is expected to be supported by high rates of investment associated with ongoing privatization and the upgrading of production facilities; and a recovery in investment is also expected in Central Europe, especially in Poland, where financial conditions in the corporate sector are improving. Monetary policy has been eased in a number of countries over the past year, partly in response to currency appreciations, but room for further monetary expansion seems to be limited as inflationary pressures are building. As most economies in the region have large budget deficits, fiscal policies will continue to focus on consolidation. The region's downside risks include the possibility of weakening business confidence in EU which may, however, be mitigated if it causes some EU firms to relocate some production to the region as a cost-cutting measure. A major policy challenge for each of these economies is to work out a comprehensive post-enlargement strategy that minimizes any adverse impact from the application of EU rules and regulations, entailing, for example, the need to phase out production subsidies and abolish preferential tax treatment for foreign investors.

A post-EU-accession strategy is important for many economies in Central and Eastern Europe and Baltic States

Growth in the **Baltic States** will remain robust in 2004-2005, reflecting success in broad-based structural policies and gains in macroeconomic stability. Rapid wage growth and expansion of consumer credit have contributed to strong growth in private consumption, and gross fixed capital formation is also booming. EU membership should be beneficial for these economies in the long run, but uncertainties associated with entry into EU may pose some short-term risks.

The broadening of the recovery in 2003 is reflected in an increase in the number of countries that achieved per capita output growth of more than 3 per cent and a slight decrease in those experiencing a fall in per capita output (see table I.2). The economies in transition fared even better than in 2002, with per capita output growing in every case and in the majority of countries by more than 3 per cent. Although the number of countries in Africa that increased per capita output by this amount grew in 2003, the majority of people in that region are living in countries where growth was below this long-term benchmark for meaningful poverty reduction. Almost one quarter of that region's population live in countries where per capita output fell in 2003. In Western Asia, while the overall situation improved, there was a sharper dichotomy between fuel-exporting countries and fuel-

More countries achieved acceptable growth in per capita output in 2003

Table I.2
Frequency of high and low growth of per capita output, 2001-2003

	Number of countries monitored	Number of countries					
		Decline in GDP per capita			Growth of GDP per capita exceeding 3 per cent		
		2001	2002	2003[a]	2001	2002	2003[a]
World	146	40	37	34	43	41	52
of which							
Developed economies	24	2	4	8	2	3	2
Economies in transition	27	1	1	0	22	22	22
Developing countries	95	37	32	26	19	16	28
of which							
Africa	38	11	10	11	10	6	12
Eastern and Southern Asia	18	7	3	3	4	6	7
Western Asia	15	7	7	5	4	3	6
Latin America	24	12	12	7	1	1	3
Memorandum items							
Least developed countries	41	12	14	14	12	7	11
Sub-Saharan Africa	31	10	9	11	8	6	9
	Share[b]	Percentage of world population					
Developed economies	14.3	4.7	2.4	3.0	0.2	0.3	0.2
Economies in transition	6.9	0.0	0.1	0.0	5.6	5.4	5.9
Developing countries	78.8	10.4	8.1	10.6	45.2	29.2	50.2
of which							
Africa	12.8	2.6	2.0	3.0	3.4	1.4	3.0
Eastern and Southern Asia	53.4	1.3	1.3	1.0	40.4	25.0	43.7
Western Asia	4.0	2.4	1.3	1.2	1.2	2.3	2.7
Latin America	8.6	4.2	3.5	5.5	0.2	0.4	0.7
Memorandum items							
Least developed countries	10.8	2.1	2.9	3.5	3.7	1.5	4.2
Sub-Saharan Africa	7.8	2.5	1.9	3.0	2.7	1.4	1.8

Source:
UN/DESA, including population estimates and projections from *World Population Prospects: The 2000 Revision*, vol. I, *Comprehensive Tables* and corrigendum (United Nations publication, Sales No. E.01.XIII.8 and Corr.1).

a Partly estimated.

b Percentage of world population for 2000.

importing countries, with most of the former exceeding the 3 per cent benchmark and most of the latter recording falls in output per capita in 2003. In Eastern and Southern Asia, four fifths of the population lived in countries, notably China and India, that exceeded 3 per cent growth of per capita output in 2003; the proportion living in the three countries in the region where per capita output declined was very small. In Latin America, the number of countries experiencing a decline in per capita output fell in 2003 but the proportion of the region's population affected rose: almost two people of every three were in countries where output per capita declined.

China and India are becoming important economic driving forces in the world economy

The extended rapid economic growth of the two most populous economies in the world, China and India, is reshaping the global economy in various respects (see box I.1 for the case of China). Over recent decades, both countries have gradually, but actively, integrated themselves into the world economy through a judicious mix of State intervention and gradual market-oriented reforms and other changes, but there have also been marked differences in their economic structures and in their paths towards high growth. China's growth has mainly featured rapid expansion in manufacturing with intensive inputs of raw materials and labour, whereas India's rise has manifested itself chiefly in the service sector, especially in information technology (IT)-related activities and back-office services. China has become a major importer of raw materials and oil; Indian demand for oil is also rising, but to a lesser extent. China is in direct competition with other developing economies in its exports to third markets, while India's success in IT and business outsourcing means that it is increasingly competing with skilled labour in developed economies. China's economic ties to neighbouring countries are stronger and therefore potentially more beneficial to the region than are those of India, whose main trading partners are the developed countries. However, there is potential for stronger regional economic integration in South Asia and between South and East Asia in the future.

Revitalizing employment

Employment growth is weak ...

With only a few exceptions, most economies are facing pressures from weak employment growth. There are two different employment problems. The first is a cyclical one, referring to the inability of the labour market to reverse the lay-offs during the earlier economic downturn and to absorb, at the same time, the natural increment in the labour force. As a result, unemployment rates remain much higher than normal. The second is a structural employment problem, namely, the persistently high unemployment and underemployment prevailing in many developing (and some developed) countries that are not attributable to the business cycle. Many economies are facing both problems, although the focus of policy concerns varies from country to country.

... for cyclical and structural reasons

Among the developed economies, policy concerns in the United States are mostly focused on the slower-than-expected cyclical recovery in the labour market: the unemployment rate rose from 4 per cent in 2000 to a peak of above 6 per cent in 2003, dropping only to 5.6 per cent in mid-2004.[3] In Japan, the decade-long stagnation pushed up the unemployment rate from 3 per cent in the early 1990s to about 5 per cent. This is low compared with the unemployment rate of most developed countries but Japanese unemployment is more structural in nature (although there has been some tentative improvement with the recovery of the economy). Most Western European economies are challenged by both structural and cyclical employment problems. Unemployment rates remain the highest in a few large European economies, but current levels are still measur-

Box I.1

Global implications of the rising economic weight of China

The economic weight in the world economy of China, with its growth of over 9 per cent annually for more than two decades, has been rising.[a] Although its external economic ties, if measured by trade flows, are concentrated in Asia, China's international economic linkages are more diversified if other factors are taken into account (see table).[b] With its external sector expanding more vigorously than that of the rest of the world by a wide margin,[c] China is integrating into the global economy rapidly and ubiquitously.

China's trade with the rest of the world, 2003

Percentage			
Region	Share of China's total trade	China's share of region's trade	Region's share of world gross product
Africa	2.2	6.1	1.8
Southern and Eastern Asia (including Japan)	54.7	18.0	22.9
Western Asia	3.7	6.5	2.7
Europe	18.5	2.8	30.2
Latin America	3.2	3.6	6.2
North America	15.8	5.3	34.6
Oceania	1.9	9.5	1.5

Source: UN/DESA, based on national and international data.

Like the take-off in Japan and a few Asian newly industrialized economies in earlier years, the steady growth and openness of China should be beneficial not only for the country itself, but also for the world as a whole: it is increasing global economic welfare and generating positive synergies for other economies. The same experience also suggests, however, that China's rapid integration into the world economy is likely to lead to intensified international competition in various sectors and significant relocations of resources across sectors and countries.[d] At the same time, a number of characteristics relating to China's size, structure and institutions are likely to make its global impact greater than that of the historical cases of Japan and the newly industrialized economies.[e]

Size matters. China's population, accounting for 21 per cent of the world total, is a multiple of that of Japan and the newly industrialized economies combined whereas, despite its rapid growth, China's share of GWP is only about 3.5 per cent. Historically, China was a major economic power for the first 18 centuries AD, accounting for 20 per cent or more of the world economy. The recent revival might be the beginning of China's return to its long-term average position. If this is the case, China's size alone will have wide-ranging implications in terms of global aggregate demand, supply and the international balance of goods, services and financial resources.

The impact of its size has already manifested itself. For example, China's demand for raw materials and energy has recently accelerated exponentially, driven by soaring consumption demand for housing and cars and by booming investment.[f] This, along with other factors, has caused the international prices of many commodities to surge to multi-year highs. Although China is still at an early

a China's contribution to global economic growth was about 15 per cent in 2002-2003.

b China's economic relations with the rest of the world would appear even more diversified if the distance factor was taken into account, as in "gravity" trade models.

c In 2003, China became the third largest trading nation and was the world's largest recipient of FDI.

d For example, Japan's economic emergence in the post-war period was accompanied for decades by escalating trade disputes and fears on the part of many other economies.

e Quantitative studies of this issue can be found in, for example, Yang Yongzheng, *China's Integration into the World Economy: Implications for Developing Countries*, IMF Working Paper (WP/03/245) (December 2003); Ma Jun, "China: changing the landscape of the world economy", *Deutsche Bank China Economics*, February 2003; and Global Insight, "China's impact on the world recovery", *Global Executive Summary*, February 2004.

f The ratio of electricity demand to GDP reached 1.7 in 2003; for iron and steel, above 2; for non-ferrous metals, above 2; and for cement, near 2. The world average for these ratios is normally below unity.

Box I.1 (cont'd)

stage of industrialization, it already accounts for 25 per cent of the world consumption of iron and steel, 30 per cent of world consumption of coal and 20 per cent of world consumption of cement. Furthermore, these proportions are expected to grow. China's strong demand for raw materials and energy is beneficial for many commodity-exporting countries, but the consequentially higher commodity prices are unfavourable for a number of other economies. A more profound question, however, is whether the supply of global raw materials can accommodate such rapidly growing demand from such a large economy or whether China's growth will be curbed by limited global resources.

The structural implications for the world economy are more complex, varying by countries and sectors. A prodigious low-skilled labour force, low labour costs,[g] a scarcity of arable land per capita, and high household saving rates are among the major structural features of the Chinese economy that give rise to its comparative advantage in producing labour-intensive goods in the world economy. Most developed economies will benefit from the import of low-cost manufactured goods made in China and from the export of capital- and technology-intensive products to China. Developing countries that produce raw materials and land-intensive products will benefit from the complementarity of their structure with that of China, but others, particularly those with a similarly labour-intensive structure, will face heightened competition and will be under increasing pressure for structural adjustments. Some of these adjustments, including the relocation of labour, may be costly and difficult in the short run. Meanwhile, even though China receives a large proportion of foreign direct investment (FDI) inflows, its high domestic saving rate suggests that China's dependency on external financing will be lower than that of most other developing countries, so that China will not be a major competitor for global capital.

The institutional implications are also important, both for the rest of the world and for China itself. Notwithstanding the progress over the past two decades in transforming a centrally planned economy into a market-based one, China's institutional economic framework remains different from that of other economies in such respects as its large proportion of State ownership, the direct involvement of the government in economic decision-making[h] and its underdeveloped legal, banking and financial systems. These institutional factors may lead to international frictions during China's integration into the global economy, as already reflected in various disputes on trade and intellectual property rights and the recent discussions about China's exchange-rate policy, for instance.

Facing these institutional challenges, China may have to accelerate its reforms, as occurred with its recent accession to the World Trade Organization, which, among other effects, narrowed some institutional gaps between China and the rest of the world. On the other hand, the rest of the world should be patient about the pace at which China carries out its reforms as well as wary of the potential risks associated with any possible slippages or pitfalls in these reforms. For example, a combination of the fragile financial system, the heavy direct government involvement in economic activity, and the excess investment in some sectors, if aggravated by a misstep in reforming the exchange-rate regime or the capital account, could lead to a financial crisis in China, undermining not only its growth but also that of the world economy.

The sustainability of China's growth will also be challenged by various economic as well as institutional constraints, but a stronger and growing Chinese economy should be beneficial for the global economy as a whole; conversely, a stagnant and unstable Chinese economy would be disadvantageous for the rest of the world. China's emergence also implies, however, significant challenges for many other economies, often necessitating structural adjustments. Such adjustments can be costly, but they can also be smoothed by increased international economic cooperation, such as China has been increasingly engaging in with the Association of South-East Asian Nations (ASEAN) and Africa. A continuation and strengthening of such cooperation will be important in ensuring that the world economy is not adversely affected by either the challenges of an ever-larger China in the world economy or the growing negative global repercussions should the economy of China falter.

g China's wage rate in manufacturing is about 5 per cent of that in major developed economies and less than one third of that in Mexico.

h China has undergone extensive decentralization, but the direct involvement of the provincial and local governments in economic activity remains intense, and may have become even more intense than before, replacing the reduced role of the central government.

ably lower than the peaks of the mid-1990s: the mild rise in unemployment rates in recent years because of weak economic growth seems not to have reversed the downward trend achieved by various reforms of labour markets over the past decade, but lowering unemployment further will require a continuation of the reforms.

The contrast between robust GDP growth and persistent weakness in the labour market in the United States has triggered a broad debate. Some observers have ascribed the hesitant recovery in the labour market to strong productivity growth, as businesses have continued to benefit from the rapid innovations in ICT over the past decade, allowing them to raise output without much increase in labour input. Other analysts blame the weak employment growth on increased global economic integration, arguing that the increase in imports from developing countries has led to reduced job creation in manufacturing in the United States, while outsourcing has reduced domestic job opportunities in the services sector.

Recovery of employment requires translating efficiency gains into effective demand

These explanations may be partially true at the firm or industry levels, but do not hold at the macroeconomic level where efficiency gains from either technological change or international economic integration should not harm aggregate employment as long as effective demand grows in tandem with potential output growth. Thus, the delayed recovery in economy-wide employment in the United States is not a result of the efficiency gains per se, but the consequence of a lag, or failure, in translating these gains into a sufficient effective demand.

The grave unemployment problems in most developing countries and economies in transition are partly cyclical, but mostly structural

Unemployment in developing countries and economies in transition is even more severe, in both cyclical and structural terms. So far, only a small number of countries in Asia and in the group of economies in transition have registered a cyclical recovery in unemployment rates. Even so, the unemployment rates for most Asian economies are still far above their levels prior to the Asian financial crisis of the 1990s and, despite some improvement, unemployment rates in the economies in transition are still high. The unemployment problem in a number of East Asian economies, where the degree of industrialization has already reached high levels, has been mainly cyclical; but in China and many other Asian economies, where rural areas still account for a large share of the population, the presence of large amounts of surplus labour, or repressed unemployment, in rural areas remains a long-term policy concern.

The most difficult structural unemployment and underemployment problems, however, are found in Africa and some Latin American economies. In South Africa, for example, the official unemployment rate stands at 28 per cent—a figure that, as in most developing countries, does not include those who are not officially recognized as unemployed. High unemployment and slow economic growth in these economies are creating a vicious circle within which a large proportion of the population are entrapped in perennial poverty. The structural unemployment problems in some of these economies have also been aggravated by cyclical factors and the effects of downsizing the public sector and fiscal consolidation. In addition to the unemployment resulting from the latter, there are persisting high levels of underemployment in the public sector in many countries.

The solution to the problem of high unemployment in these countries will depend on lifting their economies to a sustained path of industrialization and on continued investment in human capital to improve the quality of labour. However, a number of external measures, such as further improvements in market access in developed countries for the exports of these countries, particularly labour-intensive products, could alleviate the situation. A number of African countries that were able to use the trade preferences granted by some developed countries in the past few years have already seen salutary effects on employment, although these are generally small in relation to the overall level of employment.

The baseline forecast predicts a progressive and cyclical improvement in the employment situation in 2004-2005 as the global economic recovery solidifies further. On the other hand, the longer the delay in the recovery of employment in the developed countries, the higher the risk of a relapse in the global recovery because consumer confidence will weaken and household spending will falter. As part of the effort to avoid this situation, government policies should include mechanisms to support labour relocation, including providing training and assistance to workers who are in transition as a result of technological change or global economic integration. Although it is among the approaches sometimes proposed, international protectionism will not lead to an efficient solution of unemployment problems.

A cyclical recovery in employment worldwide is expected in 2004-2005

Restraining inflation

As global growth solidifies and excess capacity declines, the policy focus has gradually shifted from worries about global deflation towards concerns about the risks of a rise in global inflation.

Inflation concerns have been kindled mainly by a substantial rise in many commodity prices. The prices of petroleum, metals, fats and oils surged, rising 50 per cent or more in a year to reach their highest levels for several years, although some prices, notably of tropical beverages, weakened in the first quarter of 2004. Rising global demand is a common factor behind the recovery of these prices, particularly the strong growth in China's demand for raw materials and energy (see figure I.1). The substantial depreciation of the United States dollar vis-à-vis other major currencies may also have contributed to the higher prices of commodities: historically, these prices, since they are mostly quoted in

A substantial rise in commodity prices has led to concerns about inflation ...

Figure I.1
Price of Brent oil in United States dollars and special drawing rights (SDRs), January 2000-April 2004

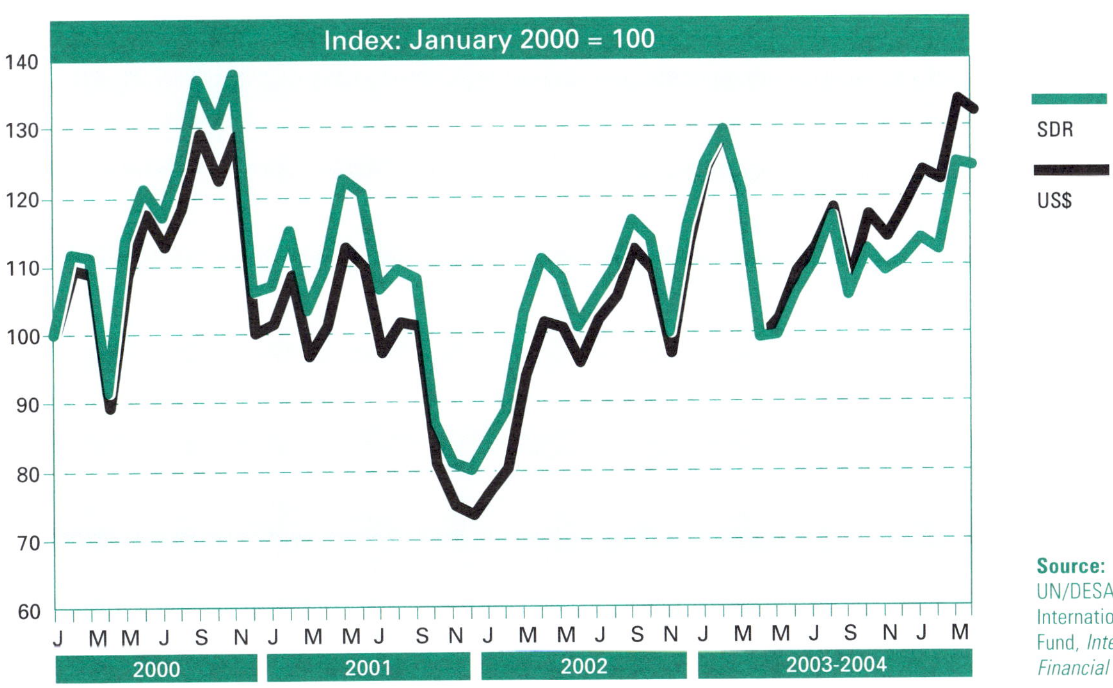

Source: UN/DESA, based on International Monetary Fund, *International Financial Statistics*.

United States dollars, tend to move inversely with the exchange rate of the dollar. At the same time, supply constraints, such as the poor soybean harvest and labour disturbances at some mineral sites, have also pushed up the prices of specific commodities.

Petroleum prices have remained persistently high for the past year, surging to their highest level in a decade. Despite the fact that the price of petroleum has been significantly above the target range of $22-$28 per barrel (pb) that it has established, the Organization of Petroleum Exporting Countries (OPEC) has continued to announce production cuts, partly in an attempt to adjust the target so as to take account of the depreciation of the United States dollar. At the same time, global demand for oil has been on the rise owing to accelerating world economic growth. In addition, geopolitical concerns have increased the pressure placed on many countries to build or replenish strategic petroleum reserves, adding further to global oil demand.

The pass-through of higher commodity prices to overall inflation has so far been minimal, suggesting that a large proportion of the rise in the prices of commodities was absorbed by producers and distributors, instead of being passed on as higher prices to consumers. Headline inflation has edged up in a large number of countries, but "core" inflation measures—excluding such volatile components as food and energy prices—remain relatively stable. Economies that previously had rapidly increasing price levels, such as a few Latin American countries and economies in transition, have reduced inflation further. In some other economies, deflationary pressures have been dissipating; in China, mild deflation for the past few years has been replaced by moderate inflation.

... although other inflationary pressures are also present

In addition to higher commodity prices, other potential inflationary factors include: the depreciation of the United States dollar, in which a large part of international trade is invoiced; the unsterilized foreign exchange interventions by central banks in a number of economies in response to the depreciation of the dollar; the relatively high and growing fiscal deficits in many countries; and overheating in some economies and exuberance in some sectors, as exemplified by higher housing prices in a number of countries and the torrid pace of fixed investment and credit expansion in China.

However, anti-inflationary forces are expected to ensure that global inflation remains benign

On the other hand, there are several forces restraining inflation, as reflected in the persistence of low rates of inflation to date. The monetary policy of many central banks is focused on controlling inflation, with the policy rules in a number of cases inherently engineered to be more aggressive in fighting inflation than in handling deflation. Macroeconomic management in many developing countries has improved. Global integration has increased international competition and thus curbed monopoly power.[4] Technological innovations have raised productivity growth. Various economic reforms, both in domestic markets and in international trade and financial systems, have reduced rigidities and barriers. As long as these factors persist and firmly anchor low inflationary expectations, global inflation should remain under control.

Monetary authorities are expected to raise interest rates gradually ...

Given this generally benign inflation environment, global monetary policy has remained accommodative, with only a few exceptions. While it appears that the three-year cycle of global monetary easing is about to end, a number of central banks have indicated that they will show restraint in raising interest rates. The baseline forecast assumes a gradual increase in policy interest rates by major central banks in late 2004, but a number of economies that are behind in the recovery cycle could maintain low interest rates for a longer period. The difficulty lies in judging the uncertain lag between the activation of monetary policy and its effects on the economy: this will require finesse by central banks, in addition to a sound policy framework. Gradualism and transparency of the policy intention will be crucial in avoiding an abrupt reaction in financial markets, which may otherwise push up long-term interest rates to levels that might dampen investment.

The difficulties for fiscal policy in many economies are even greater. Current fiscal policy stances vary substantially from country to country. Among the developed countries, fiscal policy remains the most expansionary in the United States, modestly stimulatory to neutral in most Western European economies and restrictive in Japan. Fiscal policy has been stimulatory in most Asian developing economies, mainly restrictive in Latin America, and mixed in other developing regions and in economies in transition. However, one common trend throughout the world is the widening of government deficits, accompanied by rising public debt. The exceptions are few, one being the Russian Federation, with its large budget surplus from increased oil revenues. Several Latin American economies have also made notable progress in achieving a surplus in their primary balances as a result of more disciplined fiscal policy in recent years. Most economies are expected to have to undertake fiscal consolidation in the next few years. Although only a few have started this process so far, fiscal policy in general will become less stimulatory around the world in 2004-2005.

... and fiscal policy is expected to be less stimulatory

Managing downside risks

The improved short-term prospects for the world economy are tempered by some potentially far-reaching downside risks. As the second quarter of 2004 unfolded, the spectre of international terrorism, geopolitical concerns and increased political instability was once again hovering over the world economy. None of the events triggering this development were global in scale but the increased interdependencies across countries and between the political and economic domains resulted in the translation of a number of those events into enhanced global economic uncertainty, with the possibility of a dampening of future economic growth.

This possible outcome was reflected first and foremost in the price of oil, which rose rapidly after early April 2004 to above $40 pb, its highest level in about two decades. Nevertheless, oil prices were still 30 per cent lower than the peak of the 1980s if measured in constant United States dollars. Furthermore, a large part of the increase in the oil prices has reflected the substantial depreciation of the dollar vis-à-vis other major currencies. If measured in special drawing rights (SDRs), oil prices are not much higher than in 2000 (see figure I.1).

Higher oil prices present downside risks for the world economy

Increases in oil prices redistribute income from oil consumers to oil producers and from a large number of oil-importing economies to a relatively small number of oil-exporting countries. Quantitative studies suggest that an increase of $10 pb in petroleum prices will lead to a loss of about 0.5 per cent in GWP.[5] If the shock is severe, the slowdown is likely to be aggravated by a series of indirect, but even more severe, shocks brought about by a sharp collapse of consumer and business confidence because of the higher prices. The two previous major oil shocks (1973-1974 and 1979-1980) suggest that the negative indirect consequences are likely to be larger than the direct effects. During these previous shocks (when oil consumption per unit of GDP was far higher than at present), the index of consumer confidence in the United States dropped by more than 50 per cent when oil prices stayed at their peak levels for about 6-12 months. In both instances, this loss of confidence resulted in a recession in the United States, to the detriment of growth in the world economy as a whole.[6] On this occasion, there has been no major disruption in the supply of oil. Nevertheless, the previous experiences suggest that, if the higher prices increase further or even persist for some time, global economic growth is likely to be curbed.

Higher oil prices caused by temporary mismatch between supply and demand will not have the same impact as an oil crisis

Higher oil prices will have different effects across countries

The impact of an oil price shock varies across country groups. The direct income effects of increased oil prices for net fuel-importing countries depends on the share of oil in total consumption. Most developed economies, the United States in particular, are still the largest per capita consumers of oil, but changes in the structure of output towards services, increased energy efficiency and greater use of non-oil sources of energy have made output in most developed economies less oil-intensive, reducing the direct adverse impact of any "oil shock". Meanwhile, industrialization in many developing countries during the past decade has been oil-intensive; in particular, oil consumption in Asian developing economies has increased significantly, making them more vulnerable than previously to increases in prices and, in several cases, more likely to be affected than other countries in relative terms. For instance, oil consumption per unit of GDP in China and many other developing countries is more than twice that of most developed economies. As a result, for any given oil price shock, these countries will experience a larger adverse effect than during earlier episodes. In addition, higher oil prices might trigger financial instability, for example, a currency crisis, in some fuel-importing developing countries that already have sizeable external deficits.

Some analysts have drawn a parallel between the current situation and the oil shock in the early 1970s and the subsequent collapse of the world economy. A significant difference between the two situations is that the oil crisis of the 1970s was a pure supply-side shock, involving a disruption of oil supply by the major oil-producing countries; the current rise in prices has been driven mainly by higher demand. So far, there has been no large-scale disruption of supply; to the contrary, the major oil-producing countries have indicated a willingness to accommodate the increases in demand.

The large twin deficits of the United States present risks for the world economy

A second major downside risk for the world economy is the series of large and widening global imbalances. The most threatening of these are the twin deficits of the United States, but there are also deteriorating fiscal positions in many other economies and high private debt levels in some, in certain cases accompanied by substantially appreciated housing prices. Some of these risks will be heightened when global interest rates rise, particularly if they rise abruptly as a result of either inappropriate monetary policy or panics in financial markets.

The deteriorating fiscal position of the United States poses particular global risks. The country's budget balance shifted from a surplus of above 2 per cent of GDP in 2000 to a deficit of about 4 per cent of GDP in 2003. Even the most optimistic projections show that large fiscal deficits are likely to persist for a considerable period of time unless there is a major change in policy.

By spurring domestic growth, the United States fiscal stimuli played an important role in making the United States the "locomotive" for the global economic recovery. More recently, concerns have risen regarding the sustainability of this fiscal deficit and the fact that it might lead to higher long-term interest rates in global capital markets and to a consequential dampening of global investment and growth in the longer run. Moreover, the inextricable linkages among the fiscal deficit, the external deficit and the exchange rates of the dollar vis-à-vis other currencies mean that the fiscal deficit has broader direct risks for the stability of the world economy.

Growth in the United States has been largely fuelled by foreign resources. This is unlikely to prove sustainable

In this sense, the notion of the United States as a locomotive for the world economy becomes more complex. This locomotive has been powered by resources borrowed from the rest of the world: the current-account deficit of the United States, a measure of how much of the spending by the United States is financed by borrowing from abroad, is more than 5 per cent of GDP. The sustainability of the United States economic expansion is therefore crucially dependent on the willingness of the rest of the world to continue to lend to the United States by accumulating United States assets, mostly United States Treasury bonds.[7] Such a pattern of interdependency between the United States and the rest of the world is unlikely to prove sustainable.

The emergence of new engines of growth for the world economy, such as China and India, has added resilience to, but has also raised additional risks for, the world economy and for many individual countries. These risks are associated with overheating in some sectors and a weak financial sector in China, and with the large fiscal deficit in India. Imports by these two countries have become an important component of demand in some global markets, notably commodities, and for some regions and countries (see figure I.1). The possibility that the rapid pace of growth in China, particularly in some specific sectors, will not be maintained, would result in a loss of vibrancy in China's import demand. A sudden retrenchment, especially if it permeated the whole Chinese economy, would have far-reaching negative consequences elsewhere, most notably for those countries that have benefited from the China-driven commodity boom. India's lower degree of integration into the world economy means that its performance is of somewhat lesser global concern, particularly to developing countries.

Many developing countries and economies in transition are subject to these, and other, global risks and uncertainties

Developing countries and economies in transition remain highly vulnerable to these uncertainties and risks. The anticipated increases in interest rates can have only a negative impact on developing countries that are active in international capital markets, since the overwhelming majority of these countries are net borrowers. Continued volatility in the exchange rates among the major currencies will have different net effects on individual developing countries and economies in transition, with some receiving a net benefit and others a net loss, depending on the extent to which their trade flows, external debt and international reserves are dollar-based. However, most of these countries are less well equipped than developed countries to manage volatility in exchange rates and some are likely to suffer a negative short-term shock.

Coherent policy measures worldwide are required to sustain growth in developing countries

Developing countries have very little influence on these developments in the international economy and yet they are subject to them. That it is the responsibility of the developed economies, particularly the largest among them, to take measures to ensure an orderly unwinding of the global imbalances, suggests that multilateral surveillance for the time being should focus primarily on the policies of these economies. It is particularly important to ensure that the correction of the imbalances does not disrupt the development efforts of the poorest countries. It will therefore be necessary to ensure not only a consistent approach across countries but also coherence between policies and measures intended to restore macroeconomic balance in the world economy and those intended to foster long-term growth and development in the developing countries. Particular efforts should be made to ensure that the adjustment is achieved by raising growth in those countries that are lagging, rather than by reducing global demand. Above all, there should be no relaxation in the commitments to advance development made by the developed countries in the United Nations Millennium Declaration,[8] the Monterrey Consensus of the International Conference on Financing for Development,[9] the Doha development agenda and the Plan of Implementation of the World Summit on Sustainable Development "Johannesburg Programme of Implementation".[10]

Delivering on the commitment to development

In addition to managing the short-term economic risks, global leaders need to restore the priority given to international cooperation for development. Renewed efforts are urgently required to fulfil the various commitments that were made in the first few years of the new century to improve the human well-being of the overwhelming majority of the world's population who live in developing countries.

Most developing countries are facing difficulties in achieving the Millennium Development Goals

Few developing countries—and almost none of the poorest—seem likely to achieve all of the Millennium Development Goals unless there is accelerated progress on the key domestic and international actions that have already been universally agreed. Encouragingly, however, China and India, homes to most of the world's poor people, seem likely to achieve the poverty reduction goal, largely because of their high rates of economic growth. The challenge is to ensure that other countries are able to emulate these examples.

Higher growth is required to extricate the poorest countries from their "poverty trap"

From a long-term, as well as a short-term, perspective, the priority must be to sustain the global cyclical recovery, to transform it into robust long-run growth, and to transform such growth into poverty reduction and the fulfilment of other Millennium Development Goals. Most of the countries that face the greatest challenge in achieving the Millennium Development Goals—largely the least developed countries and most countries in sub-Saharan Africa—are mired in a "poverty trap".[11] A substantial acceleration in economic growth is indispensable in most of these countries if they are to achieve the primary goal of reducing poverty by half by 2015. Not only would achieving a quantum improvement in their rates of economic growth have a direct effect on incomes and poverty but it should also transform their present vicious circle of underdevelopment into a virtuous circle that sustained growth over the longer term: higher growth itself generates additional resources that will relieve the present downward pressures on these countries and contribute to further growth.

Improving the international trading environment for developing countries should be a priority

Particularly for smaller developing economies, improving the international trading environment could provide important opportunities for accelerating growth, as recognized in the collective decision to launch a series of trade negotiations that would be development-oriented. Since that decision taken in Doha in November 2001, there has been very little progress in translating the universal good intentions into tangible results. In view of the continuing difficulties in achieving concrete progress in the key areas, negotiators need to look beyond the particulars of the individual subject areas and identify ways and means, possibly far from the approach originally envisaged, of achieving the overriding objective of ensuring that the international trading system is more conducive to the development of developing countries. Although all parties recognize the sizeable benefits that should result from successful trade negotiations and their centrality to development, these benefits are being reduced through the resort to second-best bilateral solutions because of failure at the global level. In trade negotiations possibly more than elsewhere, time is of the essence if growth in the poorest developing countries is to be raised to the level necessary to achieve the poverty objective set out in the United Nations Millennium Declaration. The aim must be to ensure that developing countries are provided with improved market access for products and services in which they have export potential.

Introduced by IMF as a new arrangement for "Support for Trade-related Balance of Payments Adjustments", the so-called Trade Integration Mechanism (TIM) is an important innovation intended to assist developing countries in meeting any short-term costs of trade liberalization; but it only is a small step in relation to the overall need to ensure that trade can contribute more extensively to growth and the reduction of poverty in developing countries. Developing countries need assistance in expanding their supply capacity for those goods and services in which they have export potential and they need to develop capacities to export before they can reduce their levels of protection. There is growing evidence that reduced levels of protection do not lead automatically to the development of export capacities and the strong links between export sectors and domestic economic activities that result in rapid economic growth.

Developing countries should mobilize additional resources to address social priorities ...

Attainment of many of the other Millennium Development Goals can be achieved largely through social policy and, above all, by interventions by the Government to provide additional institutional, physical, human and financial resources. A major constraint on achieving these goals is the overall lack of public resources. Governments of developing countries therefore need to continue their efforts to improve efficiency in the use of public resources through strengthened governance and public administration. In addition, they have to raise additional financial resources domestically through more efficient and effective systems of taxation and through improved financial intermediation to mobilize domestic savings. At the same time, success in raising the rate of economic growth should yield additional resources for development purposes, including within the private sector.

... but further debt reduction for the poorest countries is equally crucial

Particularly in the poorest countries, however, increasing the mobilization and effective use of domestic resources is unlikely to be sufficient to meet the Millennium Development Goals. For this purpose, developing countries will need additional international support. A first avenue for such support is debt relief because it immediately releases for domestic use financial resources that otherwise might be paid to foreign creditors. Completion of the Heavily Indebted Poor Countries (HIPC) Initiative is therefore of crucial importance to reviving growth in the poorest countries; every effort should be made to ensure that all eligible countries reach their completion point before the Initiative is terminated. At the same time, it is fully recognized that the debt relief provided under the Initiative has been insufficient to achieve its goal of ensuring debt sustainability in all beneficiary countries because the measure of sustainability was based on assumptions regarding economic growth, export growth and interest rates that proved to be optimistic. Development partners should ensure that, in all such cases, countries reaching the completion point are provided with the additional relief needed to ensure debt sustainability.

Debt sustainability is a multifaceted concept that, like most other aspects of development, has to be considered in the light of the circumstances of each individual country. Ongoing work in IMF and the World Bank to refine the concept of debt sustainability from this point of view is therefore welcomed. Similarly, the Paris Club's adoption of a more flexible approach to countries in debt difficulties is to be commended. The ongoing consideration of ways of introducing greater variability and flexibility into debt instruments, such as linking debt-service payments to changes in capacity-to-pay (for example, through bonds indexed to GDP or commodity prices), should also be pursued. Nevertheless, the lack of multilateral frameworks for resolution of debt crises continues to be responsible for one of the great vacuums in the international financial architecture.

ODA flows are expected to increase in the short run ...

Particularly in the poorest countries, debt relief and debt sustainability will not obviate the need for additional concessional resources for development. Flows of ODA have increased for the past few years and, on the basis of commitments already made, further increases are expected over the short term. Recent increases, however, have in part been a reflection of the depreciation of the dollar, the inclusion of debt relief and expenditures in Afghanistan and Iraq. Looking ahead, the increases in ODA that are currently foreseen, while highly commendable in themselves, are modest in relation to the volumes that are widely estimated to be required to achieve the Millennium Development Goals. Encouragingly, there are a number of proposals on how to improve the situation, including the financing of the fourteenth replenishment of the International Development Association (IDA) and the proposed international financing facility (IFF).

... but an international strategy is required to ensure adequate resources over the longer run

Over the longer term, many developed countries already face fiscal constraints. Additional demands, particularly those associated with the ageing of their populations, are likely to increase this fiscal pressure as time progresses, and to compromise ODA flows. This suggests that attainment of the Millennium Development Goals will require a strategy for identifying potential new sources of financing over the longer term. It is therefore encouraging that the Development Committee (Joint Ministerial Committee of the Boards of Governors of the Bank and the Fund on the Transfer of Real Resources to Developing Countries), at its meeting in April 2004, took a first step in this direction when it called for a report for its next session addressing "policy options and financing mechanisms for mobilizing additional resources (including examining an international finance facility, global taxation and other proposals)".[12] Hopefully, this will mark the first step towards formulating a strategy that will ensure the necessary flow of resources not only until 2015 but beyond that date so that poverty can be not only halved but eradicated.

Progress has been made on most fronts ...

The collective policy challenge is, on the one hand, daunting but, on the other hand, achievable, as reflected in the progress already made. There is universal recognition that development policy in developing countries, in all its many facets, has improved over recent years. Similar strides have been made by donor countries, not least in the recognition that country-ownership is a sine qua non for successful development policies. Despite the supposed onset of "aid fatigue", flows of ODA increased in 2002 and 2003, with commitments of further increases in the pipeline. There has been some, albeit inadequate, progress made in reducing the debt burden on developing countries, most particularly the HIPCs, and some improvements in the treatment of external debt of the middle-income countries as well.

... but more action is required to ensure that the Millennium Development Goals are achieved

These steps indicate that the necessary actions are universally recognized and are feasible, provided that there is the necessary political will. The challenge to the Governments of both developing and developed countries is to undertake such actions not only on the scale that is necessary to achieve the Millennium Development Goals but also within a time frame that ensures that the Goals are met by the target date of 2015. Anything less would be a betrayal of the faith that peoples deserve to have in their Governments and in international organizations.

Notes

1 See *World Economic Situation and Prospects, 2004* (United Nations publication, Sales No. E.04.II.C.2). Also available from www.un.org/esa/policy/index.html (accessed 14 June 2004).

2 See *World Economic Situation* ..., chap. III, for the presentation of a detailed regional economic outlook.

3 Strong growth in payroll employment was finally registered in March 2004, but a continuation in coming months is necessary to confirm a steady recovery in the labour market of the United States. Although the unemployment rate in the United States fell from a peak of 6.3 per cent in mid-2003 to 5.6 per cent in March 2004, the improvement was due mainly to a drop in the labour-force participation rate, particularly for younger people; the unemployment rate would otherwise have been about 7 per cent.

4 Increased exports from China, for example, have prevented international prices of manufactured goods from rising. At the same time, China's strong growth has contributed to higher commodity prices and given China a dual role in influencing global inflation.

5 See, for example, International Energy Agency, "Analysis of the impact of high oil prices on the global economy", May 2004, available from http://library.iea.org/dbtw-wpd/textbase/papers/ 2004/high_oil_prices.pdf (accessed 15 June 2004).

6 Most quantitative studies involve static comparative analysis and capture only the linear relationship between oil prices and the welfare loss through income and substitution effects; hence they cannot reflect the non-linear impact from the shock on confidence. A DESA simulation suggests that, if there were the same decline in consumer sentiment today, growth in the United States would decline by more than 2.5 percentage points, verging on a recession. The ripple effects throughout the world economy would reduce the growth of GWP by 2 percentage points.

7 Asian central banks are estimated to finance about half of the United States annual external imbalance by accumulating dollar-denominated reserves.

8 See General Assembly resolution 55/2.

9 *Report of the International Conference on Financing for Development, Monterrey, Mexico, 18-22 March 2002* (United Nations publication, Sales No. E.02.II.A.7), chap. I, resolution 1, annex.

10 *Report of the World Summit on Sustainable Development, Johannesburg, South Africa, 26 August-4 September 2002* (United Nations publication, Sales No. E.03.II.A.1 and corrigendum), chap. I, resolution 2, annex.

11 For a discussion of the "poverty trap", see *World Economic and Social Survey, 2000* (United Nations publication, Sales No. E.00.II.C.1), part two.

12 See Development Committee communiqué on "Concerted action needed to accelerate progress towards Millennium Development Goals", *IMF Survey*, vol. 33, No. 8 (3 May 2004), pp. 122-123, seventh paragraph.

Chapter II
International Trade

Summary

International trade is both reflecting and contributing to the global economic recovery, with the improved international economic environment proving particularly beneficial for most developing countries. Growth in the volume of world trade more than doubled to almost 6 per cent in 2003, with the developing countries accounting for most of the increase. The depreciation of the United States dollar meant that growth was even higher in nominal terms and the same factor was partially responsible for the increases in the international prices of many commodities during the year. The most notable of these was the surge in the price of oil, which continued in the early part of 2004. Oil prices are expected to retreat later in 2004, while some commodity prices had already moderated in early 2004. Nevertheless, the short-term outlook for international trade remains positive, with a further increase in the growth of the volume of trade expected in 2004.

Regional trends and outlook

Growth of international trade accelerated in 2003...

After a tentative beginning, brought about by the building up of tensions regarding Iraq as well as the outbreak of severe acute respiratory syndrome (SARS), international trade resumed its recovery, having grown by an estimated 5.9 per cent in real terms in 2003 (see table A.13). In nominal terms, it expanded by almost 15 per cent, reflecting not only increased volumes but also higher prices for commodities and manufactured goods, inter alia, as a result of the depreciation of the United States dollar. International trade is expected to continue to strengthen in 2004, when growth is anticipated to reach 7¼ per cent and to maintain that strength in 2005.

Trade performance continued to be uneven across regions and countries in 2003, although this was less acute than in 2002, when trade contracted in the developed economies. The transition economies sustained relatively high rates of growth in their trade, but it was the recovery of trade in the developing countries that largely fuelled the acceleration of world trade during 2002 and 2003. In these two years, developing countries' contribution to trade growth went well beyond their share of world trade: the share of developing countries in world exports and imports is about 31 per cent, but these economies generated over 80 per cent of the acceleration in trade in 2002 (with the remainder coming from the developed economies, in particular those of North America and Japan) and about 50 per cent in 2003. In 2004, faster growth in international trade will be brought about by the developed economies as trade continues to recover in Europe and North America but growth in international trade decelerates in developing countries as China's trade growth declines to more sustainable levels. As a result, trade outcomes will be less divergent across country groupings in 2004 (see figure II.1).

Figure II.1.
Growth in the volume of trade,[a] by major country groupings, 2002-2004

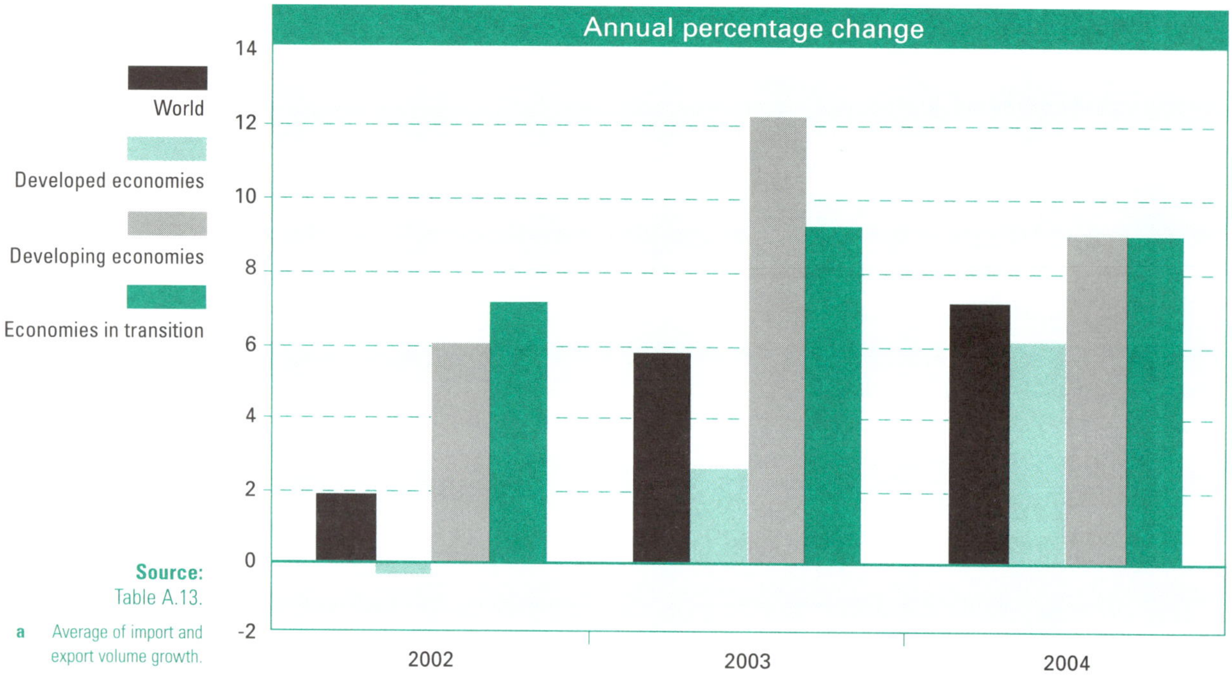

Source: Table A.13.

a Average of import and export volume growth.

... driven by developing countries, most notably China

Much of the developing countries' trade dynamism has been concentrated in East Asia—where increasing integration of production has been a noticeable feature underlying the fast growth of intraregional trade—and, in particular, in China. Owing to its buoyant economy and the improvement of the world economy, China's volumes of exports and imports grew at about 32 per cent in 2003. China's strong import demand was particularly relevant for East Asian countries, including Japan, and supported overall growth in the region. Other regions were positively affected as well. For instance, Brazilian exports to China doubled in dollar terms in the period from 2002 to 2003, making China Brazil's third most important export market in 2003. Such fast rates of growth are likely to prove unsustainable, however, and to decelerate in 2004 as measures to cool the economy take effect and supply constraints become binding. Nevertheless, China will continue to lead the world's trade expansion in 2004.

Commodity exporters benefited from the economic upturn

Latin America and Africa benefited from the growth in demand for oil and non-oil commodities. Exports of agricultural raw materials, minerals and base metals strengthened during the year as industrial production picked up in the developed countries, China and other Asian countries. In Latin America, improved export performance in 2003 was buoyed especially by increases of exports in Argentina, Brazil and the Andean countries. Conversely, Mexico—the region's largest exporter—was adversely affected by increased competition in the market of the United States of America for the third consecutive year, while disruptions in Venezuela's oil production led to yet another contraction in that country's exports. In 2004, Mexico will regain its relative importance in the trade of the region as non-oil exports recover, favoured by greater external demand, reactivating industrial and manufacturing activities. On the other hand, Brazil, whose exports grew at about 14 per cent in real terms in 2003, will witness a deceleration in its export growth, as domestic demand recovers. On the import side, import demand—albeit recovering from the deep contraction of 2002—remained constrained in the region, thus contributing to the generation of a significant trade surplus. Imports by the region will likely continue to recover, thus leading to a smaller trade surplus in 2004.

Preferential treatment sustained export growth in some developing economies

In Africa, market-access agreements with the European Union (EU) and the United States provided additional stimulus to exports in 2003. Exports to the United States under the African Growth and Opportunity Act (AGOA) increased by 55 per cent in 2003 compared with the previous year but, as in most recent years, those exports were heavily dominated by a few commodities and originated in only a few of the eligible countries (see box II.1). Higher oil prices and increased production improved export earnings in all of Africa's oil-exporting countries. Recovery of prices of several non-oil commodities from earlier lows similarly contributed to improved export earnings from a wide range of agricultural and mineral commodities. The volume of African imports grew by 5.7 per cent in 2003, driven mainly by increased consumer and public spending as a result of improved gross domestic product (GDP) and export growth. Other factors behind import growth in Africa in 2003 included increased construction activity related to the expansion of the hydrocarbon and manufacturing sectors in several countries, donor-funded projects and other development assistance and imports for post-conflict reconstruction in the Congo, Côte d'Ivoire, the Democratic Republic of the Congo and Liberia. In 2004-2005, the expansion of production of several commodities in a number of countries as a result of recent large-scale investment projects—oil in Angola and Chad; natural gas in Algeria, Egypt and Mozambique; and aluminium in Mozambique—will also contribute to export growth of the region.

Increased oil exports, particularly by Saudi Arabia, the stronger-than-expected performance by Turkey (brought about by increased competitiveness due to a rise in productivity), coupled with an export recovery in Israel, supported export growth in Western Asia, despite the drastic drop in exports by Iraq. Export growth is expected to decelerate in 2004, as slower growth is anticipated for oil exports. Import growth also accelerated in volume terms in 2003, largely owing to Turkey, as real import demand elsewhere was sluggish or contracted. This pattern will persist in 2004, when real imports are anticipated to grow by 7 per cent, largely driven by an acceleration in import demand by Turkey.

Exports by the United States recovered, but the large trade deficit will persist

Increased import demand by developing countries has impacted positively on the export performance of developed countries. After a weak performance in the past two years, exports from the United States are expected to grow in real terms by more than 10 per cent in 2004-2005. Driven by strong demand from the rest of the world, from Asian economies in particular, real exports of the United States surged by more than 20 per cent in the last quarter of 2003. Despite a notable moderation in the first quarter of 2004, forward-looking indices point to continued strong growth. At the same time, real imports are expected to grow at about 7 per cent. The depreciation of the dollar vis-à-vis other major currencies may be having some effect in curbing import demand while promoting exports. Since the current value of total imports by the United States exceeds export revenues by some 33 per cent, the anticipated faster growth in exports in the next two years will only stabilize, but not reduce, the trade deficit of about 4.5-5 per cent of GDP (see figure II.2).

The strong recovery in demand from other Asian economies, mainly the demand for capital goods and information and communication technologies (ICT)-related products, has played a similarly key role in sustaining fast export growth in Japan. The

Box II.1

Sustaining the African Growth and Opportunity Act

Signed into law in May 2000, the African Growth and Opportunity Act (AGOA) provides eligible sub-Saharan countries with additional trade preferences from the United States of America. It expands product coverage, most notably to textiles and apparel, and adds some other benefits to those already available under the United States Generalized System of Preferences (GSP) scheme. AGOA is scheduled to expire on 30 September 2008.

Country eligibility is determined annually subject to certain criteria. To be eligible, countries need to have established or be progressing towards establishing, among other things, a market-based economy, the protection of intellectual property rights, the rule of law, economic policies to reduce poverty, the protection of internationally recognized worker rights, the elimination of the worst forms of child labour, and a system to combat corruption.[a] Trade preferences are therefore an incentive for the implementation of reforms that are believed to foster development. AGOA also envisages eventual negotiations of free trade agreements with the United States. As of January 2004, there were 37 AGOA-eligible countries.

Among other things, AGOA includes specific market access provisions for textile and apparel, which can be exported duty- and quota-free, but subject to rules of origin, a regional ceiling and the establishment of a certification system attesting to the origin of inputs used. In early 2004, 23 AGOA countries were eligible for apparel benefits. Furthermore, a special rule applies to countries designated as "lesser developed", defined as those with per capita gross national product of less than $1,500 in 1998, as measured by the World Bank. These countries have the additional benefit of duty- and quota-free apparel made from yarns and fabrics from third countries. The regional ceiling, however, applies to such exports as well, and this additional benefit is expected to expire on 30 September 2004. AGOA was enhanced in 2002 (AGOA-II), expanding some benefits such as the doubling of the "regional cap" on certain apparel imports and the extending of lesser developed country benefits to Botswana and Namibia.

United States imports from AGOA countries totalled some $20 billion in 2003, an increase of 10 per cent, in value terms, over 2000. About 70 per cent of these imports entered the United States duty-free in 2003 under both GSP (5 per cent) and AGOA (65 per cent). This compares with less than 4 per cent in 2000, when only the GSP was available. Thus, while a significantly greater share of AGOA countries' exports now receives preferential treatment, the value of total merchandise exports has not increased as much.

Textiles and apparel exports, on the other hand, almost doubled from $770 million in 2000 to $1.5 billion in 2003; 77 per cent of those exports entered the United States duty-free in 2003 owing to AGOA (see figure). Lesser developed countries have been the major beneficiaries due to their additional preferences. Except for Mauritius and South Africa, AGOA countries cannot count on a well established and integrated textile sector exporting products made from local fabric. Thus, most AGOA countries would have not enjoyed greater market access if the "lesser developed country" provision had not been available. In 2003, for example, about 75 per cent of AGOA exports of apparel to the United States had been made from fabric produced in a third country while only 19 per cent used fabric from the United States or regional yarn.[b]

AGOA has been instrumental in promoting some export diversification away from traditional industries, including increased investment in countries having an undeveloped manufacturing base that would not necessarily have attracted foreign direct investment (FDI) had it not been for the possibility of increased access to the United States market. Additionally, the "lesser developed country" provision has helped such countries as Kenya, Madagascar and Swaziland to attract FDI, mainly from Asia, to their apparel industry, which has been an important source of employment-generation for these economies. In Lesotho, foreign investors—attracted not only by AGOA but also by export possibilities within the Southern African Customs Union (SACU)—are building a denim fabric mill and have announced plans for the construction of a yarn spinning plant and knitted fabric mill.

Except in the case of Lesotho, much of this investment is of a short-term nature. A possible reason could be the annual revision mechanism for country eligibility. While giving countries an incentive to proceed with reforms, the revision mechanism may discourage longer-term investment owing to uncertainties associated with a country's being able to maintain its AGOA status. Perhaps more importantly, factors

a On eligibility criteria, see Office of the United States Trade Representative, *2001Comprehensive Report of the President of the United States on U.S. Trade and Investment Policy Toward Sub-Saharan Africa and the Implementation of the African Growth and Opportunity Act*, May 2001.

b See United States Department of Commerce/International Trade Administration/Office of Textiles and Apparel, *Trade Data: United States Exports and Imports of Textiles and Apparel* (http://www.otexa.ita.doc.gov).

Box II.1 (cont'd)

United States textile imports from AGOA countries, 2001-2003

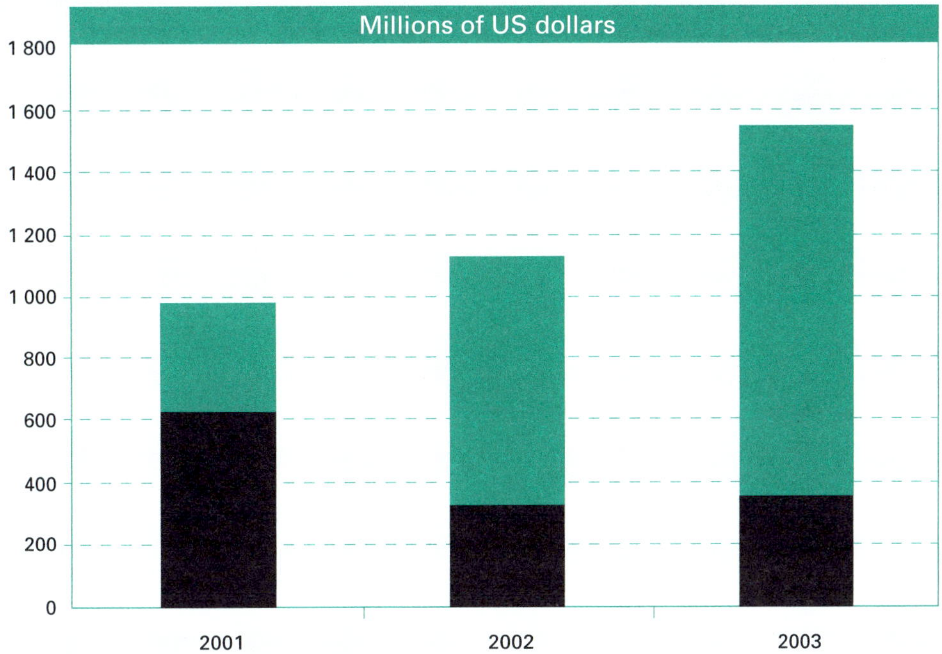

Source: United States International Trade Administration/Office of Textiles and Apparel.

a Normal Trade Relations.

b General System of Preferences.

sustaining FDI in these countries, namely, trade preferences, low-cost labour and the prevailing quotas under the World Trade Organization Agreement on Textiles and Clothing are expected to be discontinued. Although Congress is considering an extension of lesser developed countries benefits beyond September 2004, trade preferences are scheduled to expire soon, while relative labour competitiveness can quickly shift to the detriment of AGOA countries if costs rise, skills are not upgraded and productivity is not enhanced. Some assembly lines in Mauritius have been shifted to other countries owing to rising labour costs. As these assembly factories can easily migrate, AGOA countries could face higher unemployment and no lasting benefits owing to the lack of linkages with the rest of their economies, except through labour. Thus, AGOA assembling-related activities, while generating certain benefits and an initial push towards more sustainable growth, do not necessarily provide these countries with a complete answer to their development quest. Accordingly, the initiative also needs to be complemented with policy intervention at the local level in order to move to other stages of the production process and/or generate activities that would be self-sustaining once preferential treatment is removed.

The renewal of lesser developed country status would give AGOA countries more time to improve their competitiveness and address other constraints. Yet, it does not remove the bigger challenge of the expiration of the Agreement on Textiles and Clothing. The most competitive producers are expected to gain market shares to the detriment of other suppliers. It will most likely put a brake on the fast growth of garment exports by AGOA countries, as they are anticipated to lose market shares in the United States market.[c] Losing the advantage of quota-free benefits, as the other producers are no longer bound by the Agreement on Textiles and Clothing quotas, AGOA countries will still have the advantage of duty-free treatment. This, however, may not be enough to offset costs brought about by the observance of rules of origin.[d]

Despite promoting increased textile and apparel exports, AGOA benefits are unevenly balanced towards fuels and fuel-producing countries. While generating about 38 per cent of sub-Saharan African exports, fuels dominate AGOA exports (63 per cent) Nigeria and Gabon being among the largest beneficiaries of the programme. While 87 per cent of AGOA fuel exports entered the United States duty-free, only 28 per cent of non-fuel exports received preferential treatment in 2003. This imbalance raises concerns about

c United States International Trade Commission, *Textiles and Apparel: Assessment of the Competitiveness of Certain Foreign Suppliers to the U.S. Market* (Investigation No. 332-448, sent to the United States Trade Representative in June 2003), Publication 3671, January 2004.

d Aaditya Mattoo Devesh Roy and Arvind Subramanian, *The African Growth and Opportunity Act and its Rules of Origin: Generosity Undermined?* (World Bank Policy Research Working Paper No. 2908), (Washington, D. C., World Bank, October 2002).

Box II.1 (cont'd)

the developmental impact of the programme for AGOA countries, particularly in view of the challenges faced by African fuel exporters (see box III.3).

Oil exports, however, tell only part—albeit a large part—of the story. Countries with a relatively well-established manufacture base have also been able to capture benefits. For instance, South African exports of transport equipment quadrupled, in nominal terms, in the period from 2000 to 2003. Conversely, for such countries as Benin, the Democratic Republic of the Congo, Djibouti, Guinea-Bissau, Mali, Mauritania, Sao Tome and Principe, Seychelles, Sierra Leone and Zambia, AGOA has not generated additional exports. The same observation applied to the Central African Republic and Eritrea while they were AGOA-eligible. Limited response capacity to new trade opportunities could be a factor. Furthermore, difficulties in complying with required rules and procedures could be acting as a deterrent to increased exports. Another possible reason is that, except for those of the Democratic Republic of the Congo, these countries' exports already receive duty-free treatment under normal trade relations (NTR)—the United States equivalent of the most favoured nation (MFN) concept.[e] It may also be possible that some exports are still being impeded by high tariffs, the existence of some type of protectionist measure or other trade-distorting mechanisms. Thus, the list of AGOA-eligible products could be expanded further in order to include "import-sensitive items", particularly as the supply capacity of these countries, relative to the United States market, is probably limited. Some potential agricultural exports may fall into this category.

In conclusion, AGOA has brought beneficiary countries some advantages, particularly in promoting certain industries that would not otherwise have emerged, textiles and apparel being the most notable case. The sustainability of such positive impact, however, is not guaranteed. An extension of the programme, as well as increased coverage, could help cement benefits. Country response also matters. Accordingly, AGOA countries also need to look at policy interventions that would increase their capacity to benefit further from the programme while creating lasting linkages with the rest of their economies.

e United Nations Conference on Trade and Development (UNCTAD), *The African Growth and Opportunity Act: A Preliminary Assessment* (United Nations publication, Sales No. E.03.II.D.15), April 2003.

Figure II.2.
United States of America: exports and imports of goods and trade balance, 2000-2005

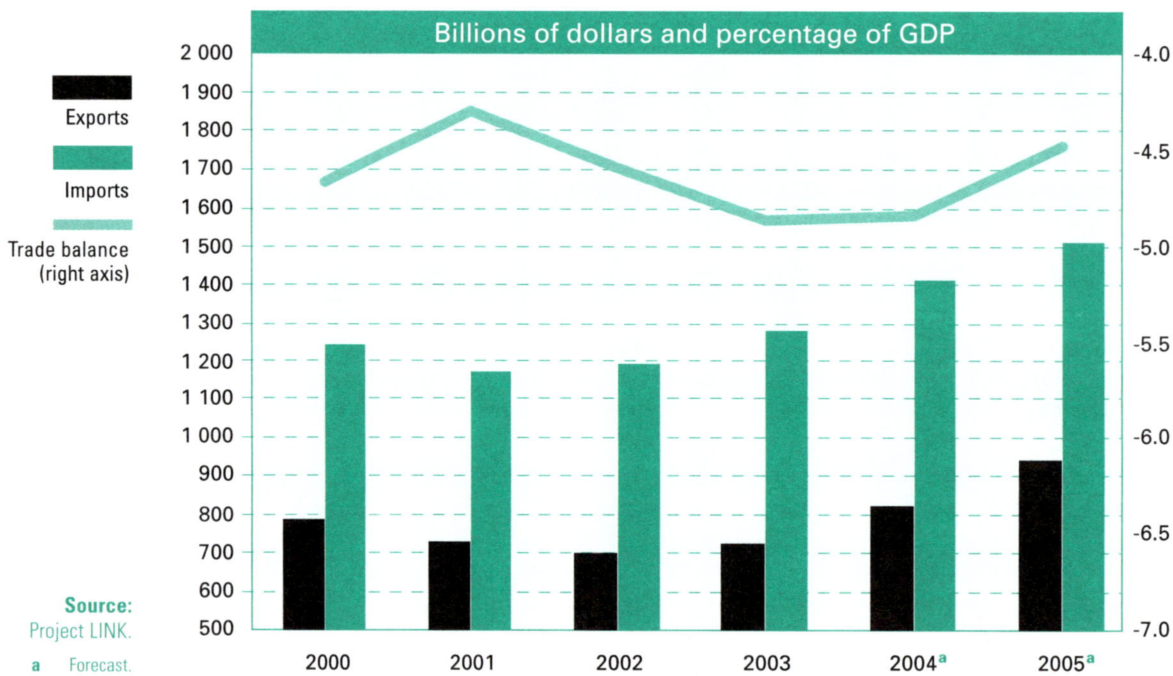

Source: Project LINK.

a Forecast.

impact of the booming Chinese economy has been particularly apparent. Japan's exports to China increased by more than 40 per cent in 2003 on top of the 35 per cent increase registered in 2002. Japan's exports to Europe have also increased steadily, but its exports to the United States declined in 2003, to some extent reflecting the different trends in the exchange rates of the yen vis-à-vis the euro and the dollar, respectively.

The full impact of major currency movements on trade flows has not yet been felt

Western Europe, which exports relatively less to developing countries (see table A.14), has been less successful in using developing countries' increased appetite for imports to offset the impact of the appreciation of the euro vis-à-vis the dollar. Export volumes in Western Europe grew by just 0.5 per cent in 2003 but are expected to rebound in 2004, growing by over 5 per cent, with some further strengthening in 2005. Generally, the income effect of expanding world demand, particularly from the United States and East Asia, is expected to dominate the price effect of the strong currency, resulting in strong growth in volume of exports, but the strength of the currency will lead to some loss in market share—depending on an individual country's exports to non-euro area countries—despite European producers' efforts to adjust prices in dollar-based markets. On the import side, volumes are expected to pick up from a rate of growth of 2.5 per cent in 2003 to a rate of growth of 5.4 per cent in 2004. This reflects the gradually improving state of domestic demand in the region, with some boost from the favourable terms-of-trade effect of the appreciation of the euro. However, the full impact of the currency appreciation has been slow to materialize.

Intra-CIS exports have show remarkable dynamism

Among the economies in transition, the economies of the Commonwealth of Independent States (CIS) also benefited from a recovery in commodity demand and prices since their export structure is highly skewed towards fuels and minerals and metals. Intraregional trade increased faster than trade with non-CIS countries, mostly owing to the continued recovery of the economies in the region (see chap. III). The depreciation in real terms of the currencies in the member States of CIS against the Russian ruble contributed to export growth within the region as well. In dollar terms, intraregional trade surged by 25 per cent on average for the region. The outlook for CIS exports is favourable, with both volume and revenue increasing in 2004, albeit at a lower rate than in 2003 as commodity price increases moderate and external demand slows down somewhat. Robust domestic demand will continue to drive imports, which are also likely to grow in value and volume.

EU enlargement will benefit the trade of the accession countries

Central and Eastern European export performance was uneven. Exports were constrained by weak import demand from EU and a loss in competitiveness experienced by some countries (the Czech Republic and Hungary) owing to labour cost increases and low gains in productivity, in contrast with other regional economies (Poland and Slovakia) that did better. Imports remained strong in response to real wage increases and credit expansion in some countries. Exports are expected to pick up in 2004 in line with stronger import demand in EU and the removal of the last trade barriers following accession of the five Central European countries of EU in May 2004. Exports of agricultural products, in particular, will become tariff - and quota-free. Strong growth in imports is also expected to continue in 2004. Following entry into EU of the five Central European countries, implementation of public infrastructure projects, and recovery of investment in general, will lead to imports of capital goods into Central Europe. Strengthening of consumer confidence, associated with the EU enlargement, will spur the import of consumer goods. Continuing strong growth in investment in Bulgaria and Romania implies that imports will remain strong there as well.

Commodity prices and markets[1]

Commodity prices recovered in dollar terms but continued to slide in SDR terms

Commodity markets experienced a recovery in 2003, with the United Nations Conference on Trade and Development (UNCTAD) index of non-fuel commodities increasing by 8.4 per cent on average during the year, while oil prices increased by some 15 per cent—both in United States dollar terms. Nonetheless, much of the price advance in some markets reflects only the depreciation of the dollar, with limited or no gain (or even further losses in some markets) when prices are measured in other currencies. When measured in special drawing rights (SDRs), non-fuel commodity prices fell on average by 2 per cent in 2003. Moreover, the terms of trade turned against commodity producers in 2003, as the combined index of non-fuel commodity prices fell by some 1 per cent in the year when deflated by the export price index of manufactures (see table A.17).

Towards the end of 2003 and during the first quarter of 2004, however, commodity prices strengthened independently of the unit of account used. That trend slowed somewhat later on, but not for fuels. In addition to the weight of Chinese demand in influencing commodity markets and acting as a price-maker for most minerals, metals and raw materials, other factors—not necessarily impacting on markets in the same way—have become increasingly influential. For instance, the world economic recovery, increased uncertainty and speculation have been pushing prices up in some markets,[2] while the strengthening of the dollar towards the end of the first quarter of 2004 and the expansion of productive capacity in some commodity sectors have acted as a deterrent to price increases in others.

Agricultural commodities

Among agricultural commodities, the prices of food failed to improve, on average, in 2003, while vegetable oilseeds and oil, as well as agricultural raw materials, echoed a strong upward trend (see figure II.3), largely owing to increased demand by China and the overall acceleration in global economic activity. Tropical beverage prices remained depressed for most of the year, reflecting prevailing conditions in the coffee market. In early 2004, most agricultural commodity markets recorded strong price increases.

A global shortage of grains persisted ...

Wheat prices rose sharply during winter 2003/04 and, after a short decline in late 2003, continued to climb in 2004. This may reflect high speculative activity as volumes on the main world cereal market—the Kansas City Board of Trade (KCBT)—were high in the first quarter of 2004.[3] Moreover, the global shortage of grains continued, with global stocks lower by 18 per cent at the end of the season.[4] The global production shortfall was caused by a drought in many parts of Europe and a poor harvest in the Russian Federation and Ukraine, partly offset by a return to "normal" production levels in North America and Australia, themselves affected by drought in the previous year. For 2004, world grain production is forecast to reach a record level owing to the assumed return of normal weather in Europe, high production incentives as a result of the high prices and – in the case of EU – a cut in set-aside obligations from 10 to 5 per cent for major field crops. At the same time, wheat demand will remain strong, in particular for feed as global income growth will increase demand for such grain-fed food products as pork, poultry and eggs. Therefore, at the global level, a major production surplus is not likely and prices are expected to remain firm in 2004. Owing to the very low stock levels, adverse weather developments could lead to sharp price increases.

Figure II.3.
Non-fuel commodity prices, monthly, January 2002-March 2004
(Indices of US dollar prices, 1985 = 100)

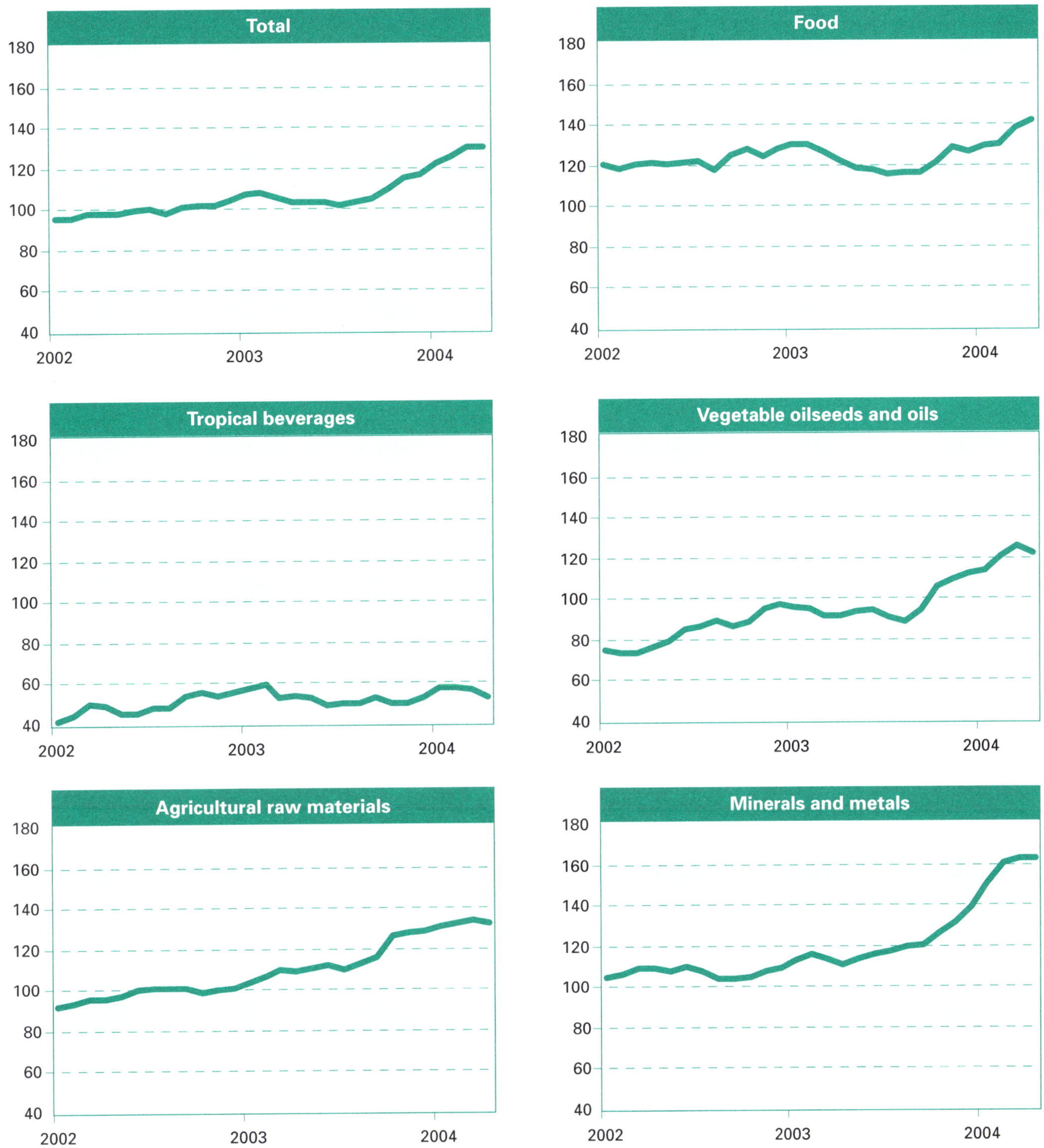

Source:
UNCTAD, *Monthly Commodity Price Bulletin.*

The prices of **rice** rose by 22 per cent between January and April 2004. Market conditions indicate continuing tight supply for the third consecutive year. The ratio of world stocks to consumption is lower than in former years, particularly in India and China. A special feature of the tight supply/demand situation is the fact that demand from Asian and South American importers might slow down owing to the expansion of production in such countries as India and in China (as a result of the larger use of hybrid varieties). World rice production is expected to grow by 3.3 per cent in 2004/05; this might not be sufficient to balance supply and demand, thus keeping some pressure on prices.

... but sugar supplies continue to increase ...

After a sharp and steady decline in **sugar** prices during 2003, a trough was reached in January 2004. Quotations on the international sugar markets subsequently improved slightly, probably owing to speculative activities, since supply continues to expand. This supposed speculative buying is probably only a temporary phenomenon and oversupply is expected to lead to a marked decrease in sugar prices later in 2004, particularly as the area under sugar beet cultivation in Europe is stable and sugar production is expected to increase in such countries as Australia, China and Pakistan.[5]

... and bananas also face overproduction

After a decline of almost 30 per cent in 2003, **banana** prices rose by 22 per cent between January and April 2004. Market fundamentals are influencing prices, in particular the growing demand in CIS and the 10 new EU member countries. China is also a promising market. The banana sector, however, faces overproduction. Ecuador, the world's largest supplier, has expanded exports significantly owing to an increase in its cultivated area. Shipments from the Philippines also increased owing to the combined effects of a larger crop, higher demand in East Asia and the devaluation of the currency against the yen and the dollar. EU will apply the revised banana transitional tariff-quota system to imports between 2004 and 2006, and in the beginning of 2006 a tariff-only system will be established. These two events will have a significant impact on producer countries, because one third of the world banana trade is currently destined for EU.[6]

Tropical beverages faced weak demand ...

The upward trend in **coffee** prices that started in 2003 continued in the first months of 2004 and largely reflected lower supply as producers cut investment and capacity owing to persistently low prices. However, prices remain too weak to indicate a recovery from the coffee crisis of recent years.

World coffee production for the 2003/04 crop year is estimated at 102 million bags, a figure nearly 15 per cent lower than in the previous year. However, this reduction depends heavily on Brazil. The country's 2004 coffee production is forecast to be 35 per cent lower than in the previous year,[7] reflecting expected lower yields, especially in the Arabica producing regions. Côte d'Ivoire, Nicaragua and Burundi will also witness further declines in their coffee production in 2004. Partly offsetting these reductions in production are increases in such key countries as Colombia, Viet Nam and Mexico. With the expected decline in global coffee production, sentiment in the coffee market has turned mildly bullish, owing particularly to additional concerns about climatic conditions in Brazil.

Three factors are particularly relevant in the outlook for coffee prices. First, coffee consumption is expected to increase only marginally. Second, coffee stocks were still high during spring 2004; and third, production in Brazil might rebound again. Accordingly, large price gains are unlikely.

After a steady decline in 2003, **cocoa** prices increased in early 2004. Prices continued to be influenced by developments in Côte d'Ivoire—the world's largest cocoa producer—which have prevented prices from falling to much lower levels. Owing to weak demand, the outlook for prices depends mainly on production in West Africa and on the political process in Côte d'Ivoire. The mid-crops of Côte d'Ivoire and Ghana are anticipated to be significantly larger this year than they were last year.[8] Moreover, cocoa production in Indonesia reached an all-time record in 2002/03 and caused a rise in stock of over 100,000 tons. This surplus will keep exerting downward pressure on prices. Additionally, demand for cocoa is weak, partly reflecting stagnating incomes in many cocoa-consuming countries and changes in chocolate processing by EU manufacturers who are now allowed to use cocoa butter substitutes in their chocolate products.[9]

Following an increase of 8.4 per cent in 2003, **tea** prices suffered a downturn during the first quarter of 2004, declining by 12 per cent. Although production is stable in many regions, increases in some countries, notably Kenya and Viet Nam, have raised global production. On the other hand, some upward pressure on prices can be expected from lower production in India owing to poor weather conditions in the south of the country. Overall, however, prices are expected to continue to decline as demand shows signs of saturation in many countries, except for the CIS countries.

... but the prices of vegetable oilseeds and oils soared in late 2003-early 2004

Vegetable oilseeds and oils experienced a strong price increase in the first quarter of 2004, largely owing to a marked upward trend in soybean oil prices. This was caused by growing demand worldwide, supported by increasing per capita incomes, especially in the middle- and low-income countries in Asia, as partly reflected in massive imports of soybean oil by China.[10] Soybean prices reached a level not seen in the past 10 years: they rose by 25 per cent in the fourth quarter of 2003 and by an additional 18 per cent in the first quarter of 2004. Besides being ascribable to increased demand, this unexpected price surge can be explained by developments on the supply side due to the successive downward revisions of the estimated soybean crops for Brazil and Argentina,[11] as well as a disappointing harvest in the United States. Meanwhile, the price of **palm oil**, the second most important product of this group, has followed a similar trend: prices increased by 27 per cent in the period from January to April 2004. One factor playing a crucial role in the palm oil market was India's decision to reduce import taxes on palm oil. India is one of the two main world importers of palm oil, China being the other.

Agricultural raw materials exhibited mixed price trends

Among agricultural raw materials, **cotton** prices declined in early 2004 after a significant increase in 2003. Over recent years, the most important determinant of annual changes in cotton prices has been China's net trade position. China has become a cotton price-maker, as it is not only the leading world producer but also, at times, a significant world importer. In 2003, for instance, world cotton imports grew by 5 per cent mainly owing to large Chinese import positions. However, an increase in stocks of 700,000 tons is anticipated for the next season as Chinese imports slow down in 2004 and production continues to rise.[12] Government subsidies in some countries still impact negatively on the cotton market by leading to overproduction and downward pressures on prices: it is estimated that the area under cotton cultivation in the United States (which exports 70 per cent of its production) could increase by 7 per cent in 2004.

Except for a temporary recovery in January 2004, **wool** prices decreased after March 2003. This development appears to have been due mostly to a decline in Chinese demand, which was affected by SARS, and by the weakness of the United States dollar (compared with the Australian dollar), which is used by Chinese buyers. In Europe, the rise of the euro against the dollar has, to some extent, limited exports. On the supply side, however, there are concerns about the adequacy of supply, as global wool production continues to decrease and has reached a 50-year low. With weak production and a slight rise in demand at the end of 2004 due to new fashion trends, wool prices might improve somewhat during 2004.

The price of **natural rubber** rose sharply during the last quarter of 2003 and continued its ascending trend during the first quarter of 2004. Among the leading producers, supply decreased in Malaysia owing to adverse weather conditions and in Thailand owing to civil unrest in the south of the country.[13] Furthermore, insufficient replanting in several producing countries will limit increases in production. Assuming that the world economic recovery continues, rubber demand should expand in 2004. Moreover, rapid growth in China—accounting for almost 20 per cent of world's rubber consumption in 2003—will sustain growth in the car industry and consequently natural rubber consumption. With oil prices at record levels, substitution of natural for synthetic rubber will also be an important factor, as the relative competitiveness of natural rubber increases. All of these factors, together with the low level of stocks, argue for continued increases in prices.

Minerals and metals

Supply reductions and stronger demand led to higher prices for minerals and metals

Minerals and metals prices have been on an upward trend in dollar terms since late 2002 (see figure II.3). During 2003, the UNCTAD price index for minerals and metals rose by 28 per cent. While the price increases up to the last quarter of 2003 were relatively modest, the trend began to accelerate in September/October of that year, reflecting higher demand in a tight supply environment, as well as declining world metal stocks. Faster growth in the United States and Japan and, above all, the continued strong growth of Chinese metals consumption drove the increase in global demand. In several cases, speculative buying also contributed to the upturn in prices. Metal prices continued to increase in the first half of 2004, with a price correction coming earlier for some metals, such as nickel, as the speculative boom in that market had exhausted itself in February. For others, the adjustment came in April/May when the Government of China announced measures to rein in economic growth and prevent the overheating of the economy. The liquidation of speculative positions by hedge funds, which had helped drive prices up earlier, also contributed to the fall in prices.

Metals prices are expected to remain high during 2004 ...

The expected deceleration in Chinese economic growth and, consequently, in metals demand, has raised the question whether metals prices will continue their recent fall and whether the price boom is over. Several factors point, however, to the decline's being a temporary correction and to prices' remaining at historically high levels at least until the end of 2004 and, in many cases, beyond. First, stock levels are low and global demand continues to exceed supply for several metals. Second, even a lower rate of growth in China would still lead to considerable growth in demand for metals, particularly since improved growth is being forecast for most of the developed world in 2004-2005. Third, while additions to production capacity have taken place and many more are under way, new capacity has a long gestation time. Additionally, in many cases, it is not clear that the new capacity will be sufficient to maintain the present tight balance between supply and demand.

... despite increased production of iron ore, ...

World **iron ore** production is estimated to have continued to increase in 2003, supported by strong demand from the steel industry. China, where iron ore imports increased by 33 per cent, was a major factor. Chinese demand continued to grow rapidly during the first quarter of 2004 and, despite measures to curb the rate of expansion of steel production in China, including higher capital requirements for new steel projects, global steel production and demand for iron ore are likely to continue increasing at historically high rates in 2004. The first results of iron ore supply contract negotiations, where prices are agreed for a year at a time, indicated price increases of about 18 per cent for 2004.

Increases of a similar magnitude are possible in 2005, particularly if the United States dollar weakens further.

World primary **aluminium** production increased by about 7 per cent in 2003. Growth in consumption paralleled that of production, as stock levels remained almost unchanged over the course of the year. As a result largely of speculation, fuelled by expectations of very rapid growth of consumption in China, prices rose by 13 per cent in 2003.[14] The continued Chinese expansion and the significant fall in stocks in early 2004 provided a stimulus to prices, which rose by 11 per cent during the first four months of 2004. Future price developments will depend to a large extent on developments in China, where the Government has taken steps to slow investment in new aluminium smelters owing to shortages of alumina and energy. Large capacity additions are already in the pipeline, however, and if these can be realized in spite of the input shortages, China should remain a net exporter of aluminium in the short-to-medium term, to some extent putting a brake on further price rises.

... aluminium ...

Copper mine production increased by 0.7 per cent in 2003, while production of refined copper fell by 0.6 per cent and copper usage increased by 2.7 per cent.[15] Stocks held in the London Metal Exchange (LME) warehouses decreased throughout 2003 and into 2004. Prices rose throughout 2003 and ended the year 25 per cent higher than at the end of 2002. The Chilean copper company Codelco, which had built up inventories to 200,000 tons in late 2003 and thereby contributed to the rise in prices, also began selling its stocks in early 2004. The shortage of copper was reflected in a backwardation, that is to say, prices for immediate delivery were higher than for delivery in three months. The price peaked in early March 2004, falling afterwards partly as a result of a slowdown in Chinese demand and partly because speculators reversed their positions. However, demand is anticipated to exceed production in 2004. The International Copper Study Group forecasts a 6.1 per cent increase in usage but an increase of only 3.7 per cent in refined metal production. Accordingly, it is unlikely that prices will fall significantly, and the possibility of new price peaks should not be excluded, particularly as growth picks up in major developed economies.

... and copper

Lead prices rose by 56 per cent in 2003 as LME stocks fell by 40 per cent. Reduced Chinese exports due to rising domestic demand have been an important factor behind the decrease in lead availability. A large proportion of lead, including almost all lead used in batteries, is recycled, and it is difficult to raise recycling rates further in the tightly regulated market that exists in many countries. Thus, scrap cannot replace primary lead in times of high prices to the same extent as for other metals, particularly since many other uses of lead are dispersive and do not allow recovery of the metal. It is possible that mines and primary refining plants that were closed during the earlier period of low prices will re-enter production and this may avert a shortage. However, prices continued rising in the first quarter of 2004 and are likely to remain at historically high levels.

Increased demand was reflected in prices of non-ferrous metals

Nickel prices rose by 97 per cent in 2003 and reached a 15-year high in January 2004, after which they fell as speculators cashed in their profits. LME stocks have remained very low. Demand continues to outpace supply, driven by rapidly increasing production of stainless steel, which accounts for the major part of nickel use. Although major capacity increases are under way, including large new mines in Australia, Canada and Indonesia, the supply deficit will probably continue for awhile and prices are not likely to return to pre-boom levels in the medium term.

Tin followed a trend similar to that of other non-ferrous metals, with prices rising rapidly in the later part of 2003 as LME stocks, which had started to decline in the second quarter, fell. Prices had increased by 43 per cent in 2003 and rose by a further 56 per cent by May 2004, when they appeared to have reached a plateau. There is little relief in sight for users, as the smelters with spare capacity are unable to obtain sufficient concentrates. A relatively large backwardation has developed, reflecting the shortage of metal. It is therefore likely that prices will remain high, at least throughout 2004.

Zinc proved somewhat of an exception in 2003, since LME stocks increased over the year, before falling in early 2004. The price, however, followed a familiar pattern, increasing towards the end of 2003, although less spectacularly than for other metals (23 per cent for the year as a whole), as sizeable closures of capacity in Europe reduced excess supply. Demand increased by 2.5 per cent, which is above average for zinc, while supply fell marginally. Future prices depend to a large extent on developments in China, which is both the world's largest producer and consumer of zinc. The rapid expansion of car production in China is a positive factor for zinc demand, since the car industry is a major consumer of galvanized steel, and the most important use of zinc is in galvanized steel production. Accordingly, it is likely that prices will remain firm in the outlook.

Do higher prices indicate a tight world oil market?

Monthly average oil prices strengthened uninterruptedly from September 2003 to April 2004 when, as measured by the reference basket of the Organization of the Petroleum Exporting Countries (OPEC), they averaged $32.35 per barrel (pb) (see figure II.4). This

Figure II.4.
Price of oil (OPEC reference basket), January 2000-April 2004

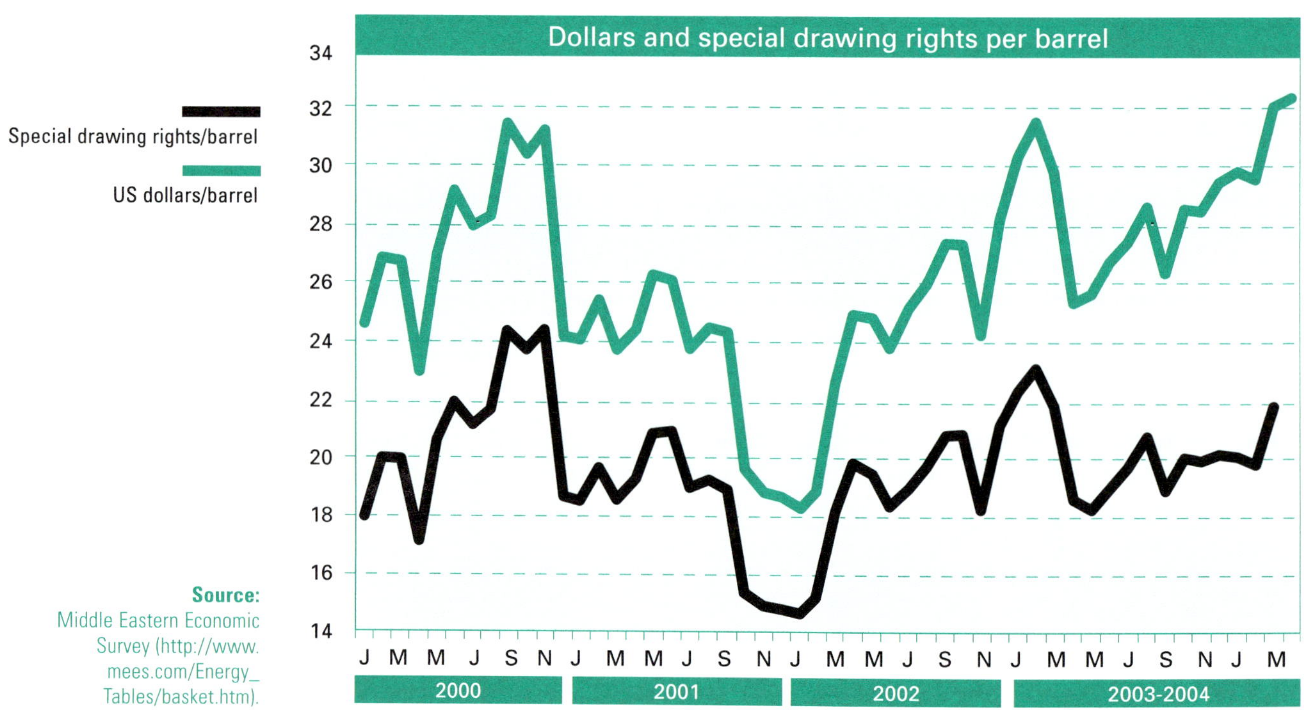

Source: Middle Eastern Economic Survey (http://www.mees.com/Energy_Tables/basket.htm).

was the highest nominal monthly average since the record of $34.32 pb in October 1990, following Iraq's invasion of Kuwait. The OPEC basket price averaged $28.10 pb in 2003, an increase of about 15 per cent over the 2002 average of $24.36. A further average increase is anticipated for 2004.

Oil prices surged owing to increased demand and mounting uncertainty

The surge in oil prices is led by market fundamentals, a great deal of speculation and a "fear premium". The first factor reflects stronger-than-expected global oil demand and lower-than-normal world oil inventories, particularly private inventories. Oil demand increased in the United States because of the cold winter and a less fuel-efficient automobile fleet. Other sources of oil demand strength were China, which has become the world's second largest oil consumer, and Japan, owing to delays in returning its nuclear power plants to full capacity. Furthermore, stocks held by Governments increased somewhat, contributing to higher demand and keeping the pressure on prices, while the fact that private inventories dropped to levels that kept refineries, particularly in the United States, dependent on fresh supplies, also maintained the pressure on prices.[16] Worldwide, oil demand increased by 2.2 per cent in 2003 and is forecast to grow by 2.4 per cent in 2004, reaching some 80.6 million barrels per day (mbd)—an increase of 1.9 mbd in relation to 2003 (see table A.18).

Markets are concerned about possible supply disruptions

Meanwhile, market sentiment since the second half of 2003 has remained strong as the global economy has entered a more definitive recovery. Additionally, market participants started to anticipate fuel shortages and other potential supply disruptions, particularly following the overall deterioration of the security situation in Iraq, the attacks on oil infrastructure in Saudi Arabia and repeated attacks and sabotage on oil installations in Iraq. As a result of such developments, some market specialists estimate the fear premium to be about $5-$8 pb.

The supply of oil, however, did not decline abruptly in 2003 or in early 2004. Saudi Arabia and other OPEC producers were able to compensate for the production disruptions in Iraq, Nigeria and Venezuela in early 2003 and a few other producers, such as the Russian Federation, were also able to expand supply. OPEC production continued to increase in the second half of 2003 and early 2004 despite official quota reductions (see figure II.5). OPEC-10 (excluding Iraq) produced 26.3 mbd in December 2003 and 26.4 mbd in January 2004, above the agreed quota ceiling of 24.5 mbd.

Iraqi production and exports resumed ...

Although a member of OPEC, Iraq is not bound to a quota ceiling. After production of only 50,000 bd in May 2003, Iraq's production had steadily risen and averaged 1.3 mbd in 2003. Oil production rose to an average of 2.0 mbd during January and February 2004, still below the 2.6 mbd pre-war level. Iraqi oil exports also remain below pre-war levels owing mainly to inadequate export outlets and infrastructure bottlenecks. Oil refineries have been operating at half capacity, forcing Iraq to import most refined products to meet domestic demand. Nonetheless, further gains in production are expected in Iraq in 2004.

... and OPEC-10 continued to produce above agreed quota

OPEC introduced a lower quota in November 2003—the second reduction of the year—in order to curb inventory replenishment that would eventually lead to a downward pressure on prices. Subsequently, in the first quarter of 2004, OPEC countries were concerned about the cyclical downturn of oil demand, which often takes place in the second quarter, the lack of compliance within OPEC with regard to the quota policy, the possible increase in Iraq's oil exports and the continued weakness of the dollar, which had been eroding the purchasing power of the OPEC oil basket.[17] Accordingly, at its meeting on 10 February 2004, OPEC-10 decided to reduce its oil production ceiling by 1.0 mbd to 23.5

Figure II.5.
World oil supply and demand, and OPEC oil production, first quarter 2000-fourth quarter 2004

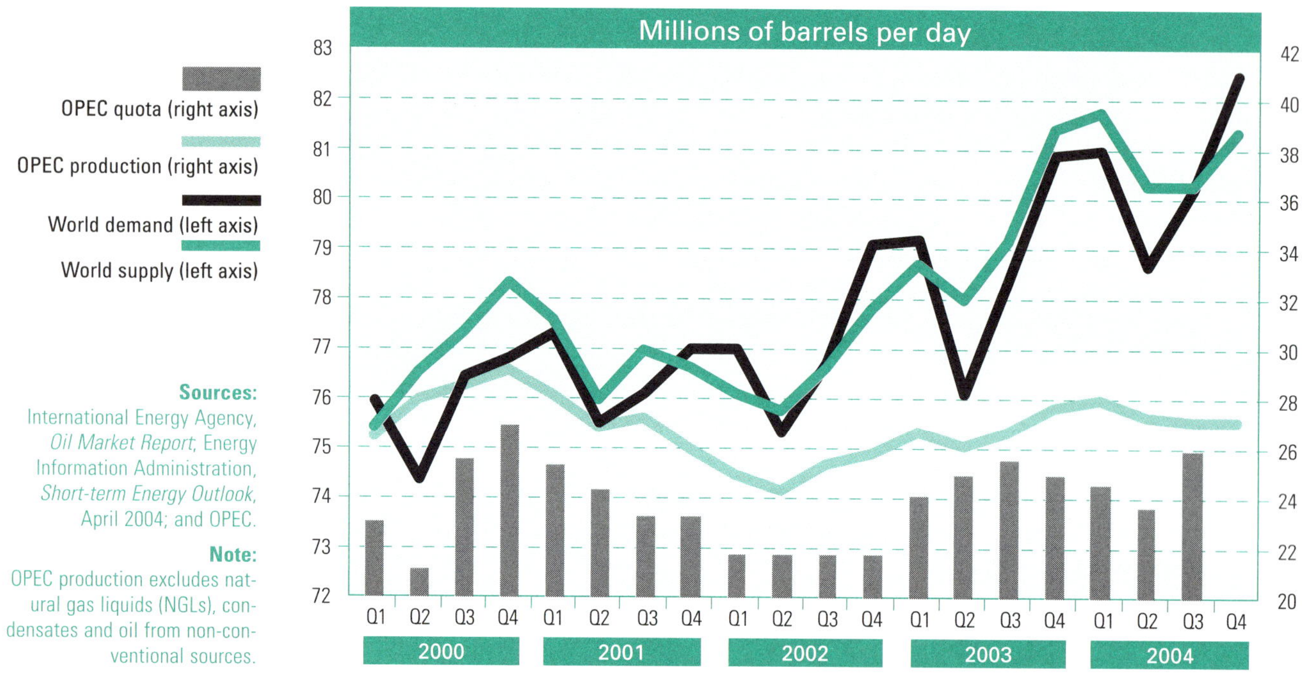

Sources: International Energy Agency, *Oil Market Report*; Energy Information Administration, *Short-term Energy Outlook*, April 2004; and OPEC.

Note: OPEC production excludes natural gas liquids (NGLs), condensates and oil from non-conventional sources.

mbd, effective 1 April 2004, and to eliminate excess production, estimated at 1.5 mbd, implying the withdrawal of 2.5 mbd from the market. This announcement provided renewed impetus to price increases, despite the fact that global production continued to expand in the first quarter of 2004. Subsequently, in view of persistently high prices, the Organization decided to raise its official oil output ceiling by 2 mbd effective 1 July 2004, and by an additional 0.5 mbd starting on 1 August 2004. Prices moderated somewhat after such announcements but remained well above the upper band of the Organization's targeted price range.

It is not clear how far OPEC members will comply with this agreement. Global oil supply exceeded global demand by some 0.8 mbd in the first quarter of 2004,[18] indicating that speculation and other concerns were underlying the price increases observed during this period. If these concerns are overcome and speculators unwind their positions in an orderly fashion, oil prices could decline in the second half of the year. However, this outlook is subject to downside risks, particularly if the security situation in major oil-producing countries deteriorates and supply is disrupted.

Prices will remain firm throughout 2004

Preliminary estimates indicate that OPEC produced above its quota in April, although output declined in a few member countries. Oil output is increasing in Algeria, the Libyan Arab Jamahiriya and Nigeria as new fields are brought on-stream. However, these additions to production are relatively small. Among non-OPEC producers, oil supply is anticipated to increase in the Russian Federation, as well as in the other oil producers in the Caspian Sea region, and in Africa. In all, global oil supply is forecast to rise by 2 per cent from 79.4 mbd in 2003 to 81.1 mbd in 2004 (see table A.18). Owing to the tight balance between supply and demand and lower oil inventories, oil prices are anticipated to remain firm over the medium term.

Trade policy developments

The multilateral sphere: the Doha negotiations

Multilateral trade negotiations have restarted after the collapse of the World Trade Organization Fifth Ministerial Conference in Cancún, Mexico, in September 2003. Since Doha, very few concrete results have emerged from two years of negotiations, although there was a notable agreement on trade-related intellectual property rights (TRIPS) and public health. For a series of negotiations that has a core development agenda, the Cancún meeting was disappointing.[19]

Trade negotiations resumed ...

After a period of soul-searching, support for the resumption of negotiations gained momentum. The World Trade Organization General Council reactivated the Trade Negotiations Committee in December 2003 and appointed chairpersons to the various negotiating bodies under the Committee in February 2004. Among others, negotiating groups on agriculture, industrial market access, trade and development, and services have met. Additional sessions have been scheduled, attesting to members' willingness to continue with the negotiations. Negotiating groups opted for a more informal negotiating approach, with delegations dealing directly with one another, without much intervention from the Chair, in order to promote more intensive and productive dialogue. The aim is to reach an agreement on a negotiating framework by July 2004. Any convergence of views, however, has remained elusive.

... but agriculture remained a challenge

Negotiations on market access in agriculture continued to be challenging, as countries' divergent priorities have prevented them from agreeing on how increased access could be achieved. A "blended formula" originally proposed by the United States and the European Commission and incorporated into the draft of the Cancún Ministerial Text is currently under consideration.[20] It combines the Uruguay Round of multilateral trade negotiations formula (average reduction with a minimum reduction per tariff lines) and the Swiss formula (which narrows the gap between high and low tariffs). Additionally, a certain number of products would be duty-free. Many countries, however, oppose the blended formula owing to concerns about the flexibility the formula provides to developed countries for not reducing high tariffs by a substantial amount.

Obstacles, and conflicting interests at the domestic level, prevail in other areas of the agriculture negotiation, such as domestic support and export competition. For instance, despite providing duty-free access for cotton and textiles to least developed countries, EU was unable to advance the reform of its cotton support system far enough. In its Common Agricultural Policy (CAP) reform adopted in April 2004, EU partially (65 per cent) decoupled subsidies from production. As a result, uncompetitive cotton production will not be completely eliminated and will continue to have a negative impact on world prices.[21] On the other hand, a preliminary World Trade Organization ruling in favour of Brazil in its case against United States subsidies to cotton producers, if upheld, may provide countries with additional incentives for faster and deeper liberalization of their agricultural sectors, thereby facilitating negotiations on agriculture.

Owing to the prevailing difficulties, the Committee on Agriculture aims at first reaching an agreement on a negotiating framework and then establishing the modalities. With the limited results to date, agriculture seems likely to remain the main stumbling block to progress in the overall negotiations, as delegations are reluctant to advance in other areas without knowing the extent of the concessions in agriculture.

Difficulties in market access negotiations persisted

Divergent views also persist in the negotiations on non-agricultural market access (NAMA). One group of countries, largely developed economies with already relatively low tariffs, favours ambitious tariff reductions in this area and supports a non-linear 4approach to tariff reduction, bringing rates to a harmonized international rate. Conversely, many developing countries, usually with higher tariffs than their industrialized counterparts, argue that they would be making greater concessions if this approach was adopted and that this would be in contradiction to the Doha provision for less than full reciprocity. Furthermore, for many developing countries, aggressive liberalization in industrial goods may compound challenges already being faced by their—in many instances, incipient—manufacturing sector and could have a negative impact on their development strategies.[22]

Erosion of preferences is a source of concern

A complicating factor is the concern of the least developed countries and other low-income countries about the erosion in preferential access to the markets of developed countries as the overall level of tariffs in the latter falls. Yet, recent studies have suggested that many available trade preferences are not fully utilized, mainly because of stringent rules of origin, accounting system requirements, and complex sanitary and phytosanitary measures.[23] Greater trade opportunities could be further exploited under current arrangements, particularly if some of the requirements are redesigned and simplified by taking into account the capacity constraints of least developed countries. Additionally, technical assistance could be enhanced in this area so that these countries could meet the required standards. Finally, financial support could be extended to countries facing trade-related adjustment difficulties. In this regard, the new International Monetary Fund (IMF) policy instrument, the Trade Integration Mechanism (TIM), is a welcome development (see below).[24]

The Committee on Trade and Development agreed to focus its attention on special and differential treatment (S&D) and bridging existing differences, which are, however, considerable. Additionally, members have yet to decide on the future of the proposals that were agreed in principle, forwarded to Cancún, but never adopted by the meeting. While most developed countries are concerned with issues of eligibility, including possible differentiation among developing countries, compliance and graduation, developing countries are pressing for greater flexibility in rules application and a non-discriminatory approach. The most difficult issue to be tackled may be the differences of approach that also exist: developed countries would like to discuss the principles and objectives of S&D measures before strengthening them, while developing countries invoke the Doha mandate of reviewing, strengthening and making existing measures more effective rather than reconsidering them which, they fear, could imply a renegotiation of such measures.

Initial offers in services considered unsatisfactory

Negotiations on services are more advanced than in other areas. However, only a limited number of delegations have been able to submit initial offers and those submitted were not considered comprehensive enough.[25] Part of the difficulty can be attributed to developing countries' limited negotiating capacity, which prevents them from identifying their priorities in this area, properly assessing the consequences of potential liberalization in specific subsectors of services and evaluating requests and offers received. While technical assistance could remove some of these constraints, its impact in the short-term would be limited as capacity takes time to build up. Furthermore, technical assistance may not provide these countries with all the requirements they need in order to face the difficulties in this area. Lack of progress in the agriculture negotiations may have also contributed to the limited results so far.

Meanwhile, developing countries, which attach particular importance to the liberalization of Mode 4 (movement of natural persons), have been disappointed by the limited opening proposed in the offers received. In many instances, offers on Mode 4 were determined by or linked to Mode 3 (commercial presence). Most developing countries, however, face comparative disadvantage in setting up a commercial presence abroad.[26]

Developing countries have also great interest in Mode 1 (cross-border trade). While developing countries have always recorded a deficit in their service balance and have been traditional suppliers of such services as travel, a few of them have been able to grasp new opportunities brought about by the emergence of the ICT industry, for instance, and have been able to increase exports of business services in the past few years. Brazil, China, India and Israel are cases in point (see table II.1). Nonetheless, the increasing presence of developing countries in offshore information technology (IT) software and services outsourcing—particularly in a period of slow global economic growth and rising unemployment—has raised protectionist sentiments in some developed countries. For instance, the United States Senate has passed a bill that prevents private companies from using offshore workers to bid on some government contracts despite the widely recognized positive overall welfare gains promoted by increased trade liberalization and the detrimental effects of protectionist measures. In the particular case of the United States, research has indicated that global outsourcing promotes cost savings, lowers inflation and increases productivity, thus contributing to GDP growth. Accordingly, despite displacement of some IT workers, total employment increases as a result of increased economic activity.[27]

All in all, the resumption of negotiations in the World Trade Organization is a positive development as members work to reduce their differences over a wide range of issues. However, it has not yet been enough to give a definitive push to the conclusion of the Doha negotiations. For that, greater political will as well as deeper understanding and consideration of developing countries' developmental needs and aspirations is necessary so that a rules-based multilateral trading system can be supported and shared by all, thereby maximizing the benefits trade can bring for growth and development worldwide.

Renewed efforts are still required for a successful conclusion of the negotiations

Table II.1.
Exports of business services from selected developing countries, 1995-2002

	Millions of dollars		1995-1996 = 100
Reporter	Average 1995-1996	Average 2001-2002	Average 2001-2002
Brazil	1 416	4 466	316
China	5 300	9 433	178
India	2 131	16 878	792
Israel	2 239	6 156	275
Memorandum item:			
Total developed countries	77 547	111 084	143

Source: IMF, *Balance of Payments Statistics.*

Termination of the Agreement on Textiles and Clothing

Conceived as a transitional instrument, the Agreement on Textiles and Clothing[28] is set to expire by the end of 2004. Textiles and clothing will be fully integrated into World Trade Organization rules and disciplines and subject to the principles of non-discrimination and transparency. Thus, textiles and clothing will no longer be the only manufactures excluded from multilateral rules and some developed countries will no longer receive a form of special and differentiated treatment in this sector.

Agreed liberalization of textiles and clothing delayed until final months

As a result of the Uruguay Round of multilateral trade negotiations, textiles and clothing trade was to be regulated by the 10-year Agreement on Textiles and Clothing, which had established a progressive schedule of product incorporation into General Agreement on Tariffs and Trade (GATT) rules—as not all textiles and clothing products are ruled by the Agreement—and quota liberalization. Nonetheless, despite formal World Trade Organization notification by Canada, EU and the United States on their intentions to fully comply with Agreement provisions, the bulk of liberalization will be occurring in 2004, as a great deal of backloading has occurred and most quotas have remained in place. Additionally, countries included in the list of products to be liberalized items that had not previously been subject to quotas. Liberalization that took place during the past nine years was de facto very modest.

Adjustment costs will likely feed protectionist sentiments

The elimination of quotas is expected to lead to shifts in the allocation of resources, with capacity expanding in developing countries, particularly in Asia, and production contracting in developed countries as imports increase. For some exporters, as well as domestic producers in major importing countries (see table II.2), such changes will involve sudden adjustment costs, which the relatively long implementation of the

Table II.2.
Leading world exporters and importers of textiles and clothing, 2002

	Percentage share of world total			
	Textiles		Clothing	
	Exports	Imports	Exports	Imports
Bangladesh	..	..	2.1	..
Canada	..	2.4	..	1.9
China	13.2	8.1	20.6	..
European Union	49.4	39.6	33.4	64.5
Hong Kong SAR[a]	..	..	4.1	..
India	3.7	..	2.8	..
Japan	4.0	2.8	..	8.4
Korea, Republic of	7.0	2.0	..	1.0
Mexico	..	4.0	3.9	1.9
Pakistan	3.1	..	..	..
Russian Federation	..	..	..	1.8
Switzerland	..	..	..	1.6
Taiwan Province of China	6.3	..	..	..
Turkey	..	1.8	4.0	..
United States of America	7.0	10.8	3.0	31.7

Source: World Trade Organization.
a Special Administrative Region of China.

Agreement on Textiles and Clothing was expected to phase over time. Thus, an abruptly liberalized market may impose heavy costs in the short run as imports, at possibly significantly lower prices, surge in 2005.[29] Accordingly, producer associations in some of the restraining countries have been pressing for an extension of the existing arrangement. Meanwhile, a group of major developing-country exporters of textiles and clothing, worried about the possibility of massive anti-dumping initiations, have proposed a two-year grace period during which no anti-dumping investigations on imports of textiles and clothing from developing countries would be initiated.[30] Increased anti-dumping investigations, if realized, would reduce the positive impact of liberalization, as increased uncertainty would deter investment in the sector and constrain trade.

Net gains are expected at the global level

There is unanimity among experts that the end of the Agreement on Textiles and Clothing would lead to an increase in global welfare as resources are more efficiently allocated and consumers benefit from lower prices in the long run. Yet, there is disagreement on the magnitude of such welfare gains—owing to different methodologies and assumptions used in the models—as well as on the distribution of these gains.[31] The quota system had introduced severe distortions in the textiles and clothing market by promoting an inefficient global allocation of production and introducing rents. The former followed the availability of quotas and protected the higher-cost (often domestic) producer. Additionally, the end of the quota system can potentially bring important benefits for developing countries, many of which have a competitive advantage in this sector, particularly in garments. It may also provide incentives for the development of the manufacturing sector in the developing countries as the industry, largely based on the availability of low-cost labour, is often a catalyst in the early stages of industrialization.

Small producers in developing countries will suffer ...

Among developing countries, smaller producers, usually relatively less efficient, are anticipated to lose markets that were formally guaranteed by quotas.[32] Of particular concern is the situation of countries enjoying preferential status in certain markets, as the advantage of duty-free treatment, in a quota-free environment, may not offset higher costs deriving from rules-of-origin requirements (see box II.1). For example, Mexico and Caribbean countries have already lost market shares in the United States to competitors not bound by rules of origin. Furthermore, smaller producers often lack a vertically integrated textiles and clothing manufacturing base, which is considered an advantage by international buyers owing to the flexibility and time-saving benefits it offers. Consequently, these producers are likely to lose some space in major markets.

... although probably less than initially anticipated

Nonetheless, losses in some cases may not be as large as initially feared. Other factors, such as proximity to markets, business climate and good infrastructure (in terms of communication systems, logistic support, trade facilitation and the like), are also relevant. In this sense, although it is expected that producers such as China will enjoy increased market shares in major importing markets, the recent fast rate of Chinese import penetration in these markets is most likely not sustainable. Although China has a definite competitive advantage in this sector, the fast growth of its textiles and clothing exports has been facilitated by the country's entry into the World Trade Organization in 2001 as well as by the liberalization that has taken place in the specific subsectors of textiles and clothing, where China enjoys competitive advantage. Finally, buying companies tend to diversify their sources of supply in order to minimize risks of supply disruption, partially offsetting the underlying forces towards concentration in this sector.

Mushrooming of regional and bilateral initiatives

The slow progress in the multilateral negotiations has been paralleled by renewed interest in bilateral and regional trade liberalization, with several initiatives being launched and new agreements concluded in the past few months.

Free trade agreements burgeoning in number and diversity

A few trends characterize the recent regional/bilateral liberalization wave. First, countries that heretofore have preferred the multilateral approach are also embarking on regional/bilateral arrangements.[33] Japan is a case in point. While still fully committed to the strengthening of the multilateral trading system, the country is pursuing closer economic integration with other nations through free trade agreements (FTAs). It concluded its second FTA in early 2004 (with Mexico) and has launched negotiations with the Republic of Korea, Malaysia and Thailand. Second, developing countries have shown renewed interest in seeking FTAs among themselves, particularly between existing regional arrangements (for example, the Southern Common Market (MERCOSUR) and the Andean countries) or between an existing regional trade agreement (RTA) and individual countries (for example, MERCOSUR and India). Individual developing countries have also forged new bilateral FTAs (for example, Chile and the Republic of Korea). Third, and emerging from the above, FTAs are no longer necessarily restricted to neighbouring countries and are increasingly established across regions (for example, those between EU and South Africa; the United States of America and Australia; and EU and MERCOSUR). Nonetheless, some new regional initiatives, such as the signing of the South Asian Free Trade Area (SAFTA) agreement in January 2004, have also been launched. Fourth, large industrialized countries continue to negotiate FTAs with smaller developing countries, either individually (for example, United States with South Africa; and Japan as mentioned above) or with groups of countries (for example, Free Trade Area of the Americas (FTAA), Central American Free Trade Agreement (CAFTA), EU Economic Partnership Agreements (EPAs)).

Agreements between unequal partners may not increase market access

Negotiations of an FTA between a developing and a developed country do not, however, necessarily entail greater market access for the developing country. For instance, in the case of CAFTA, Central American countries were already enjoying preferential treatment in the United States market, on a non-reciprocal basis, on a wide range of products under the Caribbean Basin Initiative and its successor programme. In this sense, these countries will not enjoy greater access (with the exception of modest increases in some quotas of agricultural products), while they will now have to extend preferential treatment to United States imports. On the other hand, access and related benefits—once the agreement is approved by their respective legislatures—will be sustainable whereas, under the previous arrangement, country and product eligibility was subject to revisions.

There is evidence that, independently of the previous trade relationship a developing country has had with a developed country, large countries often extract greater trade concessions from smaller countries: large increases in market access by a developed country in a developing country market do not generate equally large access by the developing country.[34] Issues of imbalances in bargaining power are often present, even more so when developing countries are negotiating with a major donor, and are thus simultaneously in the conflicting position of trade partner and aid recipient.[35] Asymmetries in market size and dependencies also contribute to this outcome of imbalanced reciprocity. Developing countries depend much more on developed markets than the latter depend on them. Nonetheless, the importance of developing countries' markets for developed countries has been increasing lately (see table A.14).

Imbalances in reciprocity may emerge

A feature of FTAs between an industrialized and a developing country is that the large country lowers some of its trade barriers in exchange for concessions in non-trade areas. Subjects other than market access that do not have consensus at the World Trade Organization (investment, competition policies and the like) and even others outside the disciplines of the World Trade Organization (such as labour) are often included in such bilateral agreements. As a result, countries may be locking themselves into a rigid policy environment that may limit their options for policy interventions in the future. Meanwhile, agricultural trade—of particular interest to developing countries—is usually excluded, and its liberalization remains dependent on multilateral negotiations.

Studies of FTAs and their impact on multilateral trade have not reached a unanimous conclusion on whether such arrangements promote trade diversion or trade creation or whether they contribute to or impede multilateral trade negotiations. Some authors have highlighted the benefits of FTAs in taking liberalization beyond what trading partners are able to accomplish in the multilateral sphere, thus allowing for deeper integration. Others have argued that FTAs divert scarce human resources from multilateral negotiations and result in a complex web of rules and regulations. Recently, using tariff data of the United States, it was shown that FTAs involving unequal partners generate a strategic motive for the larger country to maintain some of its multilateral tariffs on imports from the preferential trade partner relatively higher than those on similar imports from elsewhere.[36]

Free trade agreements remain a second best

The above suggests that developing countries have more to gain from multilateral trade liberalization than from bilateral arrangements with larger partners. FTAs remain a second-best option for the world economy. It is only through multilateral negotiations, where all partners' interests are taken into account in a balanced way and development concerns can be addressed, that global welfare will be maximized.

Notes

1 The present section was drafted in part by the Commodities Branch of the Division on International Trade in Goods and Services, and Commodities, of UNCTAD.

2 Speculative activities were intense for some non-fuel commodities (such as coffee, sugar and wheat) as well, but these are often of a different nature than those prevailing in oil markets. In the case of non-fuel commodities, speculation often corresponds to a traditional behaviour by market agents during particularly important periods of the production cycle of a given commodity (for example, harvesting time). Speculation has also been supported by uncertainties regarding the sustainability of fast growth by China.

3 In April 2004, for instance, the number of futures contracts negotiated almost reached 291,000, a 51 per cent increase over the volumes negotiated in April 2003 (source: *Les Echos,* 6 mai 2004).

4 Food and Agriculture Organization of the United Nations (FAO), *Food Outlook,* No. 1 (Cereal Supply/Demand Roundup), Rome, April 2004.

5 A record production of 3.8 millions tons is forecast in Pakistan for the 2004 harvesting season.

6 This will affect all banana producers. Currently only bananas from the African, Caribbean and Pacific Group of States (ACP Group) are allowed to enter the single European market free of any tariff or charge.

7 International Coffee Organization, *Market Report,* January, February and March 2004.

8 Some industry sources forecast a record production in Côte d'Ivoire of 1.4 million tons of cocoa in 2004 (source: Radio France Internationale (RFI), 24 May 2004).

9 In 2000, EU adopted Directive 2000/36/EC, to take effect from August 2003.

10 The Public Ledger, *World Commodity Weekly*, 17-23 November 2003.

11 Soybean production forecast for 2003/04 in Brazil and Argentina, respectively the second and third world producers, was cut by 9 per cent (The Public Ledger, *World Commodity Weekly*, 26 April–2 May 2004).

12 International Cotton Advisory Committee, press releases, January-May 2004.

13 Insecurity in the South of Thailand might affect 10 per cent of the production of the region (RFI, 29 April 2004).

14 Unless otherwise indicated, figures for metal prices refer to monthly averages of the London Metal Exchange cash price.

15 International Copper Study Group, press release, 19 May 2004.

16 Robert Kaufmann, "The forecast for world oil market", paper prepared for the Project LINK Spring Meeting 2004, New York, 14-16 April 2004 (www.un.org/esa/policy/link/index.html). Path: Agenda and meeting documentation (accessed 9 August 2004).

17 The last of those factors may explain why OPEC has not adhered to its price mechanism. At its March 2000 meeting, OPEC created a price band mechanism, which would guide member countries in responding to change in world oil market conditions. An OPEC reference basket price was to be kept within a $22-$28 price range. OPEC countries would automatically adjust their production if oil prices exceeded the upper band of $28 pb for 20 consecutive trading days or were below the lower band of $22 for 10 consecutive trading days. However, the price band mechanism was activated only once, on 31 October 2000, when OPEC increased production to reduce the rise in oil prices.

18 International Energy Agency, *Oil Market Report*, 12 May 2004.

19 Factors leading to the meeting's failure have been extensively analysed elsewhere. See *World Economic Situation and Prospects, 2004* (United Nations publication, Sales No. E.04.II.C.2; and note by the UNCTAD secretariat entitled "Review of developments and issues in the post-Doha work programme of particular concern to developing countries: the outcome of the Fifth Ministerial Conference" (TD/B/50/8), 29 September 2003.

20 See "Annexes to the draft Cancún Ministerial Text: Annex A: Framework for Establishing Modalities in Agriculture", available from http://www.wto.org/english/thewto_e/minist_e/min03_e/draft_decl_annex_e.htm (accessed 6 August 2004).

21 EU is, however, a minor producer. Nevertheless, under certain assumptions, subsidies by smaller producing countries are disproportionately harmful to some suppliers. For instance, under a fragmented market assumption in which countries can trade only with existing trade partners, the EU cotton subsidies account for 38 per cent of the loss of earnings in West and Central Africa. Under a

unitary market assumption, however, that figure falls to 9 per cent. See Ian Gibson, *Understanding the Impact of Cotton Subsidies on Developing Countries and Poor People in Those Countries* (working draft), March 2004 (http://www.odi.org.uk/iedg/cotton_report.pdf).

22 For example, through public finances which, in some cases, have been adversely affected by trade liberalization as tariff cuts have reduced fiscal revenues.

23 On existing preferential treatment and its use, see UNCTAD, "Trade preferences for LDCs: an early assessment of benefits and possible improvements" (UNCTAD/ITCD/TSB/2003/8). On the specific case of preferential treatment by the United States for sub-Saharan African countries, see box.II.1.

24 IMF, "Fund support for trade-related balance of payments adjustments", prepared by the Policy Development and Review Department (in consultation with other Departments), 27 February 2004, available from http://www.imf.org/external/np/pdr/tim/2004/eng/022704.htm (accessed 6 August 2004).

25 World Trade Organization, Special Session of the Council for Trade in Services, "Report by the Chairman to the Trade Negotiations Committee" (TN/S/15), 14 April 2004.

26 Workers' remittances represent an important source of foreign currency and finance for development, particularly for countries that do not have access to international capital markets and where foreign direct investment (FDI) inflows are limited or non-existent. Official records indicate that workers' remittances flows to developing countries reached $93 billion in 2003 (a much higher figure is possible owing to existing informal channels), representing the second largest source of private finance for these countries after FDI.

27 Global Insight (USA), Inc., "Executive Summary: The Comprehensive Impact of Offshore IT Software and Services Outsourcing on the U.S. Economy and the IT Industry", Lexington, Massachusetts, March 2004.

28 The Agreement on Textiles and Clothing is the successor to the Multifibre Agreement (MFA), which operated from 1974 to 1994 and consisted of a quota system negotiated bilaterally between importers and exporters. See World Trade Organization Textiles Monitoring Body, "The Agreement on Textiles and Clothing" (http://www.wto.org/english/tratop_e/texti_e/texintro_e.htm).

29 Dan Ikenson, *Threadbare Excuses: The Textile Industry's Campaign to Preserve Import Restraints*, Trade Policy Analysis, No. 25, Washington, D.C., (Cato Institute Center for Trade Policy Studies, 15 October 2003).

30 World Trade Organization, General Council, "Anti-dumping actions in the area of textiles and clothing: proposal for specific short-term dispensation in favour of developing members following full integration of the sector into GATT 1994 from January 2005" (WT/GC/W/502), 14 July 2003.

31 Welfare gains range from $6.5 billion to $324 billion. See Organization for Economic Cooperation and Development (OECD) (Working Party of the Trade Committee), "Liberalising trade in textiles and clothing: a survey of quantitative studies" (TD/TC/WP(2003)2/FINAL), 2 May 2003.

32 United States International Trade Commission, *Textiles and Apparel: Assessment of the Competitiveness of Certain Foreign Suppliers to the U.S. Market (Investigation No. 332.448, sent to the United States Trade Representative in June 2003)*, Publication 3671, January 2004.

33 World Trade Organization Secretariat, "The changing landscape of RTAs", paper prepared for the Seminar on Regional Trade Agreements and the World Trade Organization, Geneva, 14 November 2003.

34 Caroline Freund, *Reciprocity in Free Trade Agreements*, World Bank Working Paper, No. 3061 (Washington, D.C. World Bank, 20 May 2003).

35 Sheila Page, *Developing Countries: Victims or Participants. Their Changing Role in International Negotiations* (London, Overseas Development Institute, 2003).

36 Nuno Limão, *Preferential Trade Agreements as Stumbling Blocks for Multilateral Trade Liberalization: Evidence for the U.S.*, University of Maryland, December 2003, available from http://www.vanderbilt.edu/econ/sempapers/Limao.pdf (accessed 6 August 2004).

Chapter III
International Finance

Summary

There was an increase in net financial flows to developing countries in 2003. Official development assistance (ODA) rose to a record level in both real and nominal terms, but this was to a large extent because of special factors and, although having increased from 0.23 to 0.25 per cent, ODA still falls far short of the target of 0.7 per cent of the gross national income (GNI) of the developed countries. For those countries that have access to international capital markets, private capital flows in 2003 increased to a level not seen since the Asian financial crisis in 1997, despite a decline in inflows of foreign direct investment (FDI). The cost of external financing was also relatively low.

Developments were less encouraging from the longer-term policy perspective. The Fifth Ministerial Conference of the World Trade Organization, held in Cancún, Mexico, in September 2003, failed to advance the trade negotiations launched in Doha in 2001 and no progress was made in the first part of 2004. Meanwhile, bilateral and regional trade agreements continue to burgeon. Looking ahead, the World Trade Organization Agreement on Textiles and Clothing is scheduled to expire on 31 December 2004, with potentially widespread consequences for many developing countries. In the financial arena, the Heavily Indebted Poor Countries (HIPC) Initiative is also due to expire at the end of 2004 and there is concern that some eligible countries possibly will not have benefited from the programme by that date. The external debt of other countries and possible means of preventing and resolving international financial crises were the other main international financial policy issues receiving attention during the year.

Financial flows to developing and transition economies

Developing countries received $93 billion in net financial flows in 2003, a substantial increase from 2002 and the preceding two years (see table III.1). These net flows were boosted by a recovery in private financial flows to the highest level since the Asian financial crisis in 1997, the result mainly of a turnaround in banking flows to developing countries after many years of net outflows. FDI remained a resilient source of net private capital inflow despite having declined to its lowest level since 1997. There was also an increase in net bond and equity flows. Net financial flows to countries with economies in transition continued to increase in 2003 but more moderately than in 2002.

Table III.1.

Net financial flows to developing economies and economies in transition, 1993-2003

Billions of dollars							
	1993-1997	1998	1999	2000	2001	2002	2003[a]
Developing economies							
Net private capital flows	163.1	47.2	66.2	30.4	2.7	20.5	92.5
Net direct investment	87.8	130.2	145.7	149.8	164.1	112.8	102.6
Net portfolio investment[b]	68.0	26.4	68.2	9.6	-90.8	-91.7	-75.8
Other net investment[c]	7.3	-109.5	-147.7	-129.1	-70.7	-0.6	65.7
Net official flows	15.9	35.6	6.8	-10.6	32.8	5.3	0.5
Total net flows	179.0	82.8	73.0	19.7	35.5	25.9	93.0
Change in reserves	-78.8	-32.9	-84.8	-93.6	-95.4	-170.3	-324.9
Economies in transition							
Net private capital flows	13.5	30.2	20.4	11.8	17.9	26.5	38.7
Net direct investment	11.2	22.7	25.5	25.2	24.9	26.5	16.7
Net portfolio investment[b]	3.0	12.0	-2.2	-3.4	-4.9	-6.9	-11.7
Other net investment[c]	-0.7	-4.6	-2.9	-9.9	-2.2	6.9	33.7
Net official flows	7.0	11.7	-0.4	-3.8	-7.1	-2.1	-5.9
Total net flows	20.5	41.9	20.0	8.0	10.8	24.4	32.7
Change in reserves	-12.9	-1.7	-7.9	-23.3	-18.1	-25.7	-39.0

Source:
International Monetary Fund (IMF), World Economic Outlook Database, April 2004.

a Preliminary.

b Including portfolio debt and equity investment

c Including short- and long-term bank lending and possibly including some official flows owing to data limitations.

Private financial flows

The recovery of global growth and sustained low interest rates increased private financial flows to developing countries in 2003

The increase in private financial flows to developing countries in 2003 was driven by the recovery of global growth, the improved prospects for growth and stability in many developing and transition economies, and sustained low interest rates. Low interest rates and ample liquidity in developed economies encouraged international investors to search for higher returns and thus to purchase higher-risk financial instruments, including high-yield corporate bonds of developed countries and the bonds and stocks of emerging markets. At the same time, investors' overall appetite for risk increased with improving prospects for economic growth and corporate profitability. As investors' general perception of credit risk had been directly associated with their perception of risk in emerging market investments since 2000, investor sentiment towards these investments improved significantly during 2003.[1] In addition to these cyclical changes, there has been a diversification by emerging markets of their investor base to include institutional investors who seek to diversify their portfolios and reduce their volatility.

The robust export revenues of many developing countries and countries with economies in transition in 2003 helped to strengthen their external account balances and there was a substantial build-up of foreign currency reserves in many countries. These developments resulted in an improvement in the external debt-servicing capabilities and creditworthiness of many of these countries. In addition, countries that had recently experienced economic and financial turmoil, such as Brazil and Turkey, made progress in adjustment and enhanced their economic and financial stability. These changes were perceived by international investors to have improved the quality of credit of emerging markets overall. International credit rating agencies upgraded the ratings of a number of sovereign borrowers during the year, raising the average credit quality of these countries to its highest level since the beginning of 1998.[2] Rising fiscal and external deficits in some economies in transition in Central and Eastern Europe, particularly Hungary and Poland, in late 2003 and early 2004 raised concerns, but these were exceptions to the overall positive trend.[3]

Fall in cost of borrowing reversed in first half of 2004

The improvement in investor sentiment towards emerging markets was reflected in the falling cost of borrowing. In particular, there was a significant tightening of the spread between the yield on emerging market bonds and that of the benchmark United States Treasury bonds during 2003 (see figure III.1). The yield spread of emerging market bonds that constitutes the Emergency Markets Bond Index Plus (EMBI+) fell by 3.47 percentage points in the year. Among developing countries, the compressions in yield spreads were particularly sharp on bonds of a number of Latin American countries and Turkey, which had been pushed to very high levels early in the year by financial crises and geopolitical concerns. Among the economies in transition, yield spreads on Russian bonds reached historically low levels towards the end of 2003, benefiting from continued strong

Figure III.1.
Yield spreads on emerging market bonds, 1 January 2003-11 May 2004

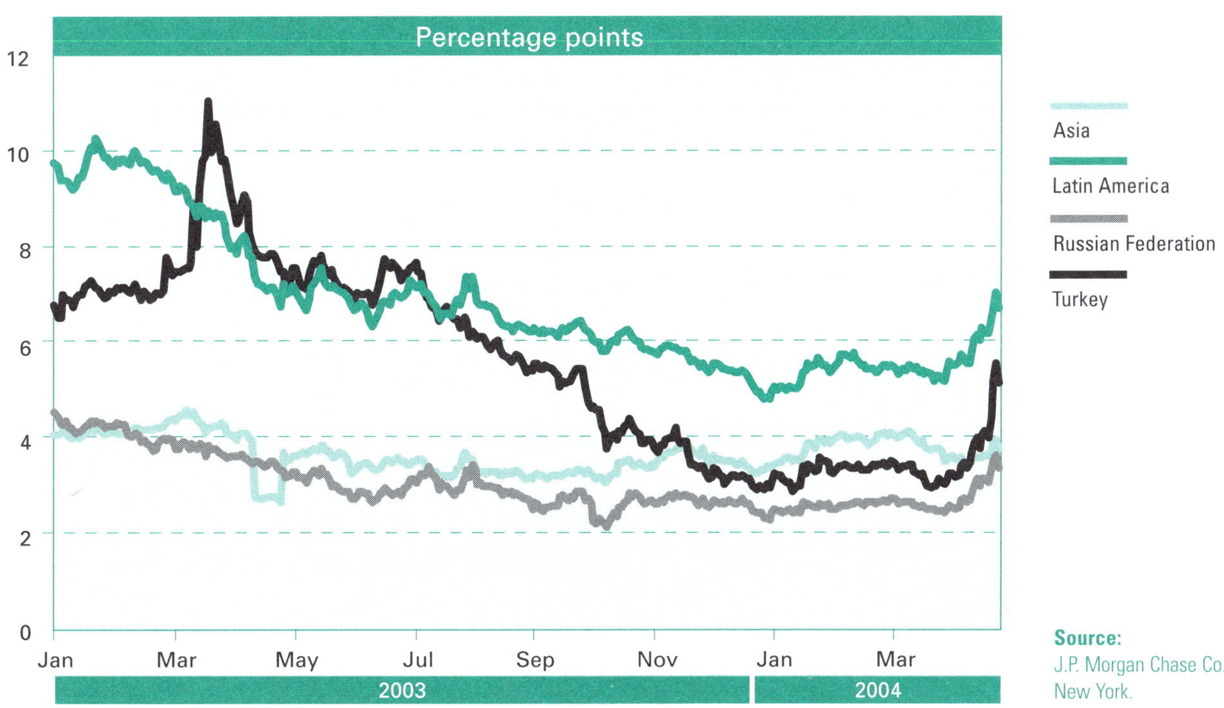

Source: J.P. Morgan Chase Co., New York.

economic growth, exports and the increase in the Russian Federation's sovereign bond rating to investment grade.

However, yield spreads on bonds of most emerging market countries widened in the first half of 2004, amid concerns about rising United States interest rates, renewed threats of terrorism and political uncertainty in some developing countries. This reversal reflects the vulnerability of these yield spreads, especially those of highly leveraged countries and countries with large external financing needs, to increases in international interest rates.

Increase in bond issuances in emerging markets in 2003

In the favourable international financial environment of 2003, net issuance of emerging market bonds increased substantially. Issuance was particularly strong in the second half of 2003, as borrowers took advantage of opportunities to raise funds at low interest rates and for longer maturities, including for debt management purposes. The increase in the issuance of sub-investment grade sovereign bonds during 2003 largely reflected the expanded access of less creditworthy developing countries to international financing. Corporate bond issuance also rebounded in 2003, with financing concentrated in Latin American countries and the Russian Federation.

The flow of new issues of sovereign bonds of emerging market countries in early 2004 slowed progressively from the surge at the beginning of the year. Issuers included countries that had not been active in international markets, such as Indonesia, Jamaica and Pakistan, as well as Brazil and Venezuela. As a result, many countries were able to prefinance a substantial portion of their 2004 funding needs. Corporate bond issues were less strong, with issuance concentrated in Brazil. High-yield local currency bonds (issued, inter alia, by Brazil, Turkey and Uruguay), some indexed to inflation, also attracted increased international funds in 2003 and early 2004, on prospects of declining local interest rates and exchange-rate appreciation.

Recovery in emerging stock markets

The surge in emerging market stock prices since early 2003 has triggered a recovery of equity issuances to a level higher than that in the few years prior to the bursting of the hi-tech bubble. Nevertheless, net equity portfolio investment remained a small proportion of total net financial flows to developing countries. There was a record level of issuance in Asia, driven mainly by increased activity in India and China, but also by that of other countries in the region. In contrast, equity issuance was low in Latin America, where there was still a net outflow of investment. Issuance was also weak in Central and Eastern Europe and CIS. In general, the strength of portfolio equity markets was supported by valuations that were still below the long-term average and prospects of continued improvement in corporate profits and debt levels.

Net bank lending turned positive

Net bank lending to developing countries, including net syndicated loans and short-term bank credit, turned positive in 2003 for the first year since the Asian financial crisis. Many borrowers in different regions took advantage of low international interest rates to refinance their debts. In addition, high domestic interest rates in some emerging market countries relative to international rates encouraged borrowing from international banks. Some corporations that could not access the international bond market also turned to international banks for credit.

Net bank inflows to Western Asia rebounded. There was also a net inflow to Eastern and Southern Asia, with an increase in net lending to India and the Republic of Korea. China received a large net inflow of short-term credit as market participants anticipated a currency revaluation. However, there were net repayments from Indonesia, the Philippines and Thailand, and sub-Saharan African countries also continued their net repayments to international banks. Latin American countries took advantage of the availability of bond financing as their main source of new credit and there was no recovery in new bank lending to the region; some countries, such as Brazil and Mexico, had large amortization payments. Among the economies in transition, new lending by European banks to the countries in Central and Eastern Europe acceding to EU increased. Net bank lending inflows to the Russian Federation also rose in response to the high quality of credit and continued strong economic growth.

Foreign direct investment stabilized in 2003 and is posed to recover

FDI flows to developing countries and economies in transition declined for a second consecutive year in 2003. The main factors behind the decline were the weak recovery in the global economy and the slower pace of privatization in many developing and transition economies. FDI was lower mainly in Latin American countries, such as Brazil and Mexico. Although inflows of FDI to Eastern and Southern Asia declined, the region was the largest recipient among emerging market countries. FDI to a number of countries in the region, notably China, India and Thailand, increased. FDI also declined in the EU accession countries in Central and Eastern Europe. Direct investment in developing countries and economies in transition is expected to recover in 2004 with improving financial stability and economic growth.

Official flows

ODA increased but net multilateral assistance flows were negligible

Net official flows continued to decline in 2003. Flows of official development assistance (ODA) from the member countries of the Development Assistance Committee (DAC) of the Organization for Economic Cooperation and Development (OECD) increased considerably, but net flows from the multilateral development and financial institutions fell to negligible levels. IMF was a net provider of $4.6 billion to the developing countries in 2003, down from $15 billion in 2002. This was offset by net repayments of a similar amount by developing countries to the multilateral development banks. The World Bank and the regional development banks, other than the Inter-American Development Bank, received net repayments. Net flows from countries with economies in transition to IMF continued in 2003, but were slightly below the level of the prior year. These declines stemmed mainly from the drop in loan packages to countries in financial crisis and were accompanied by increased repayments.

Continued repayments on IMF loans by developing countries in 2004 and the decline in IMF commitments in 2003 make it unlikely that official financial flows to the developing countries and countries with economies in transition will increase in the near term. IMF commitments to the developing countries plunged from $50.8 billion in 2002 to $17.6 billion in 2003. Although the number of commitments increased, the average size of loans declined sharply. There were only two IMF commitments of relatively substantial size, namely, the three-year $12.55 billion stand-by facility to Argentina in September to roll over other maturing credits and the two-year $2.1 billion stand-by loan to Colombia in support of its economic programme until 2004.[4] IMF commitments to countries with economies in transition slowed to $200 million as most of their multilateral financing originated from the European Bank for Reconstruction and Development (EBRD).

Concessional commitments for 2003 increased modestly and received a boost for the near term with the completion in May 2004 of the negotiations for the ninth replenishment of the Asian Development Fund, the concessional lending facility of the Asian Development Bank, covering the lending period 2005-2008. During the negotiations, donor member countries endorsed a replenishment of $7 billion (plus additional amounts for financing forgone interest on grants), a 25 per cent increase from the $5.6 billion total replenishment agreed in the eighth replenishment of the Asian Development Fund. Of the $7 billion, at least $3.7 billion will come from Asian Development Bank resources, with the remainder coming from donor and voluntary contributions. For the first time, a grants programme has been established and can account for up to 21 per cent of total operations for the lending period of the ninth replenishment of the Asian Development Fund.[5] The grants programme will, inter alia, assist poor countries in transition from post-conflict situations to peace and stability. The prospects for concessional finance could improve further with the timely completion of negotiations for the replenishment of International Development Association (IDA) resources (IDA 14) for the lending period 2004-2007 and those for the tenth replenishment of the African Development Fund, the concessional facility of the African Development Bank, covering the lending period 2005-2007.

Special factors contribute to record ODA flows

ODA from the member countries of DAC rose from $58.3 billion in 2002 to $68.5 billion in 2003 as major donors continued to deliver on their Monterrey pledges (see table III.2).[6] The increase in ODA in real terms (when the effects of inflation and exchange rates are taken into account) was 3.9 per cent and the amount was the highest ever recorded, both in nominal and in real terms. The "ODA effort", measured as the share of ODA in gross national income (GNI), rose from 0.23 per cent in 2002 to 0.25 per cent in 2003.[7] The major factors behind the rise in ODA in 2003 were the continuing growth in general bilateral grants and the start of the reconstruction aid to Iraq. It has been estimated that more than half of the increase in ODA in 2003 went into debt relief and peace and security assistance.

Net transfer of financial resources

Net financial transfer from developing countries continued to increase in 2003 ...

A net inward transfer of financial resources[8] supplements gross domestic saving and enables countries in the early and middle stages of development to raise investment levels above what could be financed by domestic saving. This might be expected as a normal pattern of development and yet developing countries as a group have made net outward financial transfers each year since 1997. In 2003, total net transfer from developing countries increased to an estimated $248 billion, surpassing the previous peak in 2002 (see table III.3). There was also a net outward financial transfer of $28 billion from countries with economies in transition.

... with increases in holdings of foreign reserves

While there were increases in net capital flows to many developing countries and countries with economies in transition in 2003, as discussed above, there were also increases in foreign reserve holdings in all developing regions, particularly in Eastern and Southern Asian countries with growing trade surpluses. The accumulation of reserves is mainly held in low-risk and low-yield government securities of developed countries. These investments have become an important source of financing for the external current-account and fiscal deficits of the United States.

The large net outward transfers of resources from Eastern and Southern Asian countries in 2003 resulted from continued strong export growth, which contributed importantly to strong economic growth and high domestic saving rates. The policies of these countries reflect the determination that the cost to large holdings of foreign reserves in terms of the domestic investment and imports forgone is outweighed by the benefits of a stable exchange rate and high export growth. Concerns have been raised, however, that

Table III.2.
Official development assistance of member countries of the Development Assistance Committee, 2003

	ODA (Millions of (dollars)	ODA/GNP (percentage)[a]	Real change 2002 to 2003[b] (percentage)
Australia	1 237	0.25	1.9
Austria	503	0.20	-20.7
Belgium	1 887	0.61	43.2
Canada	2 209	0.26	-5.1
Denmark	1 747	0.84	-12.8
Finland	556	0.34	-0.2
France	7 337	0.41	9.9
Germany	6 694	0.28	3.9
Greece	356	0.21	4.0
Ireland	510	0.41	5.1
Italy	2 393	0.16	-16.7
Japan	8 911	0.20	-8.9
Luxembourg	189	0.80	5.6
Netherlands	4 059	0.81	-1.3
New Zealand	169	0.23	9.3
Norway	2 043	0.92	4.7
Portugal	298	0.21	-24.8
Spain	2 030	0.25	-4.6
Sweden	2 100	0.70	-14.1
Switzerland	1 297	0.38	19.5
United Kingdom	6 166	0.34	11.9
United States	15 791	0.14	16.9
Total DAC	68 483	0.25	3.9
Average country effort (unweighted)	--	0.41	--
Memorandum items:			
EU countries combined	36 825	0.35	2.2
European Commission	8 147	--	1.6

Source:
Organisation for Economic Cooperation and Development, news release, OECD On-line, Paris, 16 April 2004 (www.oecd.org/dac).

a Beginning in 2001, the ratio as reported by the DAC secretariat was that of ODA to gross national income (GNI) instead of to gross national product (GNP). The change has been only in terminology, introduced with the 1993 revision of the System of National Accounts (United Nations publication, Sales No. E.94.XVII.4), inasmuch as GNI is GNP as it would currently be measured.

b Taking account of both inflation and exchange-rate movements.

Table III.3.
Net transfer of financial resources to developing economies and economies in transition, 1995-2003

Billions of dollars									
	1995	1996	1997	1998	1999	2000	2001	2002	2003[a]
Developing economies	43.6	21.2	-3.4	-36.8	-122.8	-183.3	-151.3	-203.5	-247.5
Africa	6.6	-5.0	-4.3	15.9	6.0	-23.9	-11.8	-3.4	-15.8
Sub-Saharan (excluding Nigeria and South Africa)	7.7	5.7	7.6	12.2	9.0	3.2	8.3	6.6	6.6
Eastern and Southern Asia	26.2	23.8	-28.7	-130.2	-134.1	-108.2	-107.9	-138.6	-144.6
Western Asia	11.9	0.4	4.7	31.3	-6.6	-51.0	-37.2	-30.3	-36.1
Latin America	-1.1	2.0	24.8	46.1	11.8	-0.2	5.5	-31.1	-51.1
Economies in transition	3.3	10.7	17.2	16.8	-5.9	-32.6	-20.0	-17.6	-27.8
Memorandum item:									
Heavily indebted poor countries (HIPCs)	6.9	7.3	7.8	9.6	10.0	6.5	8.3	8.7	11.0

Source:
UN/DESA, based on International Monetary Fund (IMF), World Economic Outlook, April 2004 database, and IMF, *Balance of Payments Statistics*.

a Preliminary estimate.

these economies should allow appreciation in their exchange rates and achieve more balance in growth between the tradable and non-tradable sectors.

The net outward resource transfer from Latin America in 2003 was, in contrast, a result of continued compression of domestic expenditure in adjustment to financial crisis. While export growth strengthened substantially, imports recovered only modestly. Besides being used to make debt repayments, financial outflows were also used to increase official reserve holdings for precautionary purposes.

International financial cooperation for development

Official development finance

Official development assistance

ODA continues to increase ...

Official development assistance (ODA) is projected to increase to $77 billion in 2006, a 32 per cent rise in real terms over the total recorded in 2002, as donors continue to deliver on pledges made in connection with the International Conference on Financing for Development, held in Monterrey, Mexico, in March 2002. EU reports that member States are firmly on schedule to reach, or even exceed, their target to increase collectively their average ODA from 0.33 per cent of GNI in 2002 to 0.39 per cent of GNI in 2006.[9] The

United States had also pledged in Monterrey to raise ODA by $5 billion a year by 2006, a 50 per cent increase in core development assistance over the level in 2002, through the establishment of the Millennium Challenge Account (MCA). In January 2004, the United States Government adopted the law to establish the Millennium Challenge Corporation (MCC); in February 2004, an interim chief executive officer was agreed by the MCC Board of Directors and the Board selected the first group of countries eligible for MCA assistance in May.[10]

... but needs a further substantial boost to meet Millennium Development Goals

Despite the projected increase in ODA, it is widely agreed that attainment of the Millennium Development Goals will require a substantial further increase in ODA to developing countries, estimated to be at least twice that of 2002 levels. For many of the poorer countries where the challenge is most acute, most, if not all, assistance flows will have to be on a grant basis; this, in turn, will require donors to provide a higher proportion of ODA in grant terms.

Grant finance, which was on the decline in the 1990s, seems to be recovering.[11] The IDA-13 replenishment provided for a larger share of assistance in the form of grants to eligible countries, and such initiatives as the new Global Fund to Fight AIDS, Tuberculosis and Malaria provide only grants. The international community should ensure that the increasing provision of grant assistance continues. In this regard, a substantial and timely agreement on the funding of IDA-14 will be a critical affirmation of the commitment of the international community to mobilizing the resources for its support to strong, results-oriented action by partners in the poorest countries. It is also important that the provision of assistance for peace and security purposes, such as the war on terrorism and rebuilding efforts in war-affected zones, does not crowd out development aid.

Enhancing aid effectiveness

Enhancing aid effectiveness is the focus of global and regional initiatives

In addition to increasing ODA levels, another step identified by the development community to lessen the gap between current ODA flows and the amount needed to achieve the Millennium Development Goals is to increase aid effectiveness, including reducing the administrative component of ODA disbursements through better-harmonized aid procedures and improved donor coordination. The Declaration on Harmonization, adopted at the High-level Forum of donor agencies in Rome in February 2003, involved a pledge to this effect and led to the creation of the DAC Working Party on Aid Effectiveness and Donor Practices. The Working Party has the responsibility for facilitating harmonization and alignment of donor practices with country strategies.[12]

These issues were also the focus of the Second International Roundtable on Managing for Development Results, held in Marrakech, Morocco, in February 2004. This conference focused on the need for recipient countries to manage their resources for development results, and for development agencies to give the highest priority to strengthening recipient countries' capacity. The Roundtable agreed on a set of core principles governing development partners in their development programmes.[13]

Aid effectiveness is also being addressed at the regional level. The European Commission, for instance, has put forward proposals aimed at expediting progress on the pledges made at the Barcelona Summit to achieve closer coordination of policies and harmonization of aid procedures of EU member States.[14] The Economic Commission for Africa (ECA) is engaged in a joint effort with DAC in creating an institutional framework for mutual accountability between Africa and its partners. An important function of this alliance is to conduct joint Africa/OECD reviews of the impact of partner country policies on Africa's development cooperation programmes. The New Partnership for Africa's Development (NEPAD) (document A/57/304, annex) prioritizes the development issues of the region. Its Peer Review Mechanism on economic and political governance will monitor country performance in the field of economic management, human rights, corruption and democracy from the point of view of attaining development goals. With a view to enhancing partnership with development partners, the Africa Partnership Forum was established to focus on strategic and political issues related to the implementation of the NEPAD programme of action. The Forum has identified four priorities for action, namely, peace and security, HIV/AIDS, education, and economic growth and wealth-creation, intended to lead to the achievement of the Millennium Development Goals.

Concerns about the poor prospects of many sub-Saharan countries for attaining the Millennium Development Goals have also led the United Kingdom of Great Britain and Northern Ireland to launch a Commission for Africa. The purpose of the Commission is to advance internationally agreed development goals in the region. The high-level commission, in collaboration with the United Nations, the World Bank and the academic community and building on the work of NEPAD, will assess conditions and development policies in African countries in priority areas, including trade, governance, economic policy, aid, debt relief, health and environment, and conflict resolution.[15]

In order to address the special needs of countries in or emerging from conflict, the World Bank established the Post-Conflict Fund (PCF) in 1997 to support the transition of countries from conflict and the Trust Fund for Low Income Countries Under Stress (LICUS) in 2004 to, inter alia, help poor countries ineligible for IDA funds to strengthen their institutions and build capacity for delivery of social services. For these groups of countries, timely, adequate and predictable assistance is critical to removing institutional capacity limitations and to facilitating the rebuilding effort.

Mechanisms to improve the flexibility and efficiency of existing aid flows need to be further developed. Two such challenges are to so tailor the forms and concessionality of aid as to make financing appropriate for poor countries suffering from debt problems or external shocks and to design more proactive approaches to concessionality for countries not otherwise eligible for concessional finance so as to help them achieve the Millennium Development Goals.[16]

New and innovative sources of development finance

Potential new sources of development finance receiving increased attention

Although several donor countries have pledged to increase their ODA over the next several years, it is questionable whether the volume of ODA needed to achieve the Millennium Development Goals and to meet other development needs will be reached over the medium-and-longer term. The task before the donor community, therefore, is not only to mobilize resources to meet the immediate need to speed progress towards the attainment of the Millennium Development Goals, but also to formulate a strategy that will ensure the predictable and necessary flow of resources over the long term. Even if the Millennium Development Goals were universally attained by the target date, they would reflect only partial achievement of the overall development task. Even with poverty reduced by half, poverty reduction will still be a global challenge; success in other areas will also be far from complete and a sustained flow of financial resources will continue to be required for the purpose of confronting the challenges in these areas.

The critical need for increased development finance has led to the consideration, within a number of Governments and multilateral and regional bodies, of a wide variety of possible new mechanisms for increasing the supply of international financial resources for development. Debate on, and study of, an international finance facility (IFF), the United Kingdom's proposal to frontload aid to help meet the Millennium Development Goals, are ongoing.[17] Other initiatives include a special fund jointly proposed by the Governments of France and Brazil aimed at mobilizing financing through innovative means, including selective taxation, to help reduce hunger and poverty.[18]

Pursuant to paragraph 44 of the Monterrey Consensus of the International Conference on Financing for Development,[19] which calls for the consideration of possible innovative sources of finance in the appropriate forums, the General Assembly will address the subject at its fifty-ninth session. IMF and the World Bank will jointly report on mechanisms for mobilizing additional financial resources for development at the Annual Meetings in October 2004. In light of the urgent need of developing countries for additional financial resources for development, the onus is on the international community to move expeditiously from debate and analysis of the proposed new sources of finance to decisions on feasible proposals to be implemented.

Multilateral development cooperation

Poverty Reduction Strategy Papers (PRSPs)

More countries prepare Poverty Reduction Strategy Papers (PRSPs) focused on achieving the Millennium Development Goals ...

A shared vision of development by national and international authorities is key to coherent policy formulation and international cooperation efforts. In this context, there has been increasing recognition that countries with different structural conditions can take diverse but still successful approaches to achieving sustained development and that there needs to be effective country ownership of development strategies. In low-income countries, the Poverty Reduction Strategy Paper (PRSP), a document that describes a country's near-term economic and social programmes to promote sustainable growth and reduce poverty, has become a key vehicle for designing and implementing programmes through which to reach the Millennium Development Goals. International financial institutions and other multilateral development organizations increasingly use PRSPs as decision-making tools, inter alia, in the formulation of the United Nations common country assessments and United Nations Development Assistance Frameworks (UNDAFs), in the design of the World Bank's country assistance strategies and in decisions relating to the provision of aid and debt relief by multilateral and bilateral institutions. As of end-January 2004, 35 countries had completed and were implementing PRSPs and 18 countries had prepared interim PRSPs; of the total, 30 countries were in Africa. With growing experience of PRSPs, they are increasingly focused on the achievement of the Millennium Development Goals. Government ownership of PRSPs has improved, as shown by more engagement by parliaments and improved dialogue between PRSP teams and line ministries. There are signs of a shift in spending priorities towards those that are poverty-reducing.[20]

... but challenges remain

Notwithstanding these gains, challenges remain in the preparation of PRSPs.[21] For instance, the PRSP process must be more integrated with the decision-making process, including, particularly, the budget; similarly, the involvement of sectoral ministries and representative bodies, such as parliaments, must be expanded. Similarly, although the implementation of PRSPs has become a more open and participatory exercise, some non-governmental organizations remain dissatisfied with the process. The links of country strategies and macroeconomic policies to the Millennium Development Goals should be deepened and the financial, policy and institutional constraints on the achievement of medium-term development goals need to be addressed. In particular, enhancing country ownership requires the full incorporation of country development priorities into PRSPs, including prioritization of the main national objectives. Supporting capacity-building, including data collection and analysis, is needed to enable the preparation of strategies that are truly country-driven.

Heavily Indebted Poor Countries (HIPC) Initiative and debt sustainability in low-income countries

The HIPC Initiative progresses slowly ...

There has been growing concern that the Heavily Indebted Poor Countries (HIPC) Initiative has been slow in bringing countries to their "decision points" and then to their "completion points". As of April 2004, and almost five years after the Initiative was enhanced, only 27 HIPCs out of the 38 countries potentially eligible for assistance under the Initiative had reached their decision point and are receiving debt relief. Of the 27 countries, 13 had reached completion point, where full debt relief was accorded.[22]

The delays in reaching the decision point have been attributed to problems in preparing PRSPs or meeting fiscal targets and in the international financial institutions' evaluations of the success of the HIPCs in establishing a track record of implementing sound economic policies. Reaching this phase has been especially challenging for the 11 countries that have been considered for the HIPC Initiative but have not yet reached their decision point. Some have not yet begun to establish a track record under a Fund-supported programme. With the HIPC Initiative set to expire by end-2004, there is concern that some countries might not benefit from the programme. In this regard, options concerning extension of the date of the expiration of the HIPC Initiative are being studied and the staffs of the World Bank and IMF will present their recommendations to their respective Boards by September 2004.

... and some completion point countries continue to have unsustainable debt levels

Despite having reached their completion point, some HIPCs have not achieved debt sustainability. With hindsight, it appears that this is because of unrealistic assumptions about interest rates, exports and economic growth used in the calculation of the amount of relief needed for them to reach a sustainable debt level.

The need for additional debt relief beyond the HIPC Initiative was reaffirmed by some creditor Governments at the High-level Dialogue on Financing for Development held in October 2003 at United Nations Headquarters when they agreed on the need to revisit the issue of "topping up", a mechanism to provide additional debt relief to a HIPC that is found to need additional relief to meet its debt sustainability target at the completion point. It was noted, however, that this was only part of the solution and, for many low-income countries, maintaining debt sustainability required significantly increased assistance in the form of grants. It has also been suggested that the HIPC Initiative include measures to overcome external and natural disaster shocks, which would encompass, inter alia, making available quick-disbursing contingency financing by the international financial institutions, based on annual reassessments of debt sustainability and policy adequacy.

A new framework for debt sustainability is proposed

In April 2004, the Development Committee of the World Bank and IMF expressed broad support for the principles underlying a proposed framework for debt sustainability in all low-income countries, while acknowledging that the modalities and operational implications remained to be clarified.[23]

It also underlined the need for a consistent and coordinated approach among borrowers, creditors and donors, to ensure that resources were provided to low-income countries on appropriate terms, including the degree of concessionality and level of grant financing. The Development Committee also welcomed the work of the Bank and the Fund on measures and instruments to assist low-income countries in dealing with exogenous shocks (see the discussion below) and urged them to accelerate their work for early consideration by their Boards.

Financial cooperation for middle-income countries

About two thirds of the world's poor (as measured by those living on less than US$1 a day) are in the middle-income countries. Most of these countries have set priorities for policies and investments that aim to reduce poverty by helping poor people contribute to economic growth and share in the benefits. Social spending has been increased and has become better targeted. Nevertheless, poverty has risen in a number of these countries. Efforts to combat poverty have been thwarted in many middle-income countries by a vicious circle of low economic growth and persistent inequality. It is therefore urgent to explore what could and should be done at the national and international levels to achieve effective results in the fight against poverty.

New forms of international financial cooperation explored

At the national level, to achieve faster sustained growth and poverty reduction, middle-income countries need to further strengthen their social, structural and sectoral policies with a special emphasis on reducing inequality. Despite having greater physical, financial and human resources than low-income countries for social and anti-poverty programmes, middle-income countries need strong international support to meet Millennium Development Goals. These countries are facing some specific problems, including vulnerability to volatile capital flows. Effective international mechanisms are needed to respond quickly to help these countries protect the poor and maintain ongoing reforms in the event of external shock or major changes in a country's condition. In May 2002, the World Bank introduced the "deferred drawdown option" (DDO) to protect core structural programmes, should a country face reduced access to international financial markets. Several countries have already arranged DDO facilities.[24]

In many countries, the maintenance of sustainable macroeconomic balances, especially fiscal positions, is constraining investment in infrastructure, education, health and housing. To address this problem, the Rio Group proposed discussing possible innovative financial mechanisms to ease the financial constraints that confront the member countries in their efforts to alleviate poverty and secure the long-term economic and social development of the region without undermining macroeconomic stability.[25] Although there has already been a gradual move towards setting targets for the government primary balance (that is to say, excluding interest payments), consideration should be given to the possibility of applying other improved or adjusted concepts of the fiscal target. In particular, the exclusion of capital investment expenditures from the fiscal target should be considered as these expenditures both contribute to the accumulation of assets—which can offset liabilities—and have a counter-cyclical potential during crises and adjustment. Such exclusion would imply a move towards balance-sheet accounting. In addition, the treatment of the financial results of public enterprises should be more akin to that applied to private sector enterprises. This may imply excluding the financial results of such enterprises from fiscal targets, as already practiced in EU and taken into account by the Stability and Growth Pact. This initiative reflects a general change in thinking about development finance.

Continuing reform of the international financial architecture

Crisis prevention activities

In crisis prevention, the major focus in the year under review was on the early identification of vulnerabilities, first debt-related vulnerabilities, enhancement of the pro-growth orientation of surveillance and its impact, and better coordination of multilateral and regional surveillance. Also, new incidents of corporate fraud and mismanagement renewed concerns about corporate financial reporting, auditing and governance, especially in developed countries.

IMF surveillance

Multilateral surveillance of national economic and financial policies, as well as of developments in global markets, particularly by IMF, is the chief global tool for promoting macroeconomic and financial stability, and thereby contributing to the prevention of financial crises. In addition to macroeconomic policy, IMF surveillance addresses structural and institutional policies, the transparency of countries' policies, the observance of various standards and codes, and financial sector soundness. Along with expanded surveillance coverage, there have been efforts to increase the transparency of IMF assessments of member countries via increased publication of Article IV surveillance reports and related documents, as well as reports on the use of Fund resources.

Inadequate surveillance of developed countries is a source of concern ...

Despite progress, considerable work remains to be done on crisis anticipation and prevention. There have been concerns that Fund surveillance is asymmetric, that is to say, focused on developing countries, even though the policies of the major developed countries have the greatest global impact, a development that may require a rebalancing of the focus of vulnerability assessments towards developed countries. As these countries no longer use Fund resources, strengthening the impact of surveillance on the policies of developed economies is likely to continue to be one of the major challenges in the efforts to further improve overall surveillance.

... and surveillance of developing countries is being refined

In conducting surveillance, it is often not enough to inform the country's authorities of a problem. More importantly, surveillance has to contribute to helping countries find economically, politically and socially acceptable solutions to their difficulties. A case in point is the greater focus on improving public expenditure management in middle-income countries, where protracted fiscal adjustment in many of them has had an adverse impact on public investment, particularly in infrastructure, and hence on medium-term growth prospects. To help minimize inappropriate constraints on public investment, the Fund is now working on fiscal policy and accounting issues related to public investment, with a view to finding ways to ensure that productive public investment is given increased priority and appropriately protected during periods of fiscal adjustment.[26]

It has also been argued that, in some cases, concentration on the monitoring of the implementation of the Fund programmes has led to inadequate assessments of the overall direction of policies and that the emergence of serious imbalances has been overlooked. Accordingly, there have been calls to strengthen surveillance in programme countries, particularly in those countries that have had IMF arrangements over an extended period of time, by stepping back from monitoring programme implementation to undertake a critical assessment of policies from a medium-term perspective.[27]

In some cases, overly optimistic growth projections were an important element in the failure to identify the vulnerabilities. Hence, greater realism of macroeconomic projections and more conservative assessment of sustainable debt levels in the event of adverse circumstances are called for in vulnerability analyses. More generally, Fund surveillance has not always been able to identify vulnerabilities sufficiently early and bring about needed changes in response. In particular, not only IMF but also policy makers in emerging market countries and participants in financial markets were slow to recognize the scale of the debt build-up, the balance sheet problems and the associated risks in these countries. Excessive accumulation of debt played a critical role in most recent crisis episodes: capital account crises invariably involve the loss of creditor confidence in a country's ability to voluntarily continue to service its debts.

Increased focus on assessing debt sustainability ...

Better assessment of a country's debt burden and its ability to service that debt is seen as particularly important with regard to both crisis prevention and crisis resolution. The international community has thus sought to strengthen its understanding of debt sustainability and the policies and measures that would help borrowing countries service their debts during difficult periods without an unrealistically large contraction in national income and expenditure. Particular attention is being paid to debt sustainability assessment, balance-sheet analysis, liquidity management and financial soundness indicators.[28] These major areas of work directed towards strengthening surveillance are interlinked and centred on improved capacity to address debt problems.

In 2002, IMF introduced a new analytical framework for assessing both fiscal and external debt sustainability in countries with significant access to international financial markets.[29] This framework is now being applied both in the context of surveillance and in the use of IMF resources. It can also guide debtors and creditors in their discussions on how much debt reduction is required in order to reach a manageable schedule of repayments over time. It does not take explicit account of the social impact of debt servicing, although this could be addressed in a parallel public expenditure review.

... with new modalities introduced

The balance-sheet approach complements traditional analysis of flow variables, such as current-account and fiscal balance, by examining stocks and structures of assets and liabilities. According to IMF, the approach provides a useful analytical framework within which to detect currency mismatches (a predominance of liabilities denominated in foreign currency over assets denominated in national currency) and other balance-sheet weaknesses of an economy and its main sectors. This should help to strengthen vulnerability analysis and policy advice.[30] Unlike the debt sustainability framework, balance-sheet analysis is not yet a standard element of Fund surveillance. As balance-sheet analysis is very data-intensive, establishing the necessary database will take much time and effort in many emerging economies. Besides, like the liquidity management framework and financial soundness indicators, the balance sheet approach requires further analytical work. Moreover, given that all these approaches, including the debt sustainability framework, are targeting basically the problem of debt, it is important to assess how they relate to each other in order to form an integrated view of their implementation.

Many of the aforementioned weaknesses may have their origin in the inability of surveillance to assess individual country economies on a frequent basis. Article IV consultations, the central instrument for country surveillance, are conducted only every 12-18 months or even less frequently. Consequently, there may be a need for an enhanced framework of vulnerability assessment to better monitor developing threats to stability. This requires further improvements in data capacity.

More frequent and better-targeted assessment may be needed

A closely related issue is the proper targeting of surveillance. It is essential that surveillance be tailored to the circumstances of each country. Over the past several years, surveillance coverage has broadened significantly. However, the policy message given by the surveillance exercise must not be diluted by a formulaic approach. In many cases, simplicity and speed may produce much better results than complexity and the associated slowness of the overall process.

Regional cooperation

Regional monetary cooperation could be an important element of global financial stability

Financial crises of the 1990s have reignited efforts to promote regional monetary cooperation with a view to achieving greater regional financial stability. In this regard, the most noteworthy development has been new initiatives to further monetary and financial cooperation in East Asia. In May 2000, 10 member States of the Association of Southeast Asian Nations (ASEAN) plus China, Japan and the Republic of Korea adopted the Chiang Mai Initiative. The "ASEAN+3" countries proposed to strengthen regional cooperation through an expanded network of swap facilities among their central banks. The initiative involves extending the existing ASEAN swap arrangements and establishing a network of bilateral swap arrangements among the ASEAN countries, China, Japan and the Republic of Korea.

Since then, the ASEAN countries have agreed on the new expanded ASEAN swap arrangement. Also, a consensus has been reached over the basic framework and main principles for the bilateral swap arrangements. As of May 2004, 16 bilateral swap arrangements (out of a possible 30) had been concluded with a combined size of $36.5 billion.[31]

The countries also considered possibilities for strengthening the regional policy dialogue and cooperation in surveillance and monitoring, including of capital flows. It was decided, however, that the surveillance system that had been put in place in 1999, and was basically confined to semi-annual informal general discussion of the global and regional economic outlook was, for the time being, adequate to oversee the operations of the Chiang Mai Initiative. The efforts currently being made at the institutional level are to develop early warning systems and to monitor short-term capital flows. There is an understanding that once the network of bilateral swap arrangements is completed and if a decision is made to multilateralize the bilateral swap arrangements, a more formalized and rigorous surveillance system may be needed. In May 2004, the ASEAN+3 finance ministers agreed to review the Chiang Mai Initiative further to explore ways of enhancing its effectiveness.[32]

Policy discussions are also under way in other developing-country regional groupings including the West African Economic and Monetary Union, the Central African Economic and Monetary Community, the Eastern Caribbean Currency Union, and the group of Maghreb countries associated with EU. The proliferation of such regional arrangements raises issues of their relationship with the global governance structures. In the case of the Chiang Mai Initiative, it has been decided that the activation of loans beyond 10 per cent of the agreed bilateral lines will take place in the context of IMF-supported programmes. It has also been decided that the bilateral swap arrangements should remain complementary and supplementary IMF facilities, at least until a formal regional surveillance system is brought into existence. For its part, IMF is increasing its participation in regional surveillance groups and working towards better coordination between the discussions with regional institutions and those with individual members.

Recent developments in the area of international standards and codes, financial regulation and supervision

The eleventh meeting of the Financial Stability Forum (FSF) in Rome on 29 and 30 March 2004 discussed, inter alia, the issues raised by incidents of high-profile securities fraud and market abuses, such as the case of Parmalat, which highlighted the need to further strengthen financial reporting frameworks, as well as the implementation of existing standards. It welcomed the creation, on 5 February 2004, of a special Chairmen's Task Force by the International Organization of Securities Commissions (IOSCO) Technical Committee to look into these matters.[33] The Task Force is to identify new issues arising from the recent incidents, review implementation of existing standards and suggest responses aimed at producing appropriate regulatory incentives. The IOSCO Technical Committee also decided to assess implementation of principles relating to auditors' independence and oversight and to develop standards relating to late trading, market timing and governance in the mutual funds industry. The Council of the International Federation of Accountants (IFAC) adopted in November 2003 a set of reforms to strengthen international audit standard-setting, including the proposal to create a public interest oversight board.[34]

Efforts to prevent accounting and auditing irregularities continue

The discussions also stressed the need to improve information exchange, international cooperation, and the corresponding regulatory arrangements in dealing with large firms with complex corporate structures operating in multiple jurisdictions. In this connection, the Forum commended International Accounting Standards Board (IASB) improvements of existing standards and progress in the convergence of the standards of IASB and those of the United States Financial Accounting Standards Board (FASB). In March 2004, the European Commission also proposed a new directive on statutory audit in the EU.[35] The "fast-track" directive is expected to be adopted by mid-2005. Similar to the Sarbanes-Oxley Act in the United States, the directive would require companies to set up independent audit committees with rotating auditors, whereby all auditors and audit firms would undergo quality assurance reviews. An EU-wide audit regulatory committee and extensive cooperation between member regulators would be established.

Primary responsibility for preventing accounting and auditing irregularities in public companies lies with the Boards of Directors and management of the companies themselves. The OECD Principles of Corporate Governance thus constitute one of the 12 core sets of standards and codes whose widespread adoption the Financial Stability Forum advocates. In response to accounting scandals in industrialized countries, OECD has recently revised its Principles of Corporate Governance and has brought forward the assessment of the principles to 2004. The revised Principles envision strengthening the capacity of companies' shareholders in corporate governance. Also, in cooperation with the World Bank, OECD has established a Global Corporate Governance Forum to promote continuing dialogue on corporate governance.

On 24 March 2004, the IMF Executive Board reviewed the Twelve-month Pilot Programme of Anti-Money Laundering and Combating the Financing of Terrorism (AML/CFT) assessments. The Board also endorsed the revised 40+8 Recommendations of the Financial Action Task Force (FATF) as the new standard for AML/CFT, as well as the revised methodology to assess that standard.[36] The exercise has shown that many low-income countries face challenges in implementing AML/CFT measures owing to insufficient resources and training. Compliance with the newer eight Special Recommendations on Terrorist Financing also remains weak in many countries.

Measures against money laundering and financing of terrorism are strengthened

As part of its efforts to strengthen measures against the financing of terrorism, FATF held a special seminar on 24 February 2004, focusing on the risks posed by alternative remittance systems, cash couriers, non-profit organizations and the links between narcotics trafficking and terrorist financing. In the meantime, FATF announced in February 2004 that it had removed Ukraine and Egypt from its list of Non-Cooperative Countries and Territories (NCCTs), owing to substantial reforms in the two countries.[37]

Basel Committee agrees on new Capital Accord ...

Meanwhile, the Basel Committee on Banking Supervision (BCBS) is finalizing the New Basel Capital Accord (Basel II).[38] In May 2004, the Committee announced that it had achieved consensus on the remaining issues regarding the proposals for a new international capital standard. The final text of the new framework was scheduled to be published at the end of June 2004. The implementation of the New Accord, which is mainly designed for large, complex and internationally active banking organizations, is scheduled to take effect in member countries of the Group of Ten by the end of 2006 for the "standardized approach" and the "foundation internal-ratings based (IRB) approach" to the measurement of credit risk, and by the end of 2007 for the "advanced IRB approach".[39] Work has already begun in a number of developed and emerging market economies on draft rules that would integrate the new Basel capital framework with national capital regimes. For many developing countries, moving to the New Accord may not be a top priority; in many cases, it could be more important to address deficiencies in existing supervisory and capital adequacy frameworks and loan-loss provisioning, if necessary with assistance from the international community.[40]

... but there are concerns that it may increase the pro-cyclicality of bank lending to developing countries

One of the major concerns related to the New Accord is that its higher risk-sensitivity may increase the "pro-cyclicality" of bank lending, especially to developing countries. In this regard, the architects of Basel II note that supervisory oversight and market discipline should reinforce the incentive for banks to maintain a cushion of capital above the minimum so as to have a margin of protection in downturns. They are also urging financial institutions to adopt risk management practices that take better account of the evolution of risk over time and that are not excessively vulnerable to short-term changes. Nevertheless, the regulators' success in dealing with this problem remains a concern, as Basel II, like traditional prudential financial regulation in general, does not fully take into account the macroeconomic context. Hence, in order to prevent excessive risk-taking during boom periods, there may be a need for regulatory instruments that better recognize the connection between macroeconomic cycles and risk-taking by financial institutions.

Towards more stable debt structures

Developing countries' inability to borrow abroad in their own currencies is a source of volatility

One of the major reasons for the persistence of financial troubles in many middle-income countries seems to be the high volatility of their debt service relative to their capacity to pay. Unlike developed countries, most emerging market economies cannot borrow abroad in their own currencies even if they have sound policies and strong institutions.[41] Movements in the exchange rate therefore affect the domestic burden of debt service and this is often a more important source of vulnerability than the volatility associated with fluctuations in income. Also, even in foreign currency terms, interest rates on emerging market debt are not only higher than those on developed-country debt, but also subject to large fluctuations when markets change their assessments of the riskiness of a country's debt.

In the past, such changes have been the source of sudden and sharp increases in developing countries' debt burdens and a cause of severe external debt difficulties for some individual countries. Many emerging economies faced difficulties with debt indicators at levels that were equivalent to, or even significantly lower than, those in many developed countries. This can occur even if a country's macroeconomic policies are sound. Past experience includes several cases where countries previously viewed as having a sustainable debt situation subsequently experienced an external debt crisis.

Accordingly, along with further improvement of debt sustainability analysis, the international community is working on ways to help debtor countries better monitor their evolving debt-servicing obligations and, particularly, avoid rapid increases in such obligations during external crises. This entails prudent debt management, reserves policy, prudent use of capital account regulations, access to international liquidity, and reducing volatility at the source. Many developing countries, with support from such international institutions as the United Nations Conference on Trade and Development (UNCTAD), IMF, the World Bank and the Commonwealth Secretariat, are building capacity in sovereign debt management.[42]

New debt instruments are required to cope better with volatility

To lower the exposure to the risk of debt crises, there have been proposals to issue debt instruments whose debt-service obligations fluctuate with the countries' capacity-to-pay, including GDP-indexed bonds.[43] There is also some interest in exploring financing arrangements that include guarantee schemes and other mechanisms to reduce the cost of debt during crisis periods. Another proposal calls for international financial institutions to help develop an international market in a basket of inflation-indexed developing-country currencies to allow lending in each country's consumer price index (CPI)-indexed local currency. According to the proponents of this proposal, a more complete set of market instruments will enhance developing countries' ability to cope with volatility.[44]

Another, even more important, strategy is to foster the development of domestic-currency bond markets. The development of these markets has the potential to reduce the exposure of emerging economies to maturity– and exchange–rate mismatches and to the risks of sudden loss of access to foreign capital markets.

Asian initiatives are encouraging the development of domestic currency and bond markets

In some cases, enhanced regional cooperation may accelerate the development of bond markets by combining relatively small national markets into a deeper regional one. The process of regional bond market integration and development is most advanced in East Asia where initiatives to promote the development of local and regional bond markets include the Asian Bond Fund (ABF) and the Asian Bond Markets Initiative (ABMI). The latter is a joint project of Asia-Pacific Economic Cooperation (APEC) and ASEAN + 3 covering many areas of bond market development.

In June 2003, the Executives' Meeting of East Asia-Pacific Central Banks Group (EMEAP)[45] launched the Asian Bond Fund 1 (ABF1).[46] An initial funding of $1 billion was contributed by the 11 members of EMEAP. The purpose of ABF1 is to invest a small portion of the United States dollar reserves held by the member central banks in United States dollar-denominated bonds issued by Asian sovereign and quasi-sovereign issuers in EMEAP economies (other than Australia, Japan and New Zealand), rather than in United States Treasury bonds. The Fund is managed by the Bank for International Settlements (BIS) in accordance with specific benchmarks. As of April 2004, ABF1 was fully invested.

After the launch of ABF1, the members of EMEAP started discussions on ABF2 which will invest in participating countries' local currency sovereign and quasi-sovereign bonds. In April 2004, EMEAP announced a preliminary framework for ABF2.[47] EMEAP is aiming to design ABF2 in such a way as to facilitate investment by other public and private sector investors along with central banks. The new framework consists of a Pan-Asian Bond Index Fund (PAIF) and a Fund of Bond Funds (FoBF).The Pan-Asian Bond Index Fund is a single bond index fund investing in local currency-denominated bonds in EMEAP economies. The Fund of Bond Funds is a two-layered structure with a parent fund investing in a number of country sub-funds comprising local currency-denominated-bonds issued in the respective EMEAP economies.

The Asian Bond Fund initiative represents an important step in strengthening regional financial cooperation in East Asia and in promoting the demand for regionally issued bonds. The development of bond market infrastructure and synchronization of rules and regulations on cross-border flows is at least equally important. This includes, but is not limited to, the harmonization of tax, regulatory, legal and accounting rules and regulations; a gradual relaxation of capital controls; the development of the derivatives markets to hedge the underlying credit and currency risks; efficient clearing and settlement mechanisms; a consistent credit-rating process; and work on securitization and credit guarantees to enhance the quality of bonds. The Asian Bond Markets Initiative is addressing some of these issues to make local bond markets more accessible to Asian borrowers. Given the complexity of the issues that should be resolved, a truly integrated regional bond market in Asia will likely take some time to develop.

The modalities of official liquidity provision

The international community has a long-standing responsibility to provide adequate financial assistance to countries in undertaking appropriate economic adjustments to balance-of-payments problems. Over the past year, the focus was on trade-related financing, support of low-income countries and precautionary arrangements that could help prevent capital account crises in emerging markets.

Trade-related financing

Efforts are under way to ensure more stable access to trade financing

The World Trade Organization organized a meeting of experts in the area of trade financing in January 2004, as a follow-up to an earlier meeting convened by IMF in 2003, to discuss ways of improving developing countries' access to trade financing, particularly in periods of financial crisis, in order to minimize the adverse effect on the affected countries' trade and economic growth. It reviewed the effectiveness of credit lines or guarantees supplied by international public agencies in the light of lessons drawn from the Asian financial crisis, when targeted temporary financing had proved helpful. The experience since then has suggested that an effective strategy could be built around the trade finance facilities of multilateral development banks, complemented by a more coordinated approach by official export credit agencies. A short-term trade-facilitation "global alliance", involving nearly all regional development banks, is now being established. [48] Recent experience also suggests that the trade finance facilities of multilateral development banks can be effective in mobilizing additional private sector funding and in providing risk-pooling opportunities for providers and insurers of private and public trade credit. The trade finance operations of multilateral development banks include guarantees of trade instruments issued by local banks, providing finance to exporters backed by receivables, and loan facilities on-lent through commercial banks. They have used these facilities to support emerging markets in crisis.[49]

Trade finance not only supplies liquidity necessary for efficient trade, but also enables less creditworthy and poorer countries to access international capital markets at a lower cost.[50] The current round of negotiations under the General Agreement on Trade in Services[51] can be used to make the provision of trade-financing more secure and more readily available to developing countries. Indeed, the World Trade Organization was directed at its Fifth Ministerial Conference in Cancún, Mexico, to contribute to efforts to maintain trade finance during crises.

More predictable financial assistance is being made available to countries implementing trade liberalization

In April 2004, the IMF Executive Board approved the Trade Integration Mechanism (TIM) to assist member countries in meeting short-term balance-of-payments shortfalls related to the implementation of trade liberalization measures by other countries.[52] Payments difficulties resulting from reforms of a country's own trade regime will continue to be addressed under previously established policies. TIM is not a new lending facility but a policy aimed at making existing instruments more predictably available for supporting trade liberalization. Under TIM, a member country, within existing facilities, may request Fund financing to help cover balance-of-payments needs arising from specified trade measures of other countries. This can be a new arrangement under an appropriate facility following approval of TIM or a modification in access under the existing arrangement. IMF will be prepared to consider a subsequent augmentation in access if the effect is larger than initially anticipated. Financing terms and the conditionality under TIM will be those of the underlying facility.

There is still no adequate solution to shortfalls in export earnings resulting from volatile world commodity markets

In March 2004, IMF concluded the review of the Compensatory Financing Facility (CFF), which had been established in 1963 to help cope with temporary export revenue shortfalls caused by exogenous shocks. The Facility has not been used since 1999. For middle-income countries, the usefulness of CFF has diminished as a result of their increased access to international capital markets and the need to enter into a normal stand-by arrangement to draw on CFF, contrary to its original design and intention. Although low-income countries have very limited access to capital markets and official financing may not be flexible enough to deal with temporary shocks, CFF is not attractive for these countries because of its non-concessional nature. IMF is currently considering extending the Poverty Reduction and Growth Facility (PRGF) arrangement so that it could also serve the purposes of CFF rather than subsidizing the rate of charge for stand-by or CFF resources.[53] The suggested extension of PRGF arrangements to cope with fluctuations in commodity prices is a part of an ongoing discussion on how to better help developing countries get through difficult periods without being forced into an economic slowdown that may worsen poverty and retard development. The discussion is being focused on strengthening the efficient use of PRGF financing, including in precautionary arrangements, addressing the needs of countries emerging from conflict, and better responding to the adverse impact of exogenous shocks.[54]

Precautionary financial arrangements

Work continues on precautionary arrangements to prevent capital account crises

Over the past several years, there have been attempts to develop some form of contingent financing that can be mobilized quickly and on a sufficiently large scale to provide financial support for middle-income countries that face potential capital account crisis. The Contingent Credit Line (CCL), introduced by IMF in 1999, was intended to achieve this objective. However, the facility was never used and expired in November 2003. The key problem was that application for a CCL could be viewed by the market as a sign of weakness, thereby reducing rather than strengthening confidence in the country. Also, since the Asian crisis, most emerging markets have adopted "self-insurance policies", including heavy reserve accumulation, more flexible exchange rates, changes in liability management practices, strengthening of domestic financial institutions and implementing of international standards and codes. These measures might have lessened these countries' vulnerability to shocks, thereby reducing the demand for a CCL.

Nevertheless, the lack of such a facility is considered to be an important gap in the set of tools available for crisis prevention. IMF is thus exploring other ways to achieve the objectives of CCL. One of the possibilities is to adopt an existing instrument – stand-by precautionary arrangements that are typically used when balance-of-payments pressures are more likely to arise in the current account - to the needs of countries facing a potential capital account shock. However, a number of concerns have already been raised, mainly related to the possible impact of high-access arrangements when the need is potential rather than actual. It has been argued that such types of arrangements may exacerbate moral hazard problems, thwart efforts to foster private sector involvement, and put further strain on IMF resources. In addition, assessments of the potential need for Fund resources in capital account crises would be highly uncertain and arbitrary.

IMF is continuing discussions on the role that precautionary arrangements can play in preventing capital account crises and the access that is required for this insurance to be meaningful.[55] It is vital that the Fund have the capacity to respond quickly to financial needs of member countries that have sound policies but are nevertheless challenged by the actions of the globally integrated capital markets.

Policies on crisis resolution

Along with preventive measures, improving the overall framework for resolution of capital account crises in developing countries with significant access to international financial markets has been the core issue in the international policy agenda. The policy intention has been to insert more certainty and predictability in the process for resolving crisis situations.

The role of official financing

IMF has introduced a framework for exceptional access to its resources, but ...

The critical component of this process entails having clear parameters for official intervention. To improve clarity and predictability of official response to capital account crises, IMF introduced a framework for exceptional access to its resources. The central element of the framework is judgement about debt sustainability. The Fund is prepared to provide larger loans than normally allowed if a country meets the following criteria established in 2002: exceptionally large need; a debt burden that will be sustainable under reasonably conservative assumptions; good prospects of regaining access to private capital markets during the period of the IMF loan; and indications that the country's policies have a strong chance of succeeding. Conversely, in countries where the debt burden is clearly unsustainable, the first step should be a speedy resolution of debt difficulties with private creditors. Committing resources to countries whose debt sustainability is in question may compromise the Fund's credibility, making the process of crisis resolution more, rather than less, uncertain.

In practice, despite progress in debt sustainability analysis, it is very hard to assess the nature of financial difficulties in the middle of a crisis. More sophisticated analytical tools can better inform judgement, but not replace it. The decisions to continue or withhold international support to a country in crisis are always made under uncertainty and political pressure. Hence, it would be unrealistic to expect that the international community will not continue to make occasional judgement errors and take decisions that will prove wrong ex post.

... its application has raised questions

The experience with the application of exceptional access policy has been mixed. Thus far, the new procedure has not been able to reduce debtor countries' and market participants' heavy reliance on official financial support. As a result of programmes, and sometimes successive programmes, involving exceptional access, credit to the three largest borrowers (Argentina, Brazil, Turkey) exceeded an unprecedented 70 per cent of total credit outstanding.[56] This increased concentration has been accompanied by prolonged use of official resources by some middle-income countries with access to international capital markets. Also, in several cases involving exceptional access, borrowing countries did not meet all the criteria.[57]

By the same token, there has also been an increase in the IMF share of large borrowers' external debt. For instance, in Argentina, this ratio rose from 17 per cent at the end of 2000 to over 22 per cent at the end of 2001.[58] This is viewed by some as contrary to the concept of catalytic financing and as possibly putting at risk the preferred creditor status of the Fund.[59] Alternatively, as the recent Argentine experience indicates, it may lead debtor countries to request larger reductions of debt-service obligations from private creditors to be able to fully service their debt with the multilateral institutions, which thus maintain their preferred creditor status. Interestingly, this outcome negates some of the major assumptions regarding the "moral hazard" effects of official lending, but questions in any case the rationality of increasing such financing when countries have an unsustainable debt burden.

It is thus recognized that, when debt burdens are truly unsustainable, the support of the international community should be accompanied by orderly, predictable and effective debt restructuring. Over the past several years, the international community has made significant efforts to develop a clear strategy capable of helping insolvent middle-income countries return to long-term debt sustainability and restore access to private financing.

In this regard, it has been suggested that the implementation of the Fund's "lending into arrears" framework should be strengthened. Under this policy, the Fund will disburse loans under one of its normal facilities even if the country is in arrears to its private creditors, provided that it makes a strong effort to resolve the arrears. However, this requirement is viewed by many as not sufficiently specific. Accordingly, the development of more operational criteria for judging compliance with the good faith requirement, as well as more rigorous assessments using this criteria, is considered important. Enhanced clarity could better guide the expectations of investors and debtor countries, thereby fostering debt restructuring negotiations.

Sovereign debt restructuring

There has been important progress on collective action clauses (CACs)

In debt restructuring, progress has been made in the design and use of collective action clauses (CACs) in bond contracts under New York law that could help a debtor country reach agreement with its bondholders in future debt restructuring exercises.[60] There has been growing use of CACs in sovereign bonds issued under New York law for which, unlike bonds issued under English and Japanese law, such clauses had not previously been the market standard. During 2003 and early 2004, more than 70 per cent of sovereign issues contained CACs, compared with about 35 per cent in 2001, largely reflecting the increasing number of sovereign bonds with CACs issued under New York law. In addition to investment grade countries, many sub-investment grade countries were able to issue bonds with such clauses without any evidence of a higher premium, meaning that the market has accepted the new bond terms. In sum, CACs are on the way to becoming a general market standard without having increased the borrowing costs of the countries using them.[61]

The Paris Club has agreed on a new approach to debt restructuring

It has also been argued that there is a strong case for developing-country private enterprises to use CACs (as private firms borrowing in London already do).[62] At the same time, it is recognized that the case of private firms is less urgent because these entities have the option of debt reorganization under national bankruptcy courts.

Another development was the decision in October 2003 of the Paris Club of government creditors on a new approach aimed at addressing the debt sustainability concerns of countries that are not covered by the Heavily Indebted Poor Countries (HIPC) Initiative, as had been requested by the finance ministers of the Group of Eight (G8) at their meeting in May 2003. According to this approach, in exceptional circumstances, the Paris Club will break from its traditional practice of applying standard terms for particular classes of debtor Governments in order to better tailor its response to the specific financial situation of the country in crisis with the aim of achieving lasting debt sustainability. The new approach also calls for better coordination between the Paris Club and private creditors to ensure comparability of treatment of their respective claims.[63]

A voluntary "code of good conduct" is under consideration

As CACs still affect only a small part of the outstanding debt and there are many collective action problems that cannot be addressed by these clauses or new Paris Club practices, efforts are also under way to improve the overall process of sovereign debt restructuring in the event of a debt crisis. The international official community and a number of private sector organizations have expressed interest in developing a non-statutory framework for addressing debt-servicing problems, based on a voluntary "code of good conduct", which would broadly stipulate the roles that key parties would be expected to play in resolving a debt crisis. The code would establish a number of general, non-binding principles and guidelines regarding the exchange of information between debtor and private creditors, comparable inter-creditor treatment, and decision mechanisms in case of debt restructuring.

Work on this issue was initially led by a group of private organizations, the Banque de France and the Institute of International Finance. It is now being coordinated by the Group of Twenty (G-20), where the proposals for introducing a voluntary code are an element of the Group's work on crisis prevention. A technical working group, including Brazil, the Republic of Korea and Mexico, has been established to work with the private sector to prepare the new draft code for broader consideration. There are differences in opinion on the objectives, scope and modalities of this approach and finding common ground will be important.

Work should continue on the orderly resolution of debt crises

The earlier effort by IMF to develop a statutory approach to the comprehensive treatment of the debt of a country in crisis did not win enough support to advance further. Neither debtor Governments nor their private creditors were satisfied with the proposed sovereign debt restructuring mechanism (SDRM).[64] However, the problems that the SDRM was meant to address have not disappeared. Reaching a speedy and fair agreement with creditors that may help reduce social and economic costs of default will continue to be a major challenge. The international community should continue work on the orderly resolution of financial crises because there is no generally satisfactory set of processes. In respect of reaching a consensus on what they should be, legal complexities will not be the most difficult issue: the hardest and most important part of the problem is to identify appropriate actions and then reach broad agreement on economic and financial policies and strategies that can help dismantle unsustainable debt structures with minimum damage to the country and its people, as well as to the integrity and efficiency of international credit markets.

Enhancing the voice and participation of developing countries

The Monterrey Consensus stresses the need to broaden and strengthen the participation of developing countries and countries with economies in transition in international economic decision-making, and encourages the Bretton Woods institutions to continue to enhance the effective participation of these countries in their activities.

The process for appointing the new IMF Managing Director has again brought the concern for more democratic and transparent governance of the Bretton Woods institutions into focus. In March 2004, a group of IMF Executive Directors representing more than 100 countries called for an open and transparent selection process to attract the best candidates, regardless of nationality.[65] While many Executive Directors from developing countries expressed support for the new Managing Director, the process remains opaque and subject to criticism.

As a step towards increasing the voice of developing countries in governance of the Bretton Woods institutions, a number of measures have been recently taken to enhance capacity in some developing-country Executive Directors' offices and in the capitals of these countries. This has included creating some additional staff positions in the two very large African constituencies to make them more manageable. Also, an analytical trust fund to assist Executive Directors representing sub-Saharan countries in undertaking independent research and analysis on development issues has been proposed.

Greater political will is required to increase the participation of developing countries in international economic governance

However, progress is lacking in addressing the issue of the representation of member countries on the Executive Boards and in devising a new formula for assigning votes. These issues are complex, but critically important for the representation of members. It is recognized that changes in voting shares are likely to be addressed only in the context of an agreement to increase Fund quotas and World Bank capital and neither subject is currently under international discussion. As part of the continued efforts to build agreement on governance and representation in the Bretton Woods institutions, the Development Committee has asked the Bank and the Fund to prepare a report on all aspects of the voice issue, to be discussed by the Committee at the 2004 Annual Meetings.[66]

Notes

1 See World Bank, *Global Development Finance*, 2004: Harnessing Cyclical Gains for Development, vol. I, Analysis and Summary Tables (Washington, D.C., World Bank, 2004), box 2.1.

2 The average credit quality as calculated by the World Bank based on credit ratings by Moody's Investor Service (see Global Development Finance, 2004 …, p. 43).

3 See IMF, *Global Financial Stability Report: Market Developments and Issues,* (Washington, D.C., IMF, April 2004, box 2.2).

4 In 2003, the region of Latin America and the Caribbean accounted for 90 per cent ($15.9 billion) of total IMF stand-by commitments to developing countries.

5 The ninth replenishment of the Asian Development Fund grant framework applies only to the ninth replenishment and does not commit future replenishments.

6 The United States remained the world's largest donor, followed by Japan, France, Germany and the United Kingdom of Great Britain and Northern Ireland.

7 Five countries, namely, Denmark, Luxembourg, the Netherlands, Norway and Sweden, meet the ODA United Nations target of 0.7 per cent of GNI. See also World Bank Press Review, "Development aid still insufficient to reduce poverty", 20 April 2004.

8 The net financial transfer statistic adds together receipts of foreign investment income and financial inflows from abroad minus payments of foreign investment income and financial outflows, including increases in foreign reserve holdings. The net financial transfer of a country is thus the financial counterpart to the balance of trade in goods and services. A trade surplus is generated when the total value of domestic production exceeds domestic consumption and investment, with the excess invested abroad instead of being used domestically, and vice versa for a trade deficit.

9 EU ODA is projected to reach an average of 0.42 of GNI in 2006, in which case total ODA could exceed $77 billion. See Commission of the European Communities, "Communication from the Commission to the Council and the European Parliament: translating the Monterrey Consensus into practice: the contribution by the European Union", (SEC (2004)246), Brussels (COM(2004)150 final) 5 March 2004. See also "Commission acts to boost efficiency of EU development aid through better coordination and harmonisation", press release IP/04/MONTERREY FINAL 2, Brussels, 11 March 2004.

10 The 16 countries selected were, Armenia, Benin, Bolivia, Cape Verde, Georgia, Ghana, Honduras, Lesotho, Madagascar, Mali, Mongolia, Mozambique, Nicaragua, Senegal, Sri Lanka and Vanuatu. For further information concerning MCA, see www.mca.gov.

11 See International Monetary Fund and World Bank, *Global Monitoring Report, 2004: Policies and Actions for Achieving the MDGs and Related Outcomes* (Washington, D.C., 2004), p. 166.

12 A follow-up conference in early 2005, building on the issues of aid harmonization and alignment of donor policies with the national priorities of recipient countries, is planned.

13 See World Bank, DevNews Media Center, "Results focus sharpened", 12 February 2004.

14 See Commission of the European Communities, "Communication from the Commission to the Council …", p. 2.

15 For additional information, see www.number-10.gov.UK/output/Page5427.asp (accessed 26 February 2004).

16 Ibid.

17 See progress note prepared by World Bank staff in cooperation with Fund staff entitled "Financing modalities toward the Millennium Development Goals" (SecM2004-0107), 16 March 2004, pp. 6-7.

18 See *Common Dreams, News Center, "France, Brazil relaunch* "Lula Fund to tax arms sales and fight poverty", 30 January 2004, available from www.commondreams.org/headlines04/0130-13.htm (accessed 11 August 2004).

19 *Report of the International Conference on Financing for Development, Monterrey, Mexico, 18-22 March 2002* (United Nations publication, Sales no. E.02.II.A.7), chap. I, resolution 1, annex.

20 In a sample of 14 PRSP countries where data were available, poverty-reducing expenditures increased on average by 1.4 per cent of GDP and 3.9 per cent of total government expenditures in the period from 1999 to 2001. See *Global Development Finance, 2004: Harnessing Cyclical Gains for Development* entitled "The Changing landscape for official flows", vol. 1 …, Chap. 4, p. 117.

21 Ibid., pp. 116-117.

22 Since the publication of *World Economic and Social Survey 2003,* (United Nations publication, Sales no. E.03.II.C.1), five countries have reached the completion point: Guyana, in December 2003; Nicaragua, in January 2004; and the Niger, Senegal and Ethiopia, in April 2004.

23 See IMF and World Bank Joint Ministerial Committee of the Boards of Governors of the World Bank and the IMF on the Transfer of Real Resources to Developing Countries (Development Committee), communiqué, IMF Survey, vol. 33, No. 8 (3 May 2004), 25 April 2004, eleventh para..

24 A DDO offers the option of deferring the receipt of a single-tranche adjustment loan for up to three years provided that overall programme implementation and the macroeconomic framework remain adequate. See World Bank, "Proposal to introduce a deferred drawdown option (DDO) for use with IBRD adjustment loans" (R2001-0174), 26 September 2001.

25 The member countries of the Rio Group are: Argentina, Bolivia, Brazil, Chile, Colombia, Costa Rica, Dominican Republic, Ecuador, El Salvador, Guatemala, Honduras, Mexico, Nicaragua, Panama, Paraguay, Peru, Uruguay, Venezuela and a representative of the Caribbean Community (CARICOM). See XIII Cumbre Iberoamericano, Santa Cruz de la Sierra, Bolivia, "Comunicado especial de ayuda de emergencia a favor de Bolivia", 15 November 2003, p. 7.

26 See, for instance, IMF, "Public investment and fiscal policy", 12 March 2004 (www.imf.org).

27 See, for instance, "IMF Executive Board discusses lessons from the crisis in Argentina", Public Information Notice (PIN) No. 04/26, 24 March 2004, p. 4 (www.imf.org).

28 "IMF Executive Board reviews data provision for surveillance", Public Information Notice (PIN) No. 04/37, 12 April 2004, p. 2 (www.imf.org).

29 "IMF discusses assessments of sustainability", Public Information Notice (PIN) No. 02/69, 11 July 2002 (www.imf.org).

30 IMF, "Integrating the balance sheet approach into Fund operations", prepared by the Policy Development and Review Department (in consultation with other departments), 23 February 2004, p. 1 (www.imf.org).

31 Joint Ministerial Statement of the ASEAN+3 Finance Ministers Meeting, 15 May 2004, Jeju, Republic of Korea (www.aseansec.org).

32 Ibid.

33 "Financial Stability Forum holds its eleventh meeting", press release, 30 March 2004 (www.fsforum.org).

34 "IFAC Council adopts reforms to improve audit quality worldwide", news release, 14 November 2003 (www.ifac.org).

35 "Commission proposes Directive to combat fraud and malpractice", news release, 16 March 2004 (http://europa.eu.int/comm).

36 "IMF Executive Board reviews and enhances efforts for anti-money laundering and combating the financing of terrorism", Public Information Notice (PIN) No. 04/33, 2 April 2004 (www.imf.org).

37 "FATF strengthens global anti-money laundering and anti-terrorism financing campaign", news release, 27 February 2004. The list of NCCTs still includes Cook Islands, Guatemala, Indonesia, Myanmar, Nauru and the Philippines.

38 For a discussion of the Basel II proposal, see *World Economic and Social Survey, 2003* ..., chap. II, subject, entitled "The New Based Capital Accord".

39 "Consensus achieved on Basel II proposals", BCBS press release, 11 May 2004 (www.bis.org).

40 For a discussion of issues related to the implementation of the New Accord in developing countries, see, for instance, IMF, "Guidance for Fund Staff", IMF Staff Note on Basel II, 23 April 2004 (www.imf.org).

41 For a discussion of this phenomenon see, for instance, Barry Eichengreen, Ricardo Hausmann and Ugo Panizza, Currency Mismatches, Debt Intolerance and Original Sin: Why They are not the Same and Why it Matters, NBER Working Paper, No. 10036, (Cambridge, Massachusetts, October 2003).

42 For more details, see report of the Secretary General entitled "External debt crisis and development", (A/58/290), 15 September 2003, sect. V.E.

43 See, for instance, Morris Goldstein, *Debt Sustainability, Brazil, and the IMF*, Working Paper, No. WP 03-1 (Washington, D.C., Institute for International Economics, February 2003), p. 31.

44 See, for instance, Barry Eichengreen, Ricardo Hausmann and Ugo Panizza "Original sin: the pain, the mystery and the road to redemption", unpublished manuscript, November 2002, paper prepared for the conference "Currency and Maturity Matchmaking: Redeeming Debt from Original Sin", Inter-American Development Bank; Washington, D.C., 21 and 22 November 2002.

45 Australia, China, Hong Kong Special Administrative Region (SAR) of China, Indonesia, Japan, Republic of Korea, Malaysia, New Zealand, the Philippines, Singapore and Thailand.

46 "EMEAP Central Banks to launch Asian Bond Fund", press statement, 2 June 2003 (www.emeap.org).

47 "EMEAP Central Banks announce the initial structure of the Asian Bond Fund 2", press statement, 15 April 2004 (www.emeap.org).

48 World Trade Organization, General Council, Working Group on Trade, Debt and Finance, "Expert Group Meeting on Trade Financing: note by the Secretariat", (WT/GC/W/527), 16 March 2004.

49 *Global Development Finance 2004*, vol. I …, p 132.

50 Trade finance spreads averaged 28 basis points lower than spreads on other bank loans over 1996-2002 for a sample of countries with data on comparable transactions, (ibid., p 127).

51 The full text of the General Agreement on Trade in Services is available from http://www.wto.org/english/tratop_e/serv_e/gatsintr_e.htm (accessed 6 August 2004).

52 "IMF Executive Board approves Trade Integration Mechanism", press release No. 04/73, 13 April 2004.

53 "IMF concludes review of the Compensatory Financing Facility", Public Information Notice (PIN) No. 04/35, 7 April 2004, p. 3 (www.imf.org).

54 See, for instance, IMF, "The Fund's Support of low-income countries: considerations on instruments and financing", prepared by the Finance and Policy Development and Review Departments (in consultation with other departments), 24 February 2004 (www.imf.org).

55 "IMF needs to do far more to help countries learn from each other's success and failures: interview with Mark Allen", *IMF Survey*, vol. 33, No.7, (12 April 2004), p. 101.

56 In 1980, in contrast, 16 debtors had accounted for 70 per cent of credit outstanding.

57 See, for instance, Michael Mussa, Senior Fellow, Institute of International Economics, Washington, D.C., statement to the Senate Banking Subcommittee on International Trade and Finance, Hearing on the Argentine Financial Crisis, 10 March 2004, available from http://www.senate.gov/~banking/_files/mussa.pdf (accessed 6 August 2004).

58 Guillermo Nielsen, Secretary of Finance, Argentina, "An update on Argentina", Latin American Investor Conference, Merrill Lynch, 27 March 2004, p. 2 (www.emta.org).

59 See, for instance, statement by Mr. Per-Kristian Foss, Minister of Finance, Norway, to the International Monetary and Financial Committee at its ninth meeting, 24 April 2004 (www.imf.org).

60 For a discussion of CACs, see *World Economic and Social Survey, 2003* …, chap. II, subsect. entitled "Sovereign debt restructuring".

61 Bond issues under the German law continue to lack CACs. However, the German Government is working on a comprehensive reform of the indenture law that will explicitly enable borrowers to use CACs in sovereign bond contracts issued under German law.

62 See, for instance, Barry Eichengreen, Kenneth Kletzer and Ashoka Mody, *Crisis Resolution: Next Steps*, IMF Working Paper, No. WP/03/196, (Washington, D.C., IMF, October 2003), pp. 38-39.

63 For a more detailed description of the new approach, see *World Economic Situation and Prospects, 2004* (United Nations publication, Sales No. E.04.II.C.2), pp. 40-41, including box II.2.

64 For a discussion of the SDRM proposal, see *World Economic and Social Survey, 2003* …, chap. II, subsect. entitled "Sovereign debt restructuring".

65 Statement by a Group of IMF Executive Directors on the Selection Process for a New Managing Director, press release No. 04/55, 19 March 2004 (www.imf.org).

66 Development Committee communiqué, Washington, D.C., 25 April 2004, IMF Survey, vol. 33, No. 8 (3 May 2004) twelfth para. (also available from www.imf.org).

Chapter IV
The Situation in the World's Economies

Summary

Growth in most countries gained momentum as 2003 progressed and is expected to accelerate further in 2004, before moderating somewhat in 2005. After three years of sub-par performance, growth in most countries will be close to its long-term potential by the end of 2004.

The United States of America was the initial driving force behind the recovery but prospects for continued global economic expansion have been strengthened by the emergence of additional poles of growth, mostly in Asia. In particular, China's extended period of rapid growth has now propelled that economy onto the world economic stage as an engine of growth, especially, but far from exclusively, for Asia and for developing countries. China's growing appetite for raw materials, in particular, gives its economy a newfound global role. With its sustained high growth, India is also beginning to assume a greater global economic position. In addition, Japan, the world's second largest economy, grew more rapidly than anticipated in 2003 and seems more likely to be able to sustain the higher growth than on previous occasions in the past decade when an end to its stagnation appeared imminent.

The economies in transition continue to be the fastest growing of the three major country groupings. The prospect and, in 2004, the implementation of the accession of five of these economies to the European Union (EU) have been an important stimulus to growth in the countries of Central and Eastern Europe and the Baltic States, while rapid growth in the Russian Federation has performed a similar function for the other members of the Commonwealth of Independent States (CIS).

Although most developing countries are also participating in the global recovery, growth outside Asia has been less dynamic. After its setback in 2002, Latin America achieved positive, but modest, growth in 2003. Growth in Africa improved but also only to a minor extent and remains far short of the level required to extricate the continent from its "poverty trap". The uncertainties in Iraq continue to cast a shadow over economic activity in West Asia. In contrast with all other developing regions, Eastern and Southern Asia continues to grow strongly.

Developed market economies: the recovery takes hold

The recovery strengthens ...

The recovery in the developed market economies continues to accelerate and broaden both within and across countries, but there remain significant weaknesses. Economic activity accelerated in the second half of 2003 (see table IV.1), led by investment activity and continued strong consumption expenditure in the United States, an important impetus to global demand. Domestic demand was also a strong element in the growth of the United Kingdom of Great Britain and Northern Ireland while exports were the catalyst for Western Europe. Increasing exports also led the recovery in Japan.

... but uncertainties remain

The recovery is expected to solidify in 2004 and moderate slightly in 2005. However, questions remain. In the United States, employment creation, a requirement for resumed impetus to consumption growth and hence a maturing of the recovery, has been hesitant. In Japan, the pickup is no longer in doubt but inflation has yet to convincingly stabilize in positive territory and many financial problems remain. In Europe, activity is beginning to accelerate but consumption remains weak and employment has yet to show any signs of rebounding. In addition, there are several global imbalances: the continuing current-account imbalance in the United States (fed in part by the United States fiscal deficit), fiscal imbalances in many other countries, possible overvaluation of the housing market in some countries, and high levels of consumer debt. These imbalances were in part responsible for the volatile movements in foreign exchange markets over the past few years and remain a significant risk with respect to the smooth evolution of economic activity in the developed countries.

North America: maintaining a robust growth in the United States

Robust GDP growth in the United States in 2004 ...

After a strong recovery in the second half of 2003, the economy of the United States carried the momentum into 2004. Gross domestic product (GDP) is expected to grow by 4½ per cent in 2004, moderating to 3½ per cent in 2005 (see table A.2). Leading this strength has been an acceleration of business investment in equipment and software, buttressed by an improvement in corporate profits and historically low interest rates. Consumer spending continues to grow robustly. Exports, which were a drag on the economy in the past few years, have also revived. On the supply side, labour productivity, which has been growing at an exceptionally strong rate, continues to improve. Inflation, while rising, remains benign. Monetary policy has retained its highly accommodative stance and fiscal policy continues to be stimulatory, although less than in the previous year. However, the slower-than-expected recovery in employment, the large and widening twin deficits, and a surge in the prices of fuel and other commodities pose risks for the economy.

... will be sustained by strong business investment

Business capital spending has been growing at a double-digit pace, fully recovering to the peak level of 2000, and is expected to expand at a robust pace in 2004-2005, as the outlook for corporate profits remains optimistic. In contrast, residential investment is expected to slow, particularly because interest rates are expected to move up. Household consumption is expected to maintain solid growth, but this is contingent on the forecast of a gradual improvement in employment.

Table IV.1.
Growth, unemployment and inflation in the major developed economies, quarterly indicators, 2002-2003

	2002 quarter				2003 quarter			
	I	II	III	IV	I	II	III	IV
	Growth of gross domestic product[a] (percentage change in seasonally adjusted data from preceding quarter)							
Canada	5.8	3.8	2.7	1.6	2.5	-1.0	1.3	3.8
France	3.1	2.3	0.6	-0.4	0.6	-1.2	2.4	2.5
Germany	0.8	0.9	0.6	-0.3	-1.0	-0.7	0.8	1.0
Italy	0.8	0.9	1.1	1.7	-0.4	-0.4	2.0	0.0
Japan	-2.0	4.5	4.3	0.5	0.8	3.4	3.0	6.9
United Kingdom	1.2	1.6	3.1	2.3	0.8	2.3	3.5	3.4
United States	4.7	1.9	3.4	1.3	2.0	3.1	8.2	4.1
Major developed economies	2.4	2.4	3.0	1.0	1.2	2.2	5.2	4.1
Euro zone	1.6	2.0	0.8	0.0	0.0	-0.4	1.6	1.6
	Unemployment rate[b] (percentage of total labour force)							
Canada	7.8	7.6	7.6	7.6	7.5	7.7	7.9	7.5
France	8.6	8.7	8.9	9.0	9.2	9.3	9.4	9.5
Germany	8.0	8.1	8.7	8.9	9.2	9.3	9.3	9.2
Italy	9.1	9.0	9.0	8.9	8.8	8.7	8.6	8.5
Japan	5.3	5.4	5.4	5.4	5.4	5.4	5.2	5.1
United Kingdom	5.1	5.1	5.2	5.0	5.0	5.0	4.9	4.9
United States	5.6	5.9	5.8	5.9	5.8	6.1	6.1	5.9
Major developed economies	6.4	6.5	6.6	6.6	6.6	6.8	6.7	6.6
Euro zone	8.1	8.2	8.5	8.6	8.7	8.8	8.8	8.8
	Growth of consumer prices[c] (percentage change from preceding quarter)							
Canada	2.7	6.1	4.3	2.1	5.4	-0.5	1.5	0.5
France	2.7	3.2	0.9	1.8	3.5	1.5	1.1	2.6
Germany	4.5	0.8	0.6	-0.4	3.7	-0.4	1.2	0.3
Italy	3.5	3.0	1.9	2.7	3.3	2.9	2.1	1.9
Japan	-2.8	1.8	-0.7	-0.4	-1.6	1.8	-0.7	-0.7
United Kingdom	0.2	5.1	1.4	3.6	2.3	4.9	1.0	2.5
United States	1.4	4.4	1.7	1.3	4.1	1.5	2.0	0.1
Major developed economies	0.9	3.4	1.1	1.0	2.6	1.6	1.2	0.4
Euro zone	1.5	4.1	0.4	2.2	2.5	2.8	0.4	2.3

Sources:
UN/DESA, based on data of IMF, *International Financial Statistics;* Organisation for Economic Cooperation and Development (OECD); and national authorities.

a Expressed in annual rate. For major developed economies, weighted average with weights being annual GDP valued in 2000 prices and exchange rates.

b Seasonally adjusted data as standardized by OECD.

c Expressed in annual rate. For major developed economies, weighted average with weights being 2000 GDP in United States dollars.

The labour market holds the key to the continuation of the economic expansion. The recovery in employment has been unusually slow by historical standards. Corporate lay-offs have been declining, but most firms remain hesitant in hiring. Unemployment fell from a peak of 6.3 per cent in mid-2003 to 5.6 per cent in April 2004 (see figure IV.1) but the improvement occurred mainly because of a decline in the labour force participation rate, particularly for younger people.[1] Efficiency gains from technological innovation and increased global economic integration may have prolonged the lag. Labour productivity has been growing at an average annual rate of above 3 per cent for the past few years, much higher than in any recession-recovery phases in history, as companies have been able to squeeze existing employment and capacity to meet rising demand. Meanwhile, outsourcing and the relocation of manufacturing have also led to a slower hiring of workers in some industrial sectors, at least in the short run. Other explanations for the delay in hiring include rising costs of payroll benefits, especially health-care costs.

Recovery of the labour market will be crucial for continued economic expansion

The sluggish employment growth has two implications for the outlook. First, it suggests that the economy of the United States may grow at an above-potential rate for another couple of years without being constrained by labour shortages and without triggering an acceleration in inflation. Paradoxically, however, the necessary condition for the economy to sustain robust growth is a gradual recovery of employment, to maintain vigorous effective aggregate domestic demand, although a continued strengthening of the rest of the world is also important. From another perspective, the weakness in the labour market, if continued, bodes a downside risk for growth: the longer the delay in employment recovery, the higher the risk of faltering household spending and a waning of growth of gross domestic product (GDP).

Figure IV.1.
Unemployment rates (standardized) in selected developed economies: January 1999-March 2004

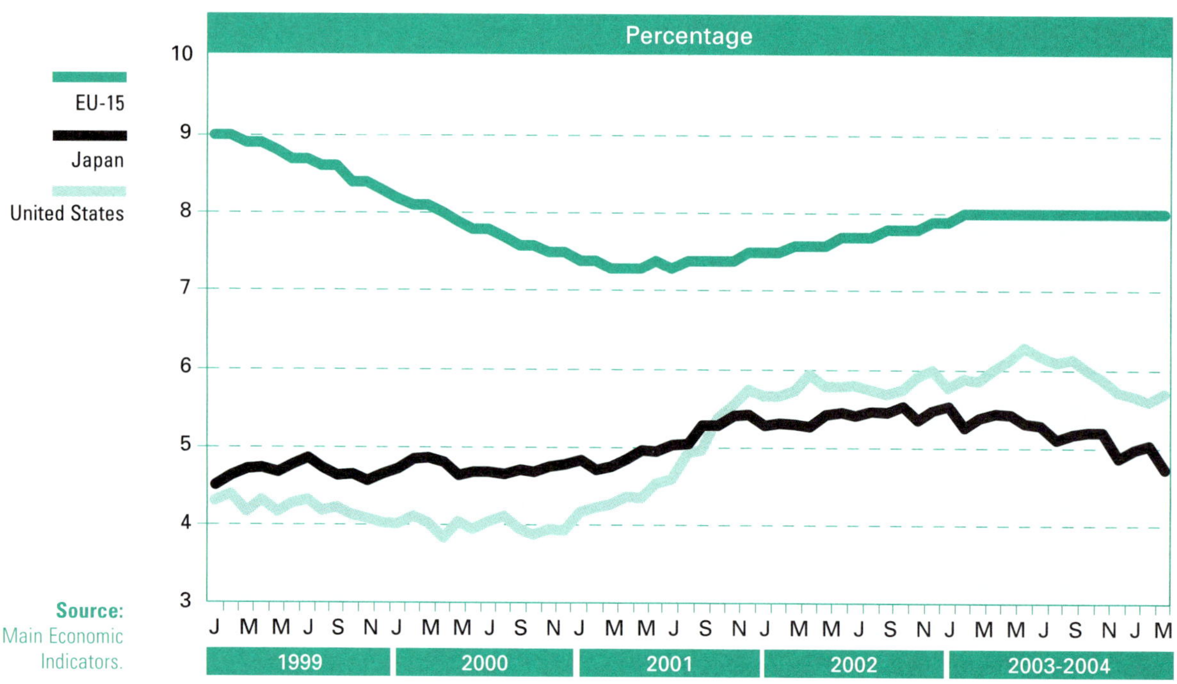

Source: OECD, Main Economic Indicators.

The inflation outlook remains benign, although the rise in the prices of many commodities, especially fuel, will continue to have adverse effects on the economy, at least in terms of the welfare losses from a lower purchasing power of consumer spending. Producer prices for core commodity goods surged at an annualized rate of near 60 per cent in the first quarter of 2004, while producer prices for core intermediate goods rose by about 7 per cent and core consumer prices rose by less than 2 per cent, indicating that a dominant proportion of the rise in commodity prices has so far been absorbed by producers. More pass-through to the prices of final products is likely if the higher prices of commodities persist; nevertheless, overall inflation will be determined primarily by such factors as monetary policy, the balance between aggregate supply and demand—particularly in the labour market—and market flexibility, including international competition. These factors remain auspicious for the inflation outlook (see table A.8).

Inflation should remain benign

Exports are expected to provide anther supporting factor for the robust GDP outlook, growing by more than 10 per cent in volume in 2004-2005. Real imports are expected to grow by about 7 per cent, boosted by the recovery in domestic demand. The depreciation of the dollar (see figure IV.2) is playing a role in boosting the competitiveness of exports and curbing import demand.

The large amount of policy stimuli has been crucial for the recovery so far, but the policy stance is expected to be less accommodative in the outlook. Given the historically low policy interest rates—1 per cent in nominal terms and slightly negative in real terms—an increase of 100-150 basis points over a two-year period would return rates to their historical average and should not be excessively restrictive. Gradualism and transparency in policy intentions will be crucial to avoiding abrupt reactions in financial mar-

Monetary policy is expected to tighten gradually ...

Figure IV.2.
Major exchange rates, January 2002-March 2004

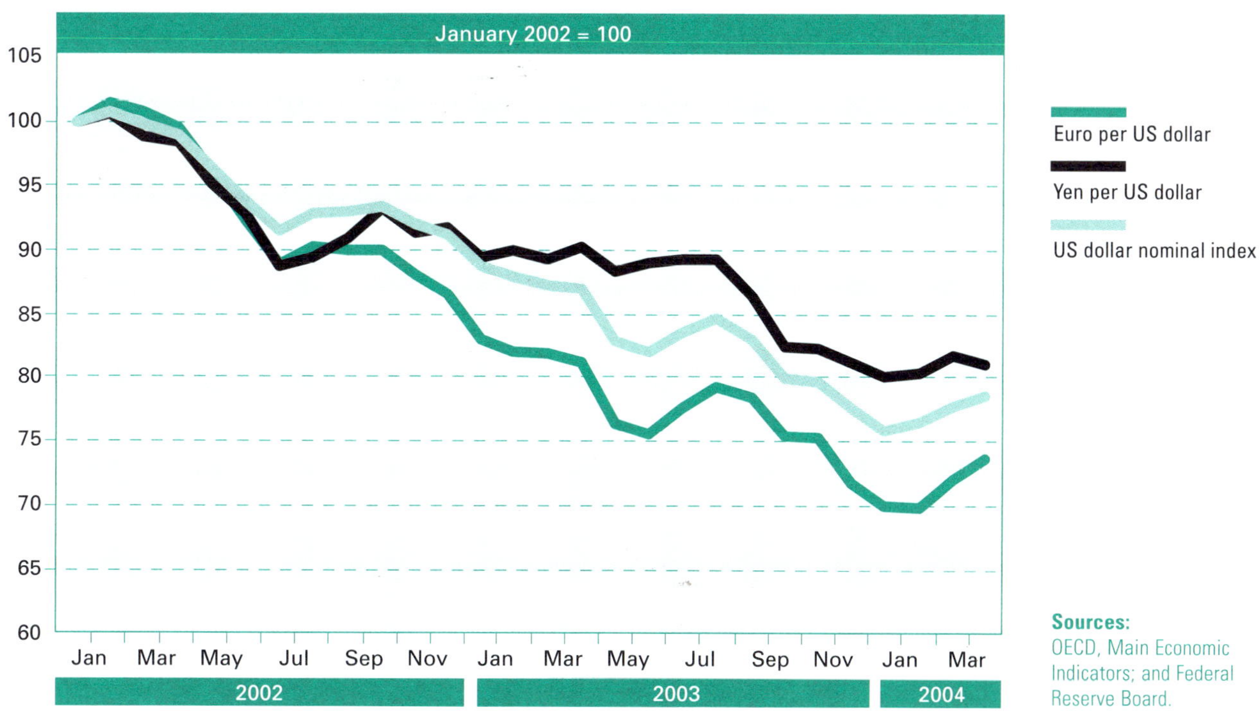

Sources: OECD, Main Economic Indicators; and Federal Reserve Board.

kets, which may otherwise push up long-term interest rates to undesirable levels. Higher interest rates present risks for growth, particularly if the increases are larger and more abrupt than anticipated. The high level of private sector debts and seemingly inflated housing prices are among the most vulnerable areas in this regard.

... but fiscal policy will remain stimulatory, at least in 2004

Fiscal policy will continue to be stimulatory in 2004; while the growth of real government spending will be lower than in 2003, it will still be higher than growth of GDP. The fiscal position of the United States has eroded rapidly over the past few years, with the budget balance swinging from a surplus of over 2 per cent of GDP in 2000 to a deficit of about 4 per cent of GDP by 2003. The deficit is expected to widen further in 2004, but to narrow slightly in 2005. Most longer-run projections, such as those of the Congressional Budget Office, point to a large deficit long into the future if there are no substantial changes in policy, leading to growing concerns about the fiscal sustainability of the United States.

A major factor behind the rapid fiscal deterioration has been the downturn phase of the business cycle. It is estimated that about half of the turnaround in the budget balance was due to the recession of 2001 and the response of the built-in "automatic stabilizers": reduced tax collections due to a smaller base in income and in capital gains—the latter resulting from the substantial decline in equity prices—and increased expenditure for income support and related programmes. The other half of the deterioration was due, roughly equally, to two other factors: increased discretionary spending, mainly military and homeland security, and changes in tax policy, including tax cuts enacted during the past few years. In the forecast, a cyclical improvement in the deficit will come mainly from the expected strengthening of the revenue base.

The United States fiscal deficit poses risks

Risks associated with the large fiscal deficit include higher interest rates, a weaker and more volatile exchange rate, and a rise in inflation expectations. The sustainability of the deficit will depend on, among other factors, the willingness of other countries to increase their holdings of United States government securities. Broader risks for the United States are mostly geopolitical uncertainties, particularly the economic implications of terrorism and the country's involvement in Iraq.

Canadian economic growth is expected to improve ...

The Canadian economy has been weaker than that of the United States. After registering growth of 1.7 per cent in 2003, GDP is expected to increase by 2¾ per cent in 2004, strengthening further to 3¾ per cent in 2005 (see table A.2). Private domestic demand will be the primary driving force, to be supported by accommodative monetary policy. A continued improvement in external demand, not only from the United States but also from Asia, along with higher prices of many commodities that Canada exports, will further boost the already robust growth of business capital spending. Meanwhile, improvements in real income will support growth in household spending. Fiscal policy is expected to remain neutral to slightly expansionary.

... but currency appreciation will put net exports under pressure

The performance of the Canadian external sector has been mixed. While the increased international demand for and higher prices of many commodities have been favourable in general, appreciation of the Canadian dollar has adversely affected exports, which declined in 2003. However, the negative impact seems to be waning, as many Canadian firms have already adopted measures to mitigate the exchange-rate pressure, such as cutting costs and improving productivity. Exports are expected to grow moderately, but the contribution of net exports to GDP growth may still be negative, as imports are expected to increase at a faster rate.

Developed Asia and the Pacific: a real recovery for Japan?

Japanese economic growth has been stronger than expected ...

The economic recovery of Japan has proved to be stronger and more enduring than expected. In the fourth quarter of 2003, GDP grew by 7 per cent, the best quarterly growth for 15 years. GDP is expected to grow by 3 per cent in 2004, slowing to 1¾ per cent in 2005 as the tax burden increases (see table A.2). The recovery was initially driven by exports, but the domestic sector has gradually gathered strength. For growth to become more self-sustaining, however, the vigour in the business sector needs to be transferred to the household sector through increases in wages and employment. For the economy to be completely extricated from its decade-long stagnation, it will be necessary to resolve a number of structural problems—the large amounts of non-performing loans (NPLs), the fragile financial positions of both the public and private sectors, and the need for corporate restructuring.

... driven by strong exports and a gradual recovery in domestic demand

Japanese exports grew by 9 per cent in volume in 2003 and are expected to remain robust in 2004 and 2005. Strong demand from other Asian economies, especially China, and mainly for capital and information and communication technologies (ICT)-related products, is the main impetus. Differing movements of the yen vis-à-vis the dollar and the euro (see figure IV.2) are boosting exports to Europe and reducing exports to the United States. Growth in the volume of imports has been weaker than for exports, but is strengthening as overall activity continues to improve.

Higher corporate profits ...

Strong exports have induced a recovery in business investment, but an increasing number of companies have also achieved positive domestic earnings. As confirmed by surveys, the improvement in corporate investment conditions is broadly based. Business capital spending has been growing briskly, particularly in manufacturing and mostly from three key machinery sectors: industrial, electrical and transport. Corporate profits have increased and the business sentiment of firms has also improved, both contributing to a better environment for business investment. Non-manufacturing firms are, however, still cautious in their investment plans. Moreover, excessive debt in the corporate sector persists, despite some improvement.

... need to be transferred to the household sector, through increases in wages and employment

The recovery in corporate profits has finally led to increases in wages, however tentative, and an improvement in labour-market conditions. Job offers have been on an uptrend and overtime hours worked continue to rise. The unemployment rate declined from a peak of 5.5 per cent in 2003 to 5 per cent at the beginning of 2004. As a result, household income is recovering gradually, although it remains weak. Consumer confidence has also been on the rise and household spending seems to be ahead of the recovery in income, reducing the savings rate to historic lows.[2] While a drop in the household savings rate could be associated with positive wealth effects from asset appreciation, the current case of Japan may reflect either an improvement in expectations of future income, raising the propensity to consume out of current income, or the ageing of the population, as the increased number of retirees consume their personal net assets.

Deflation is forecast to continue to 2005

A number of price indices have been on the rise, but it is still too early to declare the end of deflation, which has haunted the Japanese economy for several years (see figure IV.3). Driven by the surge in the international prices of commodities (see chap. II), producer prices of goods have edged up, but the prices of services continue to decline. Consumer prices, meanwhile, have halted their downturn, but some upward pressures are only temporary. Price changes are expected to remain slightly negative in 2004, turning barely positive in 2005 (see table A.8).

Figure IV.3.
Inflation in the EU-12, Japan and the United States of America, January 1999-March 2004

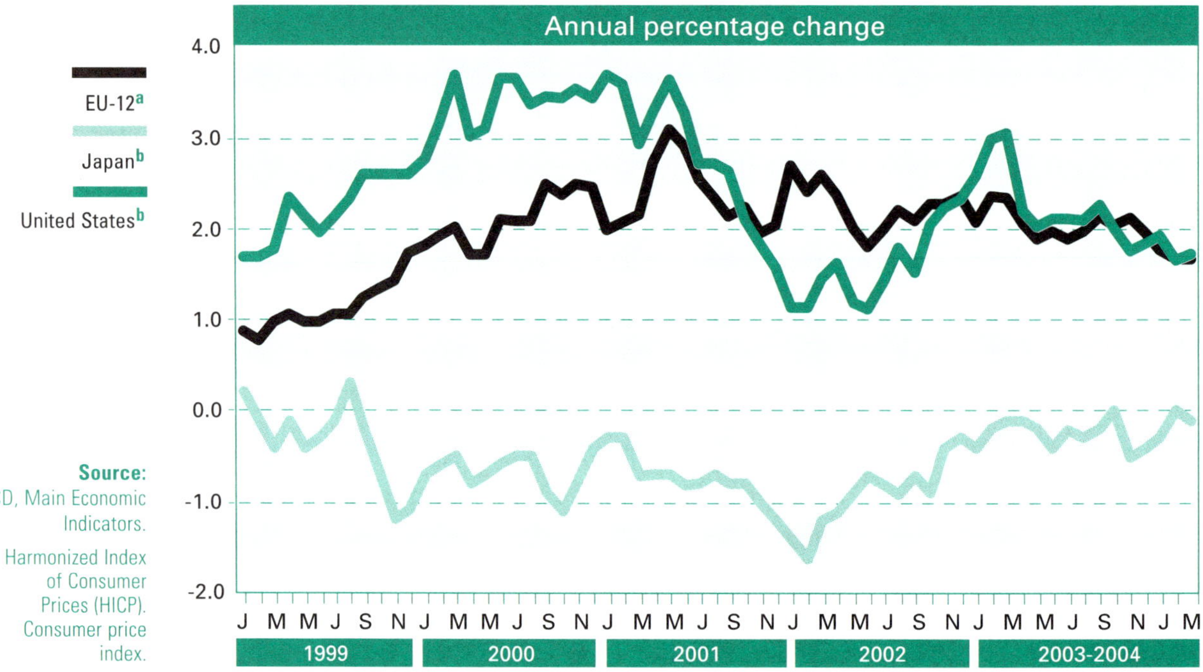

Source: OECD, Main Economic Indicators.

a Harmonized Index of Consumer Prices (HICP).

b Consumer price index.

Monetary policy is expected to remain accommodative ...

Monetary policy has been accommodative and the Bank of Japan (BoJ) is expected to maintain an easing policy stance for a considerable time. After maintaining the primary monetary policy target, the balance of current account held by the BoJ, at about 30 trillion yen for most 2003, the BoJ increased the target by about 10 per cent at the beginning of 2004. Meanwhile, the BoJ is expected to continue fighting deflation with some unconventional measures, such as outright purchases of stocks from banks and asset-backed securities from small and medium-sized firms. Although the BoJ has not adopted a formal inflation targeting mechanism, it is commonly considered that, until the annual rate of inflation, as measured by the consumer price index (CPI), reaches and stabilizes at 1 per cent, the Central Bank will not reverse its course of monetary easing. Therefore, the policy interest rate is expected to remain at virtually zero until at least 2005. However, unless the structural difficulties in banking and corporate financing, such as the NPLs, are resolved, the transmission of monetary policy to the real sector will continue to be poor, as indicated by the persistent decline in lending by commercial banks and the minuscule growth of the broad money supply, in spite of the high growth in the monetary base.

... and fiscal policy restrictive, while difficult structural reforms will continue

Facing a large amount of public debt, fiscal policy has been restrictive for the past few years, and will continue to be so in the outlook. According to the latest budget plan, government general expenditure, as share of GDP, will be maintained below the level of 2002 until 2006, aiming at a gradual reduction of the primary balance deficit, which stands at 5.5 per cent of GDP. Meanwhile, fiscal structural reforms are expected to accelerate, including such measures as a programme to resolve the problems of NPLs, regulatory reforms to encourage private investment, plans to promote the ICT sector, and measures to support job training, labour mobility and job assistance for school graduates. The tax reforms and pension reforms that are already in progress will continue to be implemented. In general, however, fiscal policy in Japan continues to face formidable challenges.

Strong economic growth in Australia is forecast to moderate in late 2004 and 2005 as the heat goes out of the housing market

The Australian economy is expected to grow by 4 per cent in 2004, stronger than the 2.6 per cent achieved in 2003, but a significant moderation is expected in late 2004 and 2005 (see table A.2). Household consumption is expected to continue to be a critical growth driver, supported by increased household borrowing, ongoing positive wealth effects, due largely to rising house prices, and rural incomes' recovering from the severe drought of 2003. Dwelling investment has peaked, but is likely to fall only slightly in 2004, with the risk of a sharp decline in 2005 being high. Business investment should continue its strong growth, given continuing low interest rates, rising corporate profits and robust corporate balance sheets.

Exports, which have been weak for the past few years, are likely to rebound in 2004, as world demand continues to grow, particularly in the United States and Asia; the emergence of China as a critical trade partner may provide a significant boost to demand for a range of commodity exports. The mining sector has increased capacity and appears well placed to respond to a pickup in global demand. One adverse factor for the export outlook has been the appreciating Australian dollar. Imports are forecast to grow further in 2004, but at a more moderate rate than in 2003. The current-account deficit is forecast to be about 5 per cent of GDP in 2004, down slightly from 2003.

Employment growth in 2004 is likely to be slower than in the previous year, but rural employment will grow strongly with the expected recovery in farm and agri-business production. The unemployment rate is expected to remain about 6 per cent over most of 2004 (see table A.6).

Since late 2003, the Reserve Bank of Australia has embarked on a phase of tighter monetary policy. The Bank, concerned about the higher housing prices of recent years, may increase interest rates further to above the neutral point. Meanwhile, defence and national security spending is expected to keep overall public expenditure at high levels during 2004, although growth is likely to be less than in 2003.

New Zealand's five years of strong growth will also moderate, as private consumption slows to correct the unusually low savings rate

In New Zealand, after above-trend growth for the past five years, averaging 3.7 per cent annually, performance is expected to moderate in the second half of 2004 and in 2005 (see table A.2). The driving forces over the past few years have been mainly favourable international prices for New Zealand's agricultural products and the phenomenon of an unexpectedly large number of immigrants (more than 100,000) which propelled housing prices and construction. Stimulated by relatively low real interest rates and buoyant consumer confidence, private consumption, boosted by wealth effects, has reached historic highs in terms of disposable income. The converse of the strong consumption growth has been a decline in the saving rate, reaching -10 per cent of current disposable income. With such a negative saving rate, there is a risk of a significant slowdown in private consumption if house-building continues to increase while net immigration slows and housing prices reverse.

The labour market has been tight over the past three years, with wages drifting upward. Meanwhile, despite overheated property prices and high rates of capacity utilization, inflation has remained at the low end of the target range set by the Central Bank, as a decline in the prices of tradable goods resulting from the appreciation of the New Zealand dollar offset a rise in the prices of non-tradables. The outlook for inflation remains within the target range (see table A.8).

The Central Bank has raised interest rates slightly over the past year, but the appreciation of the currency has made monetary conditions more restrictive than indicated by the policy interest rate. Given an expected moderation in domestic demand, the current monetary stance is expected to be maintained. However, if the risk of a "hard landing" increases, monetary easing may become necessary in 2005.

The fiscal position improved notably in 2003 as government revenues increased unexpectedly and there was a surplus of 4 per cent of GDP. Fiscal policy is expected to be stimulatory in 2004-2005, as government expenditure is set to increase.

The appreciation of the New Zealand dollar poses some downside risk. In the past few years, the exchange rate moved from exceptional undervaluation to extreme overvaluation. History indicates that a long time elapses before the full impact of a change in the exchange rate materializes in the real economy: the current-account deficit has already deteriorated as exports have slowed, but further weakening is expected in 2004-2005.

Western Europe: recovery yet to solidify

Recovery in Western Europe continues ...

The recovery of economic activity in Western Europe is continuing but has yet to show signs of acceleration to more robust levels of growth. So far, it is overly dependent on the revival of world economic activity and remains sensitive to the fluctuations in exchange-rate markets. The downturn was led by investment, and investment spending is a major driver of the recovery. However, consumption has yet to show much vigour and employment remains depressed. Within the region, the United Kingdom leads the recovery and displays the strongest performance. Germany and Italy are lagging, with France marginally stronger.

... driven by exports and investment

The recovery started in the third quarter of 2003 and was driven primarily by a surge in exports. In the fourth quarter, the driving force shifted to inventories and fixed investment, with net exports playing a restraining role as the strength of the euro dampened exports and boosted imports. Downside risks stemming from the appreciation of the euro and the lack of vigour in consumer spending remain. Industrial production rose in the second half of 2003, but weakened slightly at the beginning of 2004 (see figure IV.4). The most strength was in the intermediate, energy and capital goods sectors, consistent with the initial impetus from exports. Service sector activity was much weaker, reflecting the continued weakness in consumer spending. Survey evidence indicates that the sharpest improvement was in industrial confidence, which rose above its long-term average, although it stagnated in the first quarter of 2004, in part owing to concerns over the strength of the euro. Service sector confidence manifested a sustained upturn, but remained below its long-term average, again reflecting the weakness in consumer spending. Consumer confidence surveys also show sustained improvement since March 2003, but have yet to regain their long term-average.

The outlook is for a continuation of the gradual rebound in activity, led by a strong expansion in exports and in investment spending. Consumption is expected to pick up, but remain subdued. GDP in the EU-15 (euro zone) is expected to grow by 2 (1¾) per cent in 2004 after 0.7 (0.5) per cent in 2003 and to accelerate to 2¼ (2¼) per cent in 2005 (see table A.2).

Consumption is lagging ...

The moderate outlook for growth stems largely from the lack of dynamism in private consumption expenditure, a distinguishing characteristic of many of the underperformers in the region. The poor evolution of real disposable income, and uncertainties arising from geopolitical developments, as well as over the implications of continuing reforms, have restrained consumption. The rebound in equities and rising house prices have pro-

Figure IV.4.
Industrial production, excluding construction, in selected developed economies: January 1999-March 2004

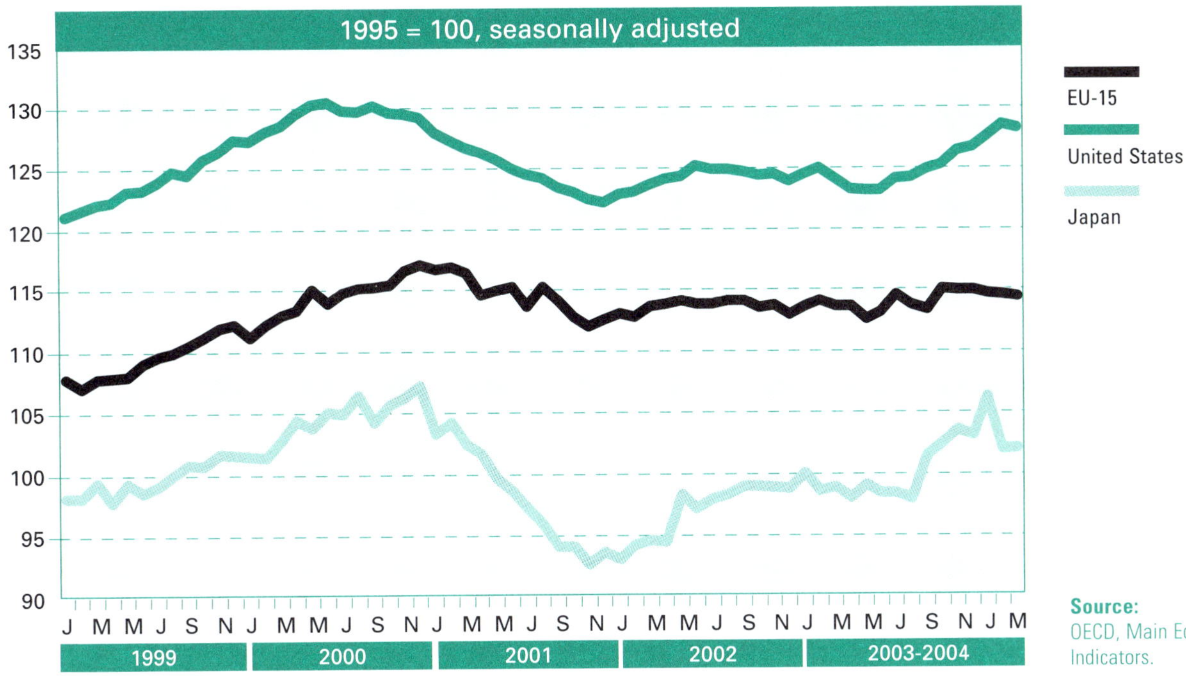

Source: OECD, Main Economic Indicators.

vided support in some countries, but not in others. Only moderate acceleration is expected in 2004 and 2005.

... but will be supported by currency appreciation, tax cuts, low interest rates and wealth effects

Consumption expenditure should largely follow the evolution of real disposable income, which is expected to pick up in line with the lagging and gradual improvement in employment and supported by moderate increases in nominal wages. The strong currency appreciation should also play a positive role, boosting nominal income via terms-of-trade effects and real income through its eventual pass-through into prices.[3] Some countries are still experiencing a boost from previously enacted tax cuts and some previously announced cuts have yet to come into force. Low interest rates continue to reduce debt burdens, but also encouraged households to take on more debt in 2003, particularly through housing purchases. Wealth should play a supporting role: equity markets have recovered from their lows in 2003 and house prices have risen in some countries, although there are questions of sustainability. Part of the weakness in consumption stems from increases in household savings rates, due in part to low confidence. The high rate of unemployment has led to more caution by consumers, exacerbated by uncertainty over reforms of pensions and social security (which will almost certainly require cuts in benefits) and the lingering effects of geopolitical uncertainty.

Government consumption expenditure continues to be a positive factor but will be withdrawn over the course of 2004 and 2005 as budgetary constraints continue to push for consolidation. One of the keys to the more robust performance of the United Kingdom during the downturn was the substantial fiscal stimulus that was enacted, made possible by good budgetary performance in the prior years. Many other countries in the region did not have such leeway, and so were severely constrained in applying a fiscal stimulus.

Investment has finally rebounded ...

After three consecutive quarters of decline, and a number of years of weakness, investment expenditure rebounded at the end of 2003 and is expected to continue to be a driving force behind the expansion. Financing conditions appear favourable: profits are improving and the cost of external finance is low. Improved profitability is coming from increased corporate earnings and continued cost-cutting by firms. Some difficulty results from the strength of the euro, which puts pressure on profit margins as companies struggle to maintain market share. It also reduces the value of the earnings of the United States affiliates of European firms when repatriated. Nominal interest rates are low and are expected to remain so and, with inflation at 2 per cent and forecast to decline only moderately, real rates will also remain low. Balance-sheet constraints continue to diminish, helped by rising equity prices. Corporate spreads have narrowed significantly. The banking sector is improving and lending is increasing. Much of the excess leverage incurred during the 1990s has been worked off. However, corporate debt levels remain high in some sectors, particularly telecommunications and automobiles. Overall, the extent to which firms have access to external financing is unclear. On the demand side, capacity utilization is still low in many sectors so that further expansion of investment spending will require a sustained improvement in overall demand. Foreign demand, particularly from East Asia in the capital goods sector, where capacity utilization is already high, has been a major driving force, but it has also been sensitive to exchange-rate developments. Further acceleration of investment will eventually require an improvement in domestic demand.

... boosted by strong foreign demand

Exports are expected to continue to play a major role in the upturn, particularly through their impact on investment expenditure. Despite the strength of the euro, which appreciated by 28 per cent in nominal trade-weighted terms between its low in September 2000 and March 2004 (see figure IV.2), the income effect of strong world demand has outweighed the price effect from the currency appreciation and the resulting weakened competitive position of euro area producers. It has led, however, to some loss of market share. At the country level, the impact has depended on export exposure to non-euro zone countries and on the sensitivity of the country to the export sector. Germany, for example, has a large share of output in manufacturing and its manufacturing sector is highly dependent on foreign demand. The rebound in activity, together with the improved terms of trade from exchange-rate developments, has led to a recovery in imports, which is expected to continue. While exports are a driving factor in the outlook, net exports are not expected to add significantly to growth.

Inflation hovers stubbornly around 2 per cent, with wide disparities across countries

In the light of the many downward pressures associated with the long period of subdued economic activity, as well as the appreciation of the euro, inflation underwent a very marginal decline vis-à-vis 2002, remaining close to 2 per cent throughout 2003 (see figure IV.3).[4] To some extent, this stickiness can be attributed to the volatile components of the index: unprocessed food prices were pushed up by the summer 2003 heatwave, processed food prices were boosted by increases in tobacco taxes, and energy prices exerted pressures at the beginning of 2003. However, price stickiness may also reflect some inertia in adjusting to changing economic conditions. There have also been differences across countries, with a difference in inflation between France and Germany of more than 1 percentage point opening up over the course of 2002, for example. Inflationary pressures are expected to continue to subside gradually. Cost pressures are subdued and producer price increases are expected to remain moderate. The oil price increases have been largely offset by currency appreciation. Wage increases are expected to be moderate and to be coupled with some improvement in labour productivity. The pickup in demand is not expected to exceed potential output in the forecast and continued pass-through of the cumulative currency appreciation of the past two years should exert downward pressure on prices (see table A.8).

The labour market held up well during the downturn. Unemployment started to increase in the latter half of 2001, in the EU-15, from a low point of 7.3 to 8.0 per cent from early 2003 (see figure IV.1). This compares favourably with the slowdown in the early 1990s, when unemployment in the EU-15 had increased by about 2.5 percentage points to more than 10 per cent. This suggests that the recent gains in performance have been durable, although there was considerable diversity across countries. Portugal, Belgium and Luxembourg suffered increases of 2 percentage points or more, followed by the Netherlands, Germany and Denmark, with increases of at least 1.5 percentage points. On the other hand, the long period of improvement in Italy continued with a further decline in unemployment of about 1.3 percentage points. The United Kingdom and Finland also saw minor declines. This generally improved resilience can be traced in part to the successful implementation of reforms in the latter half of the 1990s: increased use of part-time contracts and other flexible arrangements, cuts in non-wage labour costs and moderate wage settlements; but some of this improved resilience may be a sign of continuing inertia, due to incomplete reforms. Firms may have been hoarding labour, owing to the costs of adjusting labour inputs, and waiting for activity to resume. Whatever the reason, the corollary of this resilience is that labour productivity declined over the cycle and was another source of pressure on company profits. Companies will be seeking to restore labour productivity and profits during the initial phases of the upturn, before increasing hiring. Given the modest acceleration of growth expected, employment growth will lag the recovery and any region-wide improvement in unemployment is expected to be negligible (see table A.6).

Labour markets showed improved resilience during the downturn ...

... but so far have been impervious to the recovery

The uncertain and uneven nature of the recovery, and its diversity across countries, are reflected in divergent policies within Europe. In the United Kingdom, activity has been strong enough to motivate three policy tightenings by the Bank of England since November 2003, with further moves anticipated. On the other hand, activity has been sufficiently slow in Sweden for the Swedish Central Bank to lower rates twice in early 2004. In the euro zone, policy has been unchanged since the cut in June 2003 brought short-term interest rates to 2 per cent. It was assumed that the next policy move would signal the beginning of a slow but sustained effort to return policy to a more neutral stance, but the recovery is not yet assured, with some countries still susceptible to reversal. The tightening in monetary conditions implied in the rise in the euro in the second half of 2003 and the beginning of 2004 was damaging to industrial confidence, and further currency appreciation or evidence of faltering growth could provoke additional policy easing.

No major changes in monetary policy are foreseen for 2004 ...

A major factor behind the reluctance of the European Central Bank to lower rates further has been stubborn inflation, with the Harmonized Index of Consumer Prices (HICP) running above the 2 per cent policy target for much of 2003 with only minor deceleration in early 2004. The appreciation of the currency, as well as the weakness of the recovery, has been slow to feed through into inflation. With the expected continued strength of the currency and only a moderate acceleration in activity anticipated, the inflation outlook is for continued deceleration during 2004, but not to the extent that the European Central Bank would reduce its interest rate further. The forecast assumes that monetary policy will remain unchanged throughout 2004 and will be tightened in 2005 by a total of 50 basis points (bps).

... but gradual tightening is expected in 2005

Fiscal policy is expected to become moderately restrictive in many countries in the region over the course of 2004 and into 2005, as countries attempt to consolidate budgets. With few exceptions, 2003 saw a continuation of the deterioration in budgetary

The need for fiscal consolidation will result in some tightening of fiscal policy

conditions across the region that had started in 2001. In part the decline was cyclical, owing to the workings of automatic stabilizers, but planned boosts in public spending, spending overruns, particularly on health care, and some discretionary tax cuts were also involved.[5] As a result of this deterioration, Germany and France exceeded by wide margins the 3 per cent limit for the ratio of fiscal deficit to GDP embodied in the Stability and Growth Pact. The Netherlands, Portugal and the United Kingdom were close to 3 per cent, while Italy was at 2.5 per cent. Debt levels also rose and six countries in the euro zone registered debt-to-GDP ratios in excess of 60 per cent in 2003. This led to a crisis and, in November 2003, the European Council of Finance Ministers suspended the excessive deficit procedure rather than enforce sanctions against France and Germany, on the understanding that both countries would bring their deficits into compliance by 2005. According to their Stability programmes submitted in late 2003 and early 2004, all these countries have committed to reducing their deficits, although the pace of reduction is not expected to be very rapid.

Further currency appreciation or lacklustre consumption could imperil the recovery

There are, however, downside risks, particularly in respect of the path of exchange rates. It is assumed that the euro will peak in 2004 and then depreciate. If it were to appreciate more, this could pose a risk to the recovery, particularly in Germany, by cutting exports and leading to reduced investment spending, exports and investment spending having been key to the recovery so far. Another risk is that consumption expenditure could falter. The slow improvement in labour-market conditions, coupled with the uncertainties stemming from the prospects for reforms in pensions, health care and labour markets, could cause consumers to raise savings, dampening demand.

Economies in transition

Solid growth continues

Growth prospects for the economies in transition have been boosted by the favorable external environment, improved macroeconomic stability, progress in reforms and growing consumer and investor confidence. After a slowdown in 2002, growth for the group accelerated in 2003 (see table IV.2), and a strong pace is forecast for 2004, followed by moderation in 2005. Eight countries in the group had joined EU as of 1 May 2004, reinforcing the positive outlook for the region.

The economies in Central and Eastern Europe have continued to recover gradually and will strengthen further in 2004 and 2005 as growth in Western Europe improves. The high growth rates in the Baltic economies for the past four years have been a result of reforms and prudent macroeconomic policies and the benefits are likely to be sustained in 2004 and 2005. The acceleration in the economies of CIS has been associated with the increased prices of oil and gas, along with a recovery of investment; the medium-term prospects for these economies are to some extent subject to the vicissitudes of oil prices.

Central and Eastern Europe: sustaining recovery

Economic growth in the Central and Eastern European region accelerated to 3.6 per cent in 2003 and is expected to strengthen to over 4 per cent in 2004 and 2005, in line with the improving prospects for EU. The higher regional growth in 2003, however, was to a large extent due to the economic recovery in Poland. In many other economies of the

Table IV.2.
Growth and inflation in selected economies in transition, quarterly indicators, 2002-2003

Percentage[a]	2002 quarter				2003 quarter			
	I	II	III	IV	I	II	III	IV
	Rate of growth of gross domestic product							
Belarus	4.1	5.8	4.7	5.5	5.6	4.7	7.3	8.9
Czech Republic	2.6	2.1	1.7	1.5	2.5	2.6	3.4	3.1
Hungary	3.1	3.2	3.7	3.9	2.7	2.5	2.9	3.6
Kazakhstan	10.6	7.5	9.4	11.4	10.5	9.6	7.7	9.2
Poland	0.5	0.9	1.8	2.2	2.3	3.9	4.0	4.7
Romania	3.2	5.6	4.4	5.4	4.4	4.2	5.5	4.8
Russian Federation	3.8	4.3	4.4	6.0	7.5	7.9	6.5	7.6
Ukraine	7.4	4.9	6.8	-3.0	7.9	9.3	6.6	13.4
	Change in consumer prices							
Belarus	47.2	44.6	43.1	37.4	30.8	28.3	28.3	27.0
Czech Republic	3.8	2.3	0.8	0.6	-0.3	0.2	0.0	0.9
Hungary	6.3	5.6	4.8	5.0	4.8	4.1	4.9	5.6
Kazakhstan	5.7	5.5	6.4	6.4	7.2	6.5	5.8	7.1
Poland	3.5	2.0	1.1	0.8	0.3	0.3	0.8	1.5
Romania	26.8	24.2	21.3	18.5	16.7	14.9	15.1	14.9
Russian Federation	18.0	15.8	15.1	15.1	14.6	14.0	13.5	12.5
Ukraine	3.7	0.8	-0.9	-0.5	2.2	4.5	6.5	7.8

Sources:
UN/DESA and Economic Commission for Europe.

a Percentage change from the corresponding period of the preceding year.

region, GDP growth moderated (see table A.3) despite double-digit export growth and generally buoyant private consumption. In South-eastern Europe, agricultural output was affected by adverse weather conditions. Investment in Central Europe stagnated, suggesting weaker growth prospects for some economies in the medium term.

EU accession will provide benefits but also involve costs

Five Central and Eastern European countries (the Czech Republic, Hungary, Poland, Slovakia and Slovenia) joined the EU on 1 May 2004. The accession will bring benefits, but will also involve costs, for these economies. Since most of the gains from integration through trade and production have already materialized, further benefits in these areas may not be significant in the short run, but will increase in the long run. However, uncertainties remain with respect to the short-term macroeconomic impact of the enlargement: for example, accession, and the goal of eventually joining the euro zone, will place constraints on the macroeconomic policies of the new members.

Increased foreign direct investment (FDI) flows to Central Europe are expected following the enlargement, but these countries face growing competition in attracting FDI from South-eastern Europe, as well as from Asia. Increased competition from EU is expected to enhance productivity and product quality in the new member countries, but it may also challenge some domestic producers. Transfers from EU to the new member States should have beneficial effects, particularly for public infrastructure projects, and subsidies should support the agricultural sector, which will face increased competition within the enlarged EU. Most of the assistance received from the structural and cohesion funds of EU and under the Common Agricultural Policy, however, is to be co-financed by the new members themselves.

Economic growth shifted within the region in 2003

In 2003, economic growth within the region shifted from the Central European economies to Bulgaria and Romania, as the latter benefited from strong investment and robust private consumption. Economic policy in both countries is driven by anticipated EU membership in 2007. Strong growth was also registered in Croatia. Expansion in these countries is expected to continue in 2004 and 2005 despite higher energy prices. The situation in many of the successor States of the former Yugoslavia remains difficult, constrained by a weak production base, lack of investment and potential political instability.

Inflation fell ...

Inflation in the region fell in 2003 (see table A.9), with a number of countries undershooting their inflation targets. Nominal appreciation of local currencies vis-à-vis the United States dollar, as well as low food prices in part of Central Europe, played a role in this regard. Inflation in the region is expected to rise in 2004 as a result of higher food prices, following the drought in 2003, and because of inflows of speculative capital, attracted by the interest rate differential with the euro zone. Nevertheless, wage pressure will remain low in many countries and further disinflation is expected in the region's high-inflation countries.

... allowing an easing of monetary policy

Benefiting from the low-inflationary environment, monetary policy was relaxed in the region in 2003 and early 2004, in some cases in line with the policy of the European Central Bank. Given the expected acceleration in inflation, further interest rate cuts are not likely. For the new EU members, the challenge for monetary policy will be to combine anti-inflationary policies with the adjustment of relative prices and to avoid a misaligned exchange rate prior to entering the exchange-rate mechanism ERM2.

Unemployment remains high

There was some improvement in employment in Bulgaria and Slovakia, but no significant improvement took place in other countries of the region. The highest rates of unemployment are in Poland and most of the successor States of the former Yugoslavia. The unemployment problem in the region is largely structural and does not diminish significantly with the cyclical growth of output. Since privatization of a number of loss-making State-owned enterprises, especially in South-eastern Europe, is planned, little improvement in the employment situation is expected in the short term. Moreover, competition from Asian products is putting pressure on labour costs.

Most of the countries in the region continue to run high and largely structural budget deficits and off-budget spending has only recently been reduced. In order to balance the budgets, a reform of public finances is needed (see box IV.1). The fiscal situation is better in some countries of South-eastern Europe, where improved revenue collection and lower interest payments on government debt allow targets to be met without cuts in spending.

The current accounts in the region remain in deficit. Export performance in the region in 2003 was better than expected but the repatriation of profits by foreign investors put further strain on current accounts in some countries. Exports are expected to strengthen in 2004 although, following the EU enlargement, exports of goods may be affected by new trade barriers between Central and South-eastern Europe and falling informal trade. The strong growth in imports is also expected to continue.

Box IV.1

Fiscal consolidation in the new EU member States

The budget deficits of the Central and Eastern European States that have become European Union (EU) members increased over the past decade, reaching record highs in 2003 in some cases (see table) and leading to a steady rise in public debt. The structural deficit offset all the cyclical revenue gains from gross domestic product (GDP) growth in the late 1990s.

Consolidated general government balance and gross debt in selected EU member States, 1997-2003

Percentage of GDP							
	1997	1998	1999	2000	2001	2002	2003
General government balance							
EU-(15 countries)	-2.4	-1.6	-0.7	1.0	-1.0	-2.0	-2.6
Euro zone	-2.6	-2.2	-1.3	0.2	-1.6	-2.3	-2.7
Czech Republic	-2.5	-4.2	-3.4	-4.5	-6.4	-6.4	-12.9
Hungary	-6.8	-8.0	-5.6	-3.0	-4.4	-9.3	-5.9
Poland	-4.0	-2.1	-1.4	-1.8	-3.5	-3.6	-4.1
Slovenia	..	-2.2	-2.1	-3.0	-2.7	-1.9	-1.8
Slovakia	-5.5	-4.7	-6.4	-12.3	-6.0	-5.7	-3.6
General government gross debt							
EU-(15 countries)	71.0	68.8	67.9	64.0	63.2	62.5	64.0
Euro zone	74.3	73.6	72.2	69.7	69.4	69.2	70.4
Czech Republic	12.2	12.9	13.4	18.2	25.2	28.9	37.6
Hungary	64.2	61.9	61.2	55.4	53.5	57.1	59.0
Slovenia	..	23.6	24.9	26.7	26.9	27.8	27.1
Slovakia	28.6	28.6	43.8	49.9	48.7	43.3	42.8

Sources: Statistical office of the European Communities (Eurostat) and OECD.

Both public revenues and expenditures declined relative to GDP in these economies during the transition period, but the share of public revenues declined faster because of changes in ownership and in the taxation system, as well as reductions in tariffs. On the other hand, public expenditure continued to increase (although its share of GDP declined) and is now higher than in other economies with a similar degree of openness and per capita income. Spending was primarily in the form of current public expenditures, social transfers and income redistribution rather than public investment, which was only about 5 per cent of GDP and declined in the late 1990s. A large number of quasi-fiscal activities complicated the fiscal situation.

In Poland, as a country example, the surplus at the beginning of the decade has turned into a deficit of over 4 per cent of GDP and domestic public debt has increased to about 30 per cent of GDP. Only debt forgiveness by the London and Paris Clubs in the early 1990s prevented the Government from breaching its constitutional limit on public debt of 60 per cent of GDP.

Box IV.1 (cont'd)

EU accession will have direct and indirect fiscal effects for the new members. Among the direct effects, contributions to the EU budget, co-financing of EU projects, spending to meet EU standards regarding the environment, public administration and infrastructure and the realignment of custom duties will have a negative impact on budgets. In contrast, some relief will come from the phasing out of production subsidies and tax harmonization with EU: many foreign investors in the region were granted preferential tax treatment and many taxes, such as value-added taxes (VATs), are lower than in EU.

Among the long-run indirect effects of EU accession, tax competition will have a negative effect on budgets while stronger growth, brought about by convergence within EU, and better budget institutions, will have a favourable effect. However, according to some estimates, the overall fiscal impact of the EU accession will be negative, at least in the short run, leading to a deterioration of about 1.5 per cent of GDP in the public finances of new members.[a]

a G. Kopits and I. Szekely, "Fiscal policy challenges of EU accession for the Baltics and Central Europe", in *Structural Challenges for Europe*, G. Tumpell-Gugerell and P.Mooslechner, eds. (Cheltenham, United Kingdom, Edward Elgar, 2004).

Following admission, new EU members have to implement fiscal consolidation plans as part of the EU multilateral fiscal surveillance framework. Moreover, they will eventually have to adopt the euro, since EU does not intend to allow any more member countries to opt out. At some stage, therefore, these countries will have to comply with the provisions of the Stability and Growth Pact, including reducing their budget deficits to 3 per cent of GDP, and with other Maastricht criteria.

A number of changes may be introduced into the Pact, but these changes will probably be limited to the accounting arrangements for public investment and the cyclical adjustment of budgetary balances. EU is unlikely to allow its new members with large structural deficits, especially with their current pattern of expenditure, to join the monetary union, and it seems reluctant to adopt an individual approach. Wishing to secure investors' confidence, the new EU members, on the other hand, will wish to abolish currency risk by joining the euro zone as soon as possible.

Though often used in the past, privatization receipts are no longer an option for financing fiscal deficits in these countries. Demographic trends in the region present a further fiscal challenge. These countries' rapidly ageing populations and the possibility of large outward migration of young people following the enlargement will create difficulties for the present pension system. Servicing foreign debt is also becoming a fiscal burden for these countries.

Most of these countries have already adopted plans to reform public finances and to streamline tax systems in response to these challenges, aiming at a significant reduction of their deficits by 2008 and the adoption of the euro by 2010. Meeting these targets will require a comprehensive change in the structure of public finances, because cyclical factors, such as stronger GDP growth, will not be sufficient. Balance cannot be achieved by higher taxation, owing to a ceiling on the tax level in EU and tax competition among new members. Therefore, most of the consolidation will have to focus on the expenditure side where a gradual approach will be required to avoid adversely affecting the most vulnerable groups of the population. A crucial component of this strategy should be a shift towards investment-related spending. Among other measures, the use of mandatory private saving accounts would alleviate the financial difficulties in the pension system. Increased efficiency in public services will have to be achieved without increasing expenditure. To achieve all these goals, the new EU members will also need more effective budget institutions.

In the past, the current-account deficits of most of these countries were largely covered by FDI inflows, but diminished FDI into the new EU members may force external borrowing. At the same time, transfers from EU should improve current accounts and low global interest rates will limit deficits on investment income.

The main policy challenge for the new EU members is to work out a comprehensive post-enlargement strategy, ensuring that the application of EU rules and regulations does not have an adverse impact on their economies. Bulgaria, and especially Romania, should focus on the implementation of the EU *acquis*. Most countries in South-eastern Europe need to upgrade their industries, and implement institutional changes. Further support from EU, including increased assistance and accommodative trade policies, could contribute in all these areas.

Relations with EU are key to the region's economic future

The Baltic countries: continuing fast growth

The Baltic States' average GDP growth rate of above 7 per cent in 2003 was higher than anticipated, despite the weak recovery of Western Europe (see table A.3). Reforms and prudent macroeconomic policies have generated strong domestic demand, created jobs and boosted GDP growth, resulting in a better performance than in other economies in transition. Growth is expected to moderate in 2004 and 2005 owing to a deceleration in domestic demand, but will stay robust, supported by the improved business environment and strengthening exports. With their further integration into EU structures, the prospects of these countries' will become more dependent on the recovery in Europe on the one hand and on promoting competitiveness and growth on the other.

Strong growth is forecast to moderate

Average inflation in the Baltic States decelerated in 2003 (see table A.9), but unemployment remains high, partly owing to the skill mismatch in the labour force. There was a moderate decline in 2003 (see table A.7), but continued progress needs further labour-market flexibility, supported by improved wage determination procedures.

These countries' prudent fiscal policies and their low public debt support their intentions to join the Monetary Union in the near future. To meet this goal, Estonia and Lithuania joined the EU's exchange rate mechanism (ERM2) in June 2004. Although this mechanism allows national currencies to fluctuate against the euro within a 15 per cent band, the two countries have opted to maintain their exchange rate pegs to the euro for two years prior to adopting it. Latvia has indicated its intention to adopt the euro in January 2008, a year later than the other two Baltic States. It is therefore expected that these countries will bring their economic indicators in line with the Maastricht criteria and continue their commitment to prudent macroeconomic policies.

Adopting the euro is the next economic challenge

Current-account deficits rose rapidly in 2003, reaching a double-digit percentage of GDP in Estonia, over 9 per cent of GDP in Latvia and over 6 per cent of GDP in Lithuania. These deficits are largely covered by FDI, but concerns over their sustainability remain.

Commonwealth of Independent States (CIS): the fastest growing region

Growth in the economies of the CIS region accelerated in 2003 to 7.6 per cent, underpinned by favourable external conditions, in particular increasing world demand and prices for energy and commodities, and by robust domestic demand. Macroeconomic stability and robust growth in many countries over the past five years, in conjunction with progress in transition reforms, have restored the confidence of consumers and investors, in turn reinforcing economic performance and prospects. Growth is forecast to remain robust in

Continuing robust growth is driven by both external markets and domestic demand

2004, but to moderate in 2005 as domestic demand decelerates and oil prices retreat from their highs in 2004.

The stronger-than-anticipated recovery of the region largely reflects the rebound of the economy of the Russian Federation, supported by acceleration in the large economies of Kazakhstan and Ukraine, where GDP rose over 9 per cent. The fact that, boosted by growing import demand, trade with other CIS countries increased rapidly, in turn strengthened regional performance. The upswing of many smaller economies in the region also contributed to this acceleration; in some of them, GDP grew at a double-digit annual rate (see table A.3).

Growth in the Russian Federation is heavily dependent on exports of oil and gas ...

In 2003, the economy of the Russian Federation grew by 7.3 per cent, followed by a year-on-year growth rate of 8 per cent in the first quarter of 2004. For the first time since 2000, this recovery is being driven by investment: gross fixed capital formation grew at a double-digit rate, but there was also rapid growth in household consumption and export expansion of over 10 per cent in real terms, which marks a historic high. Real incomes and consumer spending increased rapidly, as did labour productivity. Growth was relatively balanced across industrial sectors, with particular strength in fuels and ferrous metals. However, growth continues to depend heavily on hydrocarbon exports, presenting the challenge of diversification into the non-energy sector in order to reduce the country's vulnerability to world oil prices (see box IV.2).

... supported in 2003 by monetary policy and currency appreciation

The increased growth in the Russian Federation in 2003 was also supported by easier monetary policy. The refinancing rate was cut in 2003 and in January 2004, but the priority in monetary policy is often to smooth exchange-rate fluctuations. The ruble appreciated against the United States dollar in nominal terms by 2 per cent and in real terms by 14 per cent during 2003. Further moderate appreciation is expected. The Central Bank will continue to control the growing money supply, mostly due to continued inflows, and to limit the real appreciation of the ruble. Economic activity in the Russian Federation is expected to moderate only marginally in the short run, while long-term growth prospects depend on the success of broader structural reforms.

Intraregional trade is serving as an engine of growth

In 2003, rapid growth in domestic demand in the Russian Federation boosted its imports from neighbouring countries, making it a regional engine of growth. Trade of the Russian Federation with the three biggest economies in the region (Belarus, Kazakhstan and Ukraine) rapidly increased, but exports to many other CIS countries grew as well (see figure IV.5). Meanwhile, the initiative for creating a Single Economic Space (SES) among Belarus, Kazakhstan, the Russian Federation and Ukraine will foster further regional trade and growth.

Performance elsewhere shows a similar pattern

The performance of many other CIS economies has had features similar to those of the Russian economy. Household consumption in most cases has increased rapidly and the growth of investment spending has accelerated. In Azerbaijan, strong investment is associated with the construction of oil and gas pipelines in order to expand exports; in other countries, the recovery of investment has a broader base, but remains too low to support adequate growth. Exports of hydrocarbons were the main contributor to growth in such resource-rich countries as Azerbaijan, Kazakhstan and Turkmenistan, while in Ukraine it was exports of metals (see chap. II). Relying predominantly on exports of resources, however, makes growth vulnerable to the volatility of external markets, and diversifying output remains a challenge for these countries. Imports were also strong in many economies.

Box IV.2

The oil sector and economic growth in the Russian Federation

A number of factors have contributed to the recovery of the Russian economy from the financial crisis of 1998: devaluation of the national currency, higher commodity prices, in particular of oil and gas, and progress with economic reforms. Among these, dependence on oil and oil prices presents a challenge to the sustainability of growth.

Boosted by higher world oil prices and growing demand, the Russian Federation's oil output rose by 38 per cent between 1999 and 2003 (see figure) as the result of an increase in capacity utilization and a recovery in investment in the sector. The oil sector is among the fastest growing industries in the Russian Federation, having outpaced overall industrial output growth by over 4 percentage points in 2003. Although it accounts for only 9 per cent of gross domestic product (GDP) and less than 1 per cent of total employment, it has a large and growing impact on economic activity, mainly through the increase in revenues from oil exports, but also through the growth in the volume of exports, their impact on the real exchange rate and the fact that oil revenues account for 35-45 per cent of government revenues.

Output and prices of oil in the Russian Federation, 1999-2003

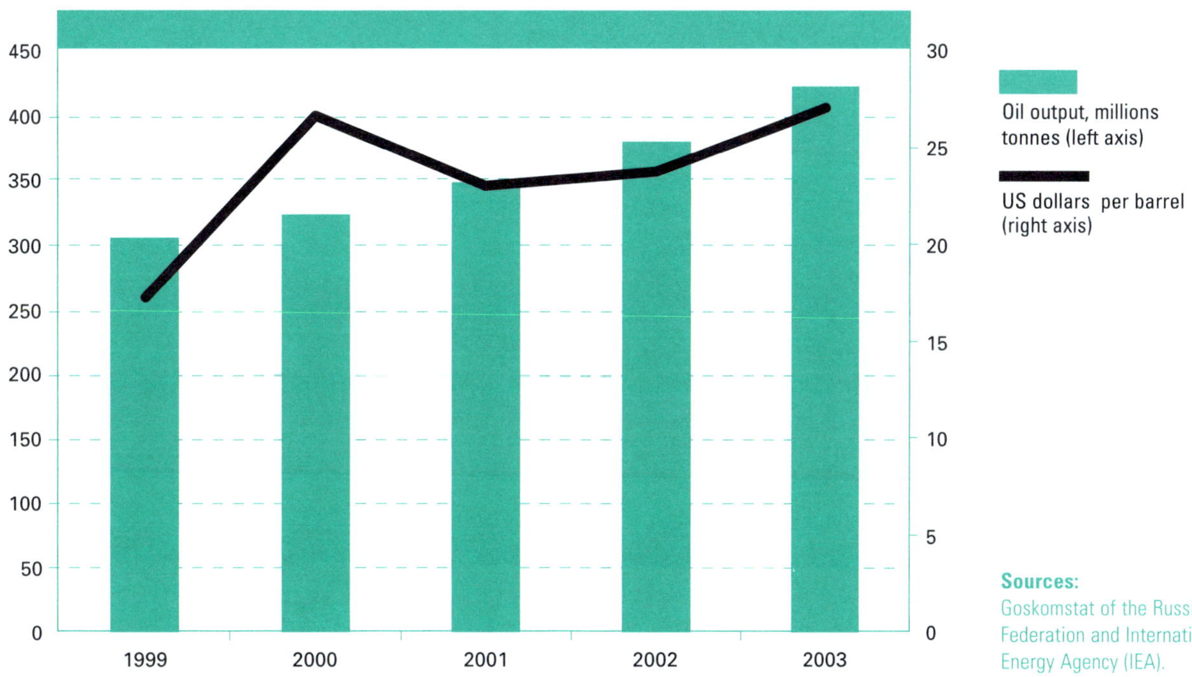

Sources: Goskomstat of the Russian Federation and International Energy Agency (IEA).

Oil revenue is subject to the short-term volatility in international oil prices. However, the role of the oil sector as a driving force for economic activity should also be viewed from a long-run perspective taking into account the relationships among GDP, the real effective exchange rate, the fiscal situation and oil prices. An empirical investigation by the United Nations Secretariat suggests that an increase of $1 in the price of Urals oil raises the Russian Federation's real GDP by 0.44 percentage points. Among other comparable oil-producing countries, only Azerbaijan, Turkmenistan, Venezuela and the Islamic Republic of Iran have a higher dependence on oil than the Russian Federation, when measured in terms of oil and gas exports as a share of total exports.[a] The study also supports the view that,

a Indicators of resource dependence are based on data from the IMF Staff Reports (various issues for the countries) and from *BP Energy Outlook*.

Box IV.2 (cont'd)

along with the increase in the price of oil, the depreciation of the rouble since 1998 has contributed to Russia's long-run growth. Both factors are driving the growth of GDP in the short run as well. Therefore macroeconomic policies, in particular, anti-inflationary policy could be used to restrain the real appreciation of the ruble.

These results underscore the importance of oil prices for the country's growth prospects and the extent to which the domestic economy is exposed to external shocks. This potential vulnerability also spills over to neighbouring countries and is therefore a downside risk for the economic prospects of the Commonwealth of Independent States (CIS) region as a whole. At the same time, there is the potential of using the windfall gains from this natural resource to diversify the economy and to improve the country's and the region's long-term prospects. A step in this direction was the establishment in 2003 of a Stabilization Fund, which started to accumulate oil-associated windfalls in 2004 and is intended to provide stability to public finance. The study indicates, however, that the beneficial impact of high oil prices on GDP could be offset by a real appreciation of the currency, as is currently happening. This suggests the need for macroeconomic policies to restrain the real appreciation of the ruble.

Oil is often regarded as a blessing, but it can also have negative economic effects on non-oil sector development, through a sequence known as the Dutch disease.[b] As a natural resource, oil's role should be not only to temporarily improve output growth, but also to transform the oil boom into sustainable long-term growth. The latter is exclusively a task for policy, not only on the fiscal side but also in terms of the macroeconomic policy required to support stabilization in conjunction with structural reforms.

b The term "Dutch disease" is used to explain a situation in an economy where exports of a natural resource raise the value of the national currency which, in turn, makes manufactured goods less competitive internationally, increasing imports and decreasing exports of such goods.

Growth fails to alleviate unemployment

The rapid economic growth in the CIS region in 2003 did not translate into many new jobs. A weakening of employment was observed almost everywhere in the region, with a few exceptions, such as Kazakhstan, where employment grew over 3 per cent. Registered unemployment remains in the range of 1.4 to 9.8 per cent (see table A.7), but the statistics may underestimate the actual level. The available labour-force survey data for some of the countries in the region indicate a higher rate of unemployment. Given the ongoing restructuring of enterprises in many countries, unemployment is unlikely to fall significantly in the short run.

Against this background, poverty and inequality remain challenges. Despite the decrease in absolute poverty in some countries, inequality is rising. The average incomes of the top 10 per cent in the Russian Federation are estimated to have been 15 times greater than those of the lowest 10 per cent in 2003.

Monetary policies are eased

Macroeconomic policy in most of these countries was supportive in 2003, mainly through a more relaxed monetary policy. In view of the inflationary expectations in such countries as Belarus, the Republic of Moldova and Tajikistan, tighter fiscal and monetary policies are needed to constrain inflation and improve debt dynamics. Refinancing rates were cut by the central banks in countries where capital inflows and export revenues from oil strengthened the domestic currency. In many cases, the continued weakening of the United States dollar throughout the period resulted in real effective depreciation of the currency. There was a reduction of the effects of world oil-price fluctuations on exchange rates and domestic markets in Azerbaijan and Kazakhstan owing to the functioning of the oil stabilization funds, and similar results are expected for the Russian Federation, as its fund goes into operation.

Government deficits decreased on average in 2003, largely owing to the cyclical effects of output, and remain lower than in other transition countries. Additional revenues from higher-than-expected prices of commodities, in particular oil and gas, in export-oriented countries contributed to this improvement. In the Russian Federation and Kazakhstan, in particular, a rapid increase in general government surpluses was due to

Figure IV.5.
Trade of the Russian Federation with other CIS countries, 2002 and 2003
(Millions of dollars)

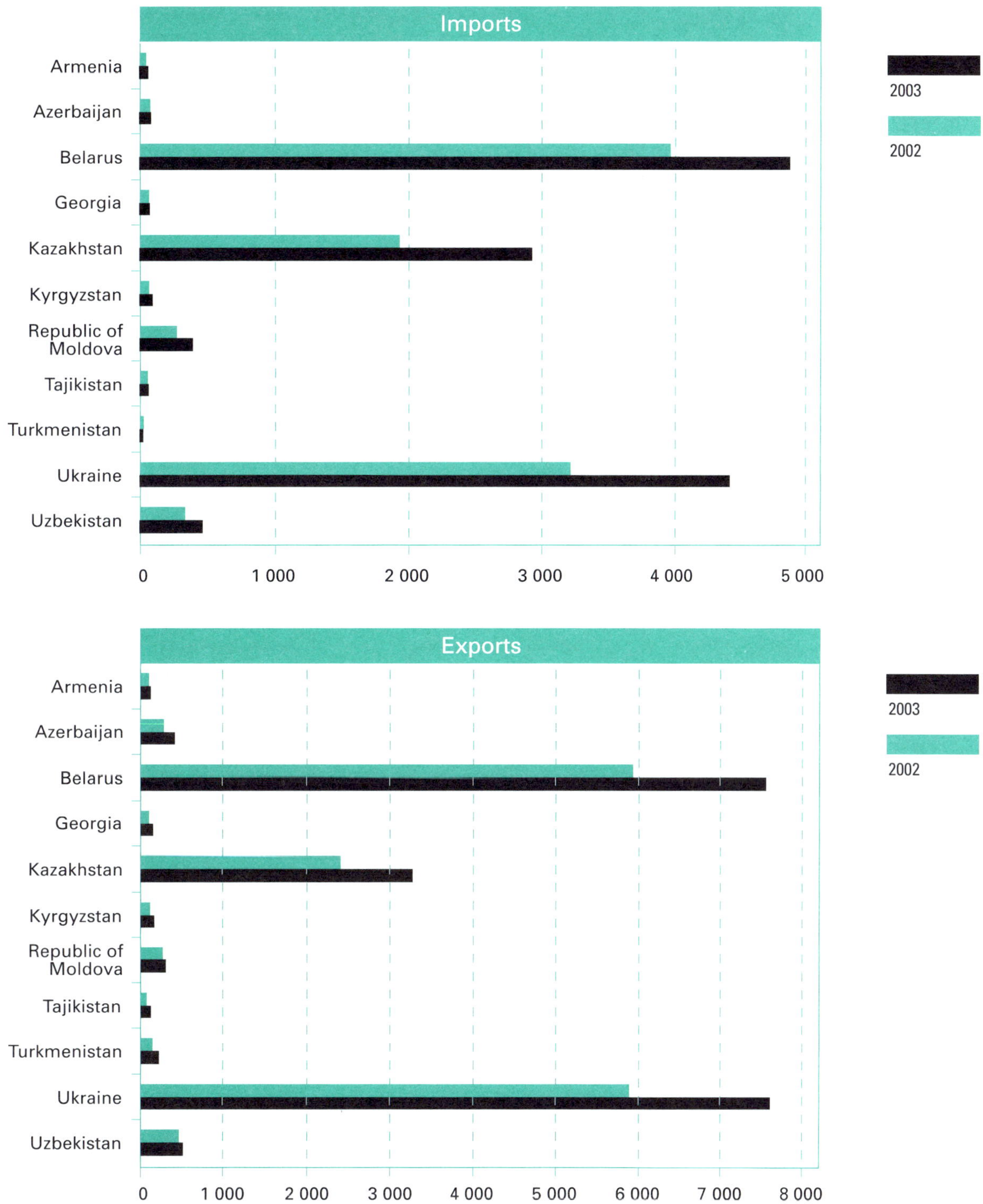

Source:
Goskomstat of the Russian Federation and Inter-State Statistical Committee of CIS.

Most fiscal balances improve ...

higher-than-anticipated revenues. There were a few exceptions, such as Armenia and Tajikistan, where growing public spending increased fiscal deficits. In countries with relatively large fiscal deficits (Armenia, Kyrgyzstan, the Republic of Moldova, Tajikistan and Uzbekistan), a further reduction is projected in 2004. Commitments to prudent fiscal policies, along with ongoing tax system reforms, are contributing to a strengthening of public finance and hence will improve overall prospects.

... but current-account balances are mixed

There was an increase in the average current-account surplus for the region in 2003, but the overall positive balance is largely a reflection of the current-account surpluses of the Russian Federation, Ukraine and Kazakhstan. Elsewhere in the region, external imbalances are the result of deficits on services and factor incomes and, given the negligible private capital inflows, external sector stability is underpinned mostly by worker remittances and official transfers. A downturn in commodity prices would worsen the external positions of the resource-rich economies. Further rapid growth in consumption and investment is also likely to narrow the current-account surpluses in the region.

Economic buoyancy, macroeconomic stability and the improved business environment in the region continued to attract foreign capital. In the Caucasian and Central Asian countries, the increase in inflows was substantial, dominated by FDI in the hydrocarbon sector. In Azerbaijan, FDI reached 46 per cent of GDP in 2003. In Ukraine and the Russian Federation, FDI inflows increased in absolute terms, but the total stock of FDI as a proportion of GDP remains low.

Commodity prices, particularly of oil and gas, are the major risks to continued rapid growth

The major risk for the CIS region is related to world prices for commodities, in particular to the prices of oil and gas, which account for a substantial part of the export revenues of the resource-rich countries. If prices go down more than anticipated by the end of the year, external imbalances might deteriorate in some of the countries and growth might moderate below the projected rate. In some countries, there also remains the risk of postponing structural reforms, including strengthening institutions (including property rights) and developing an efficient banking sector to provide financial resources for an investment-oriented growth process. Both possibilities would slow market transformation and dampen the long-term prospects of the region.

The Developing economies

The improved external environment is largely responsible for improved growth ...

Growth accelerated in the developing countries in 2003 (see table IV.3), thanks to the improvement in the international economic environment—reflected in increased capital inflows, strengthened external demand and a recovery in the prices of commodities—as well as supportive economic policies in a number of countries, notably in East Asia. Nonetheless, the employment situation continued to deteriorate and remains a source of concern in many countries. The economic outlook for developing countries in 2004 is positive, with average GDP growth expected to reach 5¼ per cent.

... because domestic policy actions are often constrained

An enabling external environment has much to contribute to developing countries' growth, but recent experience has also demonstrated the importance of countries' being able not only to maintain sustainable macroeconomic balances and to make use of counter-cyclical measures but also to count on sound regional growth to mitigate the negative effects of a global economic downturn. Most Latin American countries, for example, have been unable to use macroeconomic policies to support their economies when affected by external shocks and have thus experienced periods of unsatisfactory—in some instances, negative—growth. Policies in the region seem to exacerbate the effects of both

Table IV.3.
Growth, unemployment and inflation in major developing economies, quarterly indicators, 2002-2003

	2002 quarter				2003 quarter			
	I	II	III	IV	I	II	III	IV
	Rate of growth of gross domestic product[a]							
Argentina	-16.3	-13.5	-9.8	-3.4	5.4	7.7	10.2	11.3
Brazil	-0.6	1.0	2.4	3.7	2.0	-0.8	-1.1	-0.1
Chile	1.1	2.2	2.7	3.5	3.7	3.0	3.1	3.3
China	7.6	8.0	8.1	8.1	9.9	6.7	9.6	9.9
Colombia	-0.1	2.3	2.0	2.2	4.1	2.2	4.1	4.5
Ecuador	1.3	3.9	5.0	3.5	2.7	0.8	-2.3	4.0
Hong Kong SAR[b]	-0.6	0.8	3.4	5.1	4.5	-0.5	4.0	5.0
India	6.3	5.1	5.5	2.0	4.9	5.7	8.4	10.4
Indonesia	2.4	4.1	4.6	3.6	4.5	3.6	4.0	4.4
Israel	-2.2	-1.7	0.0	0.7	1.1	0.7	1.1	1.9
Korea, Republic of	6.5	7.0	6.8	7.5	3.7	2.2	2.4	3.9
Malaysia	1.3	4.0	5.8	5.4	4.6	4.5	5.1	6.4
Mexico	-2.2	2.0	1.8	1.9	2.3	0.2	0.4	2.0
Philippines	3.8	4.1	3.8	5.8	4.5	4.0	5.1	4.5
Singapore	-1.5	3.8	3.8	3.0	2.8	-2.8	2.6	4.9
South Africa	3.0	3.8	2.9	2.4	1.5	1.1	1.6	1.5
Taiwan Province of China	0.9	3.7	5.2	4.5	3.5	-0.1	4.2	5.2
Thailand	3.9	5.1	6.2	6.3	7.3	6.5	6.6	7.8
Turkey	2.1	8.9	7.9	11.4	8.1	3.9	4.8	5.4
Venezuela	-3.8	-9.1	-5.6	-16.7	-27.6	-9.4	-7.1	9.0
	Unemployment rate[c]							
Argentina[d]	..	21.5	..	17.8	20.4	17.8	16.3	14.5
Brazil	12.2	12.0	11.7	10.9	11.6	12.7	12.9	12.0
Chile	8.8	9.5	9.7	9.6	7.9	8.8	9.3	8.1
Colombia	16.4	15.8	15.3	15.1	15.2	14.0	14.3	13.1
Hong Kong SAR[b]	7.2	7.7	7.2	7.3	7.9	8.6	7.9	7.3
Indonesia	8.1	..	9.1	..	..	..	..	..
Israel	10.4	10.3	10.4	10.2	10.8	10.6	10.7	10.9
Korea, Republic of	3.7	3.0	2.8	2.9	3.6	3.3	3.3	3.4
Malaysia	3.7	3.8	3.2	3.2	3.8	4.0	3.4	3.2
Mexico	2.8	2.6	2.9	2.5	2.8	3.0	3.8	3.5
Philippines	10.3	13.9	11.2	10.2	10.6	12.2	12.6	10.1
Singapore	3.7	5.2	3.8	4.7	3.7	5.4	4.9	4.9
Taiwan Province of China	5.1	5.0	5.3	5.2	5.1	5.0	5.1	4.8
Thailand	3.2	2.9	1.8	1.8	2.8	2.5	1.5	1.8
Turkey	11.8	9.3	9.6	11.0	12.3	10.0	9.4	10.3
Uruguay	14.7	15.4	17.6	19.2	18.6	16.8	16.1	15.4
Venezuela	15.5	15.8	16.5	16.2	..	..	..	17.8

Table IV.3 (continued)

	2002 quarter				2003 quarter			
	I	II	III	IV	I	II	III	IV
	Growth of consumer prices[a]							
Argentina	4.2	23.3	36.0	40.3	35.7	14.5	5.2	3.7
Brazil	7.6	7.8	7.6	10.6	15.6	16.9	15.2	11.4
Chile	2.4	2.2	2.4	2.9	3.8	3.7	2.7	1.1
China	-2.8	-3.2	-2.7	-1.8	-1.6	-1.2	-2.0	-1.4
Colombia	6.6	5.9	6.0	6.8	7.4	7.6	7.1	6.4
Ecuador	14.7	13.2	12.4	9.9	9.7	8.2	7.5	6.5
Hong Kong SAR[b]	-2.6	-3.1	-3.4	-3.0	-2.0	-2.5	-3.6	-2.3
India	5.1	4.5	4.0	4.0	3.8	4.7	3.4	3.4
Indonesia	14.1	11.5	10.5	10.0	7.2	6.5	5.7	4.1
Israel	3.8	5.7	6.5	6.7	5.5	0.9	-1.8	-2.3
Korea, Republic of	2.5	2.7	2.6	3.3	4.1	3.3	3.1	3.6
Malaysia	1.4	1.9	2.1	1.8	1.3	0.9	1.0	1.0
Mexico	4.7	4.8	5.2	5.3	5.4	4.7	4.1	4.0
Philippines	3.6	3.4	2.8	2.6	2.9	3.0	3.1	3.2
Singapore	-0.8	-0.4	-0.4	0.1	0.7	0.2	0.5	0.7
South Africa	5.3	7.5	10.3	12.6	10.7	7.9	4.9	1.0
Taiwan Province of China	-0.1	0.0	-0.2	-0.5	-0.2	-0.1	-0.6	-0.2
Thailand	0.6	0.2	0.3	1.4	2.0	1.8	1.9	1.6
Turkey	70.3	47.0	39.5	31.6	27.6	30.0	25.1	19.4
Venezuela	14.6	18.9	24.8	30.6	35.5	34.2	29.5	26.3

Sources:
IMF, *International Financial Statistics;* and national authorities.

a Percentage change from the corresponding quarter of the previous year.

b Special Administrative Region of China.

c Reflecting national definitions and coverage that are not comparable across economies.

d Data are reported in May and October until 2002.

the upturn and the downturn of the economic cycle, exposing the region to marked volatility in growth. Similarly, policy constraints have prevented many African countries from breaking away from their low growth path. Conversely, East Asian countries in particular have been able to use domestic policy instruments to support their economies when confronted with adverse shocks. As domestic demand recovers in the region, these countries are switching to a more cautious policy stance in order to strengthen their fiscal positions.

Africa: growth slowly picking up

GDP growth in Africa is forecast to accelerate to 4 per cent in 2004 as many countries increase agricultural and industrial output. Higher consumer spending, increasing investment, including more FDI in several countries, and cautiously expansionary government expenditures in a growing number of countries are expected to support rising domestic demand. Moreover, the region will benefit from the more auspicious external environment, including the higher prices of commodities and increased demand for its exports. Successful transition from civil conflicts to peace and the move towards stability in several war-torn countries should also improve the economic performance of the region, especially that of sub-Saharan Africa.

Increased domestic demand and the improved international environment will continue to support growth ...

In North Africa, GDP growth is expected to be sustained at 4¼ per cent in 2004. Increased oil revenues will support the growth of both private and public consumption in Algeria, Egypt and the Libyan Arab Jamahiriya. Improved diplomatic relations with the United Kingdom and the United States and the lifting of economic sanctions are expected to pave the way for the Libyan Arab Jamahiriya's resumption of normal ties with trading partners. Substantial inflows of FDI for infrastructure development and the expansion of oil production are anticipated. Rising industrial output and services related to tourism in Egypt, Morocco and Tunisia are also expected to improve North Africa's overall growth. The forecast recovery in EU will also be a positive force for economic growth in the subregion.

GDP growth for sub-Saharan Africa, excluding Nigeria and South Africa, will accelerate to 5 per cent in 2004 from 2.8 per cent in 2003. With Nigeria and South Africa included, estimates for sub-Saharan Africa are closer to the regional average of 4 per cent in 2004, up from 2.6 per cent in 2003. Growth continues to vary widely across sub-Saharan countries.

... although currency appreciation adversely affected South Africa in 2003

South Africa achieved only 1.9 per cent growth of GDP in 2003, much lower than anticipated. The country's economic performance weakened largely because the export gains of previous years were eroded by the loss of competitiveness stemming from the sustained appreciation of the rand vis-à-vis the dollar. Growth is expected to rebound to over 3 per cent in 2004 on the basis of strong consumer demand driven by lower inflation and lower interest rates, increased investment spending and expansionary fiscal measures targeted at poverty reduction, employment creation and the fight against HIV/AIDS.

South Africa's mining and manufacturing sectors, the largest employers in the country, were hit hardest by the appreciation of the rand. Strong growth in the dollar prices of most of South Africa's commodity exports generally did not translate into price gains in national currency. The mining sector recorded no growth in the fourth quarter of 2003, with negative growth projected for 2004. Imports of low-cost consumer goods also undermined the country's labour-intensive textile and apparel industries. Large negotiated wage increases that were not matched by productivity gains compounded the sector's problems. As a result, South Africa's unemployment rate remained high, standing at 28.2 per cent in September 2003. On the other hand, the appreciation of the rand helped South African authorities to lower inflation from almost 13 per cent in the last quarter of 2002 to 1 per cent by the end of 2003 .

Nigeria launches a new development strategy

In Nigeria, higher oil-export revenues, increased public and private consumption and moderate growth in agricultural output sustained GDP growth in 2003. The same factors are expected to support a strong economic performance in 2004-2005, while the National Economic Empowerment and Development Strategy (NEEDS), the Government's economic programme launched in March 2004, should improve Nigeria's economic prospects in the coming years. NEEDS focuses on poverty eradication and places renewed emphasis on wealth and employment creation as key economic objectives. It envisions sustained improvement in the functioning of private and public sector institutions, strict adherence to fiscal discipline and diversification of production and exports to expand economic activity beyond the hydrocarbons sector.

Other oil-producing countries in sub-Saharan Africa will also continue to benefit from higher oil prices: GDP in new oil-producing countries, such as Chad and Equatorial Guinea, are growing at a double-digit pace (see figure IV.6). The same is true in Angola where new production facilities have boosted output. However, the fast growth

Figure IV.6.
Growth of real GDP in Africa, Chad and Equatorial Guinea, 2001-2004
(Logarithmic scale)

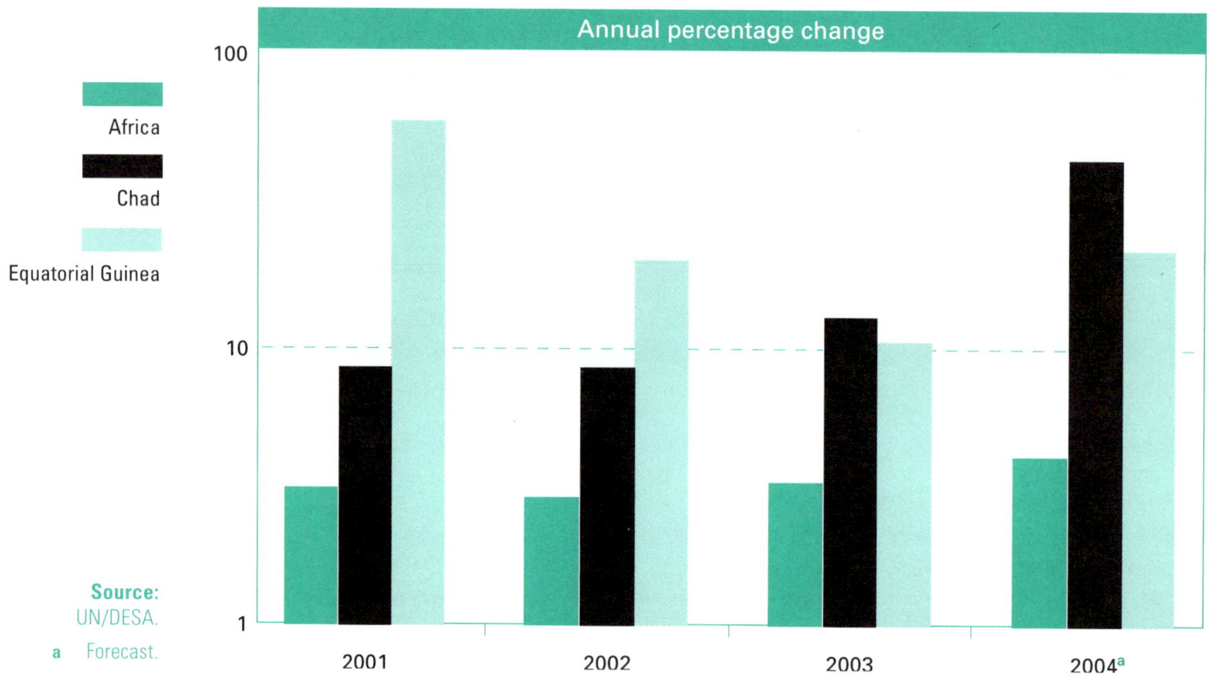

Source: UN/DESA.
a Forecast.

brought about by the oil sector is not necessarily sustainable and presents additional challenges for these countries (see box IV.3).

Improved political and economic governance has benefited many countries

Several countries that have made significant progress in political and economic reforms (Benin, Botswana, Ghana, Mauritius, Mozambique, Uganda and the United Republic of Tanzania) are expected to sustain growth rates in the range of 4-6 per cent in 2004. Countries emerging from conflict (such as the Democratic Republic of the Congo, Liberia and Madagascar) are also expected to achieve high rates of growth. Meanwhile, increased South African investment in infrastructure and in minerals and metals processing for export markets will continue to underpin growth in Namibia, Mozambique and several other countries in Southern Africa.

Conflict continues to affect growth in a few countries

Côte d'Ivoire, Ethiopia and Zimbabwe were among the few countries in Africa that suffered economic contraction in 2003. Ethiopia is expected to achieve positive growth in 2004 with the return of good weather and improved agricultural output. Economic activity resumed, haltingly, in Côte d'Ivoire after all parties involved in the conflict signed a peace agreement in January 2003 (for the text of this accord, the Linas-Marcoussis Agreement, see document S/2003/99 of 27 January 2003, annex I). However, in the early months of 2004, the country was still divided into two zones, one controlled by the Government and the other by insurgents. The peace process has been often undermined by incidents involving armed clashes and other civil disturbances. The crisis will continue to have far-reaching negative effects on the economies of neighbouring countries, especially Burkina Faso, Guinea and Mali, whose trade and financial flows with Côte d'Ivoire –particularly worker remittances– have been severely impeded since the disturbances started in September 2002. Meanwhile, Zimbabwe's economic decline, which has resulted in a cumulative contraction of economic output by over 50 per cent during the past five years, is expected to continue in 2004, albeit less severely than in previous years.

Box IV.3

Policy challenges in African oil-producing countries

The new oil-producing countries have been among the fastest growing economies in Africa in recent years. Equatorial Guinea, for instance, has grown at double-digit rates since its first oilfields came on-stream in 1992. Chad, the newcomer among African oil exporters, is expected to record the strongest GDP growth in the continent in 2004. Moreover, the promising results of preliminary explorations in West and Central Africa may add several others to the list of rapidly growing economies in the region in the near future.

The growth of the new oil-exporting countries is impressive but the sustainability of such performance and its translation into broader improvements in development are matters of debate. Almost no established African oil-producing country has been successful in achieving strong and sustainable growth. More importantly, these countries in general, have not achieved better social indicators than other countries in the region.[a] Terms-of-trade volatility, overvaluation of the real exchange rate (commonly known as the Dutch disease) and the institutional impact of oil (such as rent-seeking behaviour, corruption and public sector mismanagement) have been the usual channels of causation from oil resource abundance to disappointing long-term economic growth.[b] Improved fiscal and monetary policies could help countries to confront some of these challenges.

Fiscal expenditures in African oil-producing countries tend to increase at times of rising oil prices and remain relatively high in periods of lower prices. Consequently, the fiscal balance deteriorates and the inevitable deficit is financed by borrowing. External financing makes these countries vulnerable to interest-rate and exchange-rate fluctuations, as well as to the loss of new loans as sustainability concerns set in or investors' risk appetite declines. Domestic financing, on the other hand, is often inflationary or crowds out private sector access to credit. Mounting fiscal and external imbalances and difficulties in accessing external borrowing usually force oil-producing countries to make aggressive expenditures cuts, which undermine investment and growth. Additionally, the delivery of social services is eroded, leading to a worsening of social conditions.

The challenge of fiscal policy in African oil-producing countries is thus to avoid large swings in public spending while, at the same time, creating an enabling environment for economic growth and poverty eradication. Experience suggests that fiscal policy in these countries would benefit from the adoption of additional institutional arrangements, such as fiscal rules, legal frameworks guiding the use of oil revenues, and contingent financial instruments.[c]

The idea underpinning fiscal rules is to set a predetermined target for the fiscal balance, commonly the non-oil fiscal balance.[d] The rationale is to provide policy makers with an anchor and render difficult any attempt to pursue erratic fiscal policies in response to oil price fluctuations. This mechanism is usually accompanied by the establishment of a stabilization fund.

Chad provides an example of how a legal framework for the use of oil revenues, if effectively enforced, could contribute to addressing the challenges resulting from increased oil revenues. In 1999, Chad passed an oil revenue management law, an unprecedented legal provision in an African oil-producing country. Under this law, specific shares of oil revenues are allocated to specified uses. A Revenue Oversight Committee, comprising members of civil society, Parliament, the Supreme Court and the Government, has responsibility for ensuring the effective implementation of the scheme. It also constitutes the only institution allowed to authorize any use of oil revenues. Moreover, a decree promulgated in July 2003 envisaged a stabilization mechanism whereby a share of oil revenues will be saved and used as a buffer during periods of lower prices.

The recourse to contingent financial instruments, including futures, swaps and options, transfers the risk of oil price volatility to international markets. Oil revenues and public budgeting then become more realistic and certain. The shortcoming of this scheme for African oil-producing countries

a See Menachem Katz and others, *Improving Petroleum Revenue Management in Sub-Saharan Africa* (Washington, D.C., IMF, 23 January 2004).

b See Gylfason, Thorvaldur, "Natural resources, education, and economic development", *European Economic Review*, vol. 45, pp. 847-859.

c Report of the UNCTAD Secretariat entitled "Examination of the effectiveness and usefulness for commodity-dependent countries of new tools in commodity markets: risk management and collateralized finance", document TD/B/COM.1/EM.5/2, 24 February 1998.

d The non-oil fiscal balance is equal to the overall balance of fiscal operations less oil revenue and net interest income. It also excludes foreign-financed investment.

Box IV.3 (cont'd)

is that it requires a sophisticated domestic financial sector, or at least capacity in trading commodity-backed financial instruments; such institutional structures do not yet exist in the region.

Political acceptance of such measures, however, may be difficult to achieve. Low levels of human development, widespread poverty, poor infrastructure and the urgent need to address these challenges place pressure on public spending and make the establishment of an oil revenue saving scheme problematic. To be effective, any choice of fiscal policy should be made through deepening the dialogue between Governments and other stakeholders, including civil society. Stakeholder discussions are likely to facilitate the acceptance of cautious fiscal spending rules and also lock policy makers into an agreed position. Equally importantly, improving transparency and accountability in the use of public revenues may increase public acceptance of a stringent fiscal stance.

Nevertheless, responsible fiscal policy will not suffice to confront all the potential difficulties brought about by increased oil revenues. If converted into domestic currency, these may generate inflationary pressures; this could, for example, explain part of the rise in consumer prices in such countries as Chad and Equatorial Guinea. Achieving price stability in this context requires sterilizing foreign inflows, which means reducing the domestic component of the monetary base (bank reserves plus currency) in order to offset inflows of foreign reserves. One way of achieving this is to use open market operations whereby central banks sell treasury bills and/or other public securities, thereby removing excess liquidity.

Unfortunately, the use of open market operations in African oil-producing countries is constrained by the lack of well-developed capital markets with an adequate supply of marketable instruments, which investors are willing to hold. This is the reason why oil-producing countries in the Central African Economic and Monetary Community (Communauté Économique et Monétaire de l'Afrique Centrale (CEMAC))[e] have turned to other measures, such as reserve requirements, which the regional central bank has differentiated by country to account for their different liquidity positions. Nonetheless, even if successful, reserve requirements appear to be an implicit tax on banks and have the potential to provoke financial disintermediation, with financial activity moving outside the banking system, weakening the central bank's monetary control. Open market operations may also have two side-effects. First, they may increase domestic interest rates and trigger additional inflows if domestic capital markets are well integrated into world capital markets. Second, open market operations may generate operating losses as the funds raised domestically are reinvested in foreign assets that often generate lower returns. Because of the limited integration of African capital markets with the rest of the world, these two side-effects could be limited in African oil-producing countries and are likely to be outstripped by the benefits. One of the many challenges for these countries, therefore, is to promote the development of domestic capital markets, a precondition for successful open market operations.

e CEMAC is one of the two CFA franc zones in Africa. It comprises Cameroon, Chad, the Central African Republic, the Congo, Gabon, and Equatorial Guinea.

A cautious policy stance is followed

Fiscal and monetary policies were generally cautious in most African countries in 2003, reflecting the gains that countries had made in improving political governance and economic management in recent years. Cautious policies also reflect the need for several countries to adhere to performance criteria established by multilateral lending institutions and donor countries as underlying conditions for external financial assistance and debt relief. However, there has been fiscal expansion in several countries that have benefited from high oil revenues and improved export earnings. Increased public expenditures in such countries as Algeria, Egypt and most Communauté financière africaine (CFA) franc zone countries were largely concentrated in infrastructure development, health, education, and public works projects to combat high levels of unemployment. South Africa embarked on a third year of moderate fiscal expansion in 2003 with increased expenditures targeted at social services and labour-intensive infrastructure projects to accelerate the pace of job-creation.

Inflation remained at single-digit levels in most African countries, although sharp increases in consumer prices were recorded in countries suffering from food shortages, increased costs of imported oil and petroleum products and other inflationary effects of currency depreciation.

Improved debt financing conditions prevail in 2003

Africa's external debt situation improved as strengthened export earnings provided additional funds to meet debt-service obligations. Moreover, the appreciation of some national currencies against the dollar was beneficial for countries with external debt substantially denominated in dollars (such as most CFA countries, for example, Morocco and Tunisia). Middle-income countries with a relatively robust presence in international financial markets (for example, Tunisia) strengthened their public debt management strategies in order to reduce their exposure to adverse borrowing conditions and exchange-rate fluctuations.

Implementation of the Heavily Indebted Poor Countries (HIPC) Initiative provided either partial or full debt-relief financing to 23 African least developed countries as of May 2004 (see chap. III). However, nine African HIPC countries—Burundi, the Central African Republic, the Comoros, the Congo, Côte d'Ivoire, Liberia, Somalia, the Sudan and Togo—have not yet satisfied the governance, reform and other criteria required to receive HIPC financing. The HIPC programme is scheduled to end in December 2004 but the possibility of extending this deadline is being considered.

The near-term outlook is favourable

The short-term outlook for Africa is favourable in the absence of any major supply-side shock to domestic output, such as adverse weather conditions that would disrupt agricultural production. Expectations of a more favourable external environment in 2004-2005 have enhanced the prospects for increased export revenues from oil and non-oil commodity exports, as well as from increased exports of manufactured goods to EU and the United States under improved market access agreements.

Despite initial fears of political tensions leading to social unrest and possible disruptions of economic activity, successful presidential and parliamentary elections were conducted in Algeria, Guinea-Bissau and South Africa in early 2004. Elections are scheduled for about 20 other countries in 2004-2005 with similar apprehensions of potential downside risks. However, there is growing confidence that democracy and elections—and their contribution to peace, security and a stable economic environment—have successfully taken hold in an increasing number of African countries.

East Asia: challenges ahead

East Asia, on average, was able to sustain a fast pace of growth in 2003, despite the difficulties faced in the first half of the year when the region was affected by the uncertainties related to the war in Iraq, the sluggish international environment and the outbreak of severe acute respiratory syndrome (SARS). With the improvement in the external environment and increased domestic demand in some economies (for example, Indonesia and Malaysia), economic growth picked up during the year. Accommodative monetary and fiscal policies, as well as an upturn in stock markets, supported the economic recovery, which became increasingly entrenched towards the end of the year. For 2003 as a whole, GDP growth reached 6 per cent, which is comparable with the region's performance in 2002.

Much of this outcome was due to China, not only because of its robust economic performance and its weight in the regional economy, but also because of its role as a major market for regional exports. Excluding China, the region's GDP growth was only 3.6 per cent in 2003, a deceleration in relation to 2002 (see table A.4).

Economic growth will remain strong

GDP growth in the region is expected to accelerate to almost 7 per cent in 2004, with the majority of economies forecast to improve growth. A strong performance is anticipated for Singapore as that economy works off the negative effects of the SARS outbreak in 2003. By contrast, China and the Philippines are likely to see a modest deceleration in GDP growth in 2004 owing to contractionary monetary policy measures (see below).

Economic growth in China, at over 8 per cent, is forecast to remain the fastest in the region in 2004. China's economy continues to be driven by investment which grew by 24 per cent in 2003, with particularly strong growth in such sectors as steel, construction and real estate. China's trade volume also increased strongly in 2003, thanks to the continued recovery of the world economy and the depreciation of the dollar which, owing to the pegged currency, has contributed to the increased competitiveness of Chinese exports. This, however, generated increasing pressure on China to reconsider its foreign exchange policy (see box IV.4).

The growth of investment, together with the large increase in lending, has led to fears of an overheating of the economy. This could trigger a sudden slowdown in investment in key sectors and a fall in economic growth, possibly accompanied by difficulties in the banking sector, which has already shown some fragility owing to weak risk management. However, various policy measures by the Government to cool the economy make such a hard landing scenario unlikely.

China remains a major source of growth in the region

The strong growth of China will continue to benefit other countries in the region. In Hong Kong Special Administrative Region (SAR) of China, trade, tourism and the financial sector will profit from the easing of travel restrictions on Chinese nationals and the introduction of a free trade agreement between the two economies. Growth in Taiwan Province of China in 2004 will be based to a considerable extent on its trade linkages with China, although domestic demand is expected to play an increasingly supportive role. While China represents an important market for the Republic of Korea, Malaysia and the Philippines, competition from China in third markets may partially offset its positive impact in these economies. Meanwhile, despite the continued importance of exports, the strengthening of domestic demand will be progressively more relevant for growth in Indonesia, Malaysia, the Philippines, the Republic of Korea and Thailand.

Synchronous improvements in external and domestic demand are required to defeat stubborn unemployment

Labour-market outcomes were mixed in 2003. In Malaysia, Taiwan Province of China, Thailand and Viet Nam, improved economic conditions, combined with targeted public interventions, led to only a modest decline in unemployment, but there was no improvement in the rate of unemployment in all other economies in the region (see table IV.4). While an improvement in labour markets usually lags behind a recovery in economic activity, there are also structural and sectoral factors at play. For instance, the rise in unemployment in China is linked to the lay-offs by State-owned firms and migration of farmers to urban centres. A relatively fast growing labour force plays an important role in increased unemployment in the Philippines. In contrast, Singapore's labour market has suffered from specific sectoral weaknesses, with job losses occurring especially in the construction sector and in manufacturing.

Throughout the region, the effect of the economic upturn on employment is likely to remain limited in the short term. Any meaningful reduction of unemployment would require external and domestic demand to move more synchronously, creating more

Box IV.4

Domestic implications of China's exchange-rate regime: should China float?

China's current exchange rate regime pegs the value of the yuan at Y8.27 to the dollar, with a trading band of ±0.3 per cent. While the yuan is convertible for current-account transactions, restrictions apply for transactions on the capital account. These restrictions are asymmetric, making it easier for foreign investors—or foreign-owned Chinese firms—to conduct capital account transactions than it is for Chinese residents or firms to do so. Additionally, emphasis is placed on controlling capital outflows rather than capital inflows.

Dollar-denominated external transactions are vital for China and the peg of the yuan to the dollar reduces the exposure of the economy to the potentially large impact of fluctuations in this exchange rate. This is important because of the embryonic state of the Chinese financial market and the lack of financial instruments to hedge against exchange-rate movements. Additionally, the fixed exchange-rate regime can limit any surge in inflation resulting from China's strong economic growth.

The argument in favour of China's moving towards a more flexible currency arrangement is based on the need to improve the allocation of resources and to reduce the adverse effects of any external economic shocks. By sending the wrong price signals to economic agents, the currency regime may affect the allocation of resources not only within China but worldwide. Currently, the peg implies an undervaluation of the yuan, as it ignores the improvement in China's economic position relative to the United States. As a result, it may have led to the allocation of excessive resources to the production of exports and the country may have imported less than it otherwise would have done. Furthermore, the peg reduces the perceived exchange-rate risk and hence the associated risk premium demanded by foreign investors, making inflows of foreign direct investment (FDI) even larger than they would have been otherwise. Similarly, the undervalued currency is an incentive for speculative capital movements hoping for a revaluation. The currency peg may therefore be the source of speculative bubbles and their associated risks for the wider economy. In sum, both the perceived absence of exchange-rate risk and the perceived undervaluation of the currency can promote excessive capital inflows into China.

The fixed exchange-rate regime also makes it more difficult for China to deal with real external shocks because any adjustments have to come from changes in domestic prices or, in sectors where prices are fixed or less flexible, from changes in output and employment. During the Asian crisis, for example, downward pressure on the yuan in conjunction with the fixed exchange-rate regime was important in producing a deflationary environment in the Chinese economy.

It is also argued that a fixed exchange-rate regime constrains actions by monetary policy authorities. The need for a more independent monetary policy has become more relevant in China because of the development of capital markets in China and the increased scope that this provides for monetary policy measures. Monetary policy itself may become increasingly important because of the more stringent fiscal policy constraints that China is facing.

In China's case, however, the government has maintained a degree of autonomy in monetary policy by combining the currency peg with restrictions on capital account transactions. If there were no capital controls, the fragility of the banking sector, especially the volume of non-performing loans held by commercial banks, could lead to a run on banks and capital flight. De-control of capital flows would also allow Chinese savers to invest abroad. Their converting even a small proportion of the large amount of savings held in the Chinese banking system to foreign assets could give rise to downward pressure on the value of the yuan. Overall, the current state of the banking system and the incompleteness of capital markets suggest that the simultaneous adoption of a floating exchange-rate regime and the abolition of capital controls may not be a feasible policy option in the short term because it could destabilize both the financial sector and the real economy.

Box IV.4 (cont'd)

The foregoing suggests that decisions regarding of the exchange rate regime should be part of a broader set of carefully sequenced long-run policy measures. The move towards a more flexible exchange-rate regime should be preceded or accompanied by reform of the banking sector, the establishment of an effective and efficient regulatory framework for financial markets, a strengthening of the role of the monetary authorities and the introduction of new financial instruments. Pending the completion of such actions and as an intermediate step towards a floating exchange rate, China could introduce some greater flexibility in the present regime, for example by maintaining capital controls but widening the trading band of its current peg or by pegging the yuan to a basket of currencies, rather than to the dollar alone.

A further step would be to introduce a floating exchange-rate regime while maintaining capital controls. The strong external demand for Chinese products, reinforced by capital inflows, could lead to an appreciation of the exchange rate, dampening exports but benefiting Chinese consumers and those sectors that rely on imported inputs. Increased Chinese imports would raise growth elsewhere, especially in East Asia. In addition, currency appreciation could provide Chinese firms with an incentive to move away from a competitiveness strategy largely based on low labour costs, to one focused more on technological improvements and increases in productivity, with a positive impact on the Chinese economy in the long run.

sustainable economic growth that feeds through positively to labour markets. This is particularly true for the Republic of Korea, where an additional factor increasing employment will be the creation of a more positive investment climate through improved relations between employers and labour unions.

Subdued inflation allows for flexible monetary policies

Inflation remains subdued in the region, providing for some flexibility in monetary policy. The latter is likely to remain rather accommodative in Indonesia, Malaysia and Taiwan Province of China. Flexibility is more limited, however, in Indonesia and in the Philippines—in the former, owing to an upward pressure on interest rates stemming from the issuance of government bonds and, in the latter, owing to possible upward pressure on inflation stemming from the weakness of the currency. Meanwhile, China and Singapore will probably follow a more cautious monetary policy strategy. China will maintain its contractionary policy for the time being, in an attempt to cool credit lending and investment, while supply-side bottlenecks will continue to exert upward pressure on prices. In addition, China may opt to move away from the peg of the yuan to the dollar and align its currency with a basket of major currencies. This could lead to an appreciation of the yuan and hence contribute to monetary tightening (see box IV.4). In Singapore, where the exchange rate plays a key role in monetary policy, authorities have signalled a shift to a modest and gradual appreciation, which will help to keep inflation subdued. A more neutral monetary policy stance, possibly with some bias towards a tightening, will be maintained in the Republic of Korea and in Hong Kong SAR. The Bank of the Republic of Korea is expected to leave interest rates unchanged in the short term owing to the continued weakness of domestic demand and the appreciation of the won. Over the medium term, the expected upturn in the domestic economy is likely to lead to increased upward pressure on prices, providing the rationale for monetary policy makers to take a more cautious stance. Hong Kong SAR is expected to move out of deflationary territory in 2004, but the authorities may raise interest rates in the medium term in order to avoid pressure on the currency when the United States tightens its policy.

Table IV.4.
Unemployment in selected East Asian economies, 1998-2003

	Percentage of labour force[a]					
	1998	1999	2000	2001	2002	2003
China[b]	3.3	3.1	3.1	3.6	4.0	4.3
Hong Kong SAR[c]	4.7	6.3	4.9	5.1	7.3	8.0
Taiwan Republic of China	2.7	2.9	3.0	4.6	5.2	5.0
Republic of Korea	7.0	6.3	4.1	3.8	3.1	3.4
Indonesia	5.5	6.4	6.1	8.1	9.3	9.8
Malaysia	3.2	3.4	3.1	3.6	3.5	3.3
Philippines	10.1	9.7	11.1	11.1	11.4	11.4
Singapore	3.2	3.5	3.1	3.3	4.4	4.7
Thailand	4.4	4.2	3.6	3.3	2.4	2.2
Viet Nam[b]	6.9	7.0	6.4	6.3	6.0	5.8

Source:
Asian Development Bank, *Asian Development Outlook, 2004* (New York, Oxford University Press, 2004).

a Unemployment figures reflect national definitions and coverage that are not comparable across economies.

b Figures referring to urban unemployment.

c Special Administrative Region of China.

The continued strength of the property market and the desire to avoid a sudden and drastic fall in property prices could provide another reason for tightening monetary policy.

Improved fiscal positions are expected

Accommodative fiscal policies played an important role in allowing the countries that had experienced a contraction or a slowdown in the beginning of 2003 to experience stronger economic growth in the second half. The economic upturn has reduced the pressure on fiscal positions somewhat, a trend that is largely expected to strengthen in 2004 and 2005. Against this background, Indonesia, Malaysia, the Philippines and Taiwan Province of China are forecast to maintain a conservative fiscal policy stance, aiming at an improvement of their fiscal balances. In the case of Indonesia, a high debt burden provides an additional rationale for a more cautious fiscal approach, although political factors may override such considerations. China is expected to move towards a more neutral fiscal policy stance, combined with greater emphasis on targeting public expenditure, while the Republic of Korea is likely to adopt a more accommodative policy, at least in the short run, owing to the sluggishness of domestic demand.

The short-term economic prospects for the region depend heavily on three broad issues. First, China's economic expansion will continue to have increasingly important implications for the external trade of other East Asian economies, both in absorbing regional exports and in exerting competitive pressure in third markets. Second, the sustainability of the economic expansion in the region and its increased insulation from external shocks will depend on the strength of domestic demand, in particular of private consumption. Third, world commodity and oil prices will be influenced by the economic growth of the region, particularly of China (see box I.1), while, at the same time, they also constitute an important determinant of regional economic growth because of their impact on export revenues and input costs.

South Asia: sustaining robust growth

South Asia is among the fastest growing regions in the world. After the slowdown in 2002, largely caused by a poor harvest, regional GDP grew by 6.5 per cent in 2003. With adequate rainfalls in 2003 and early 2004, the agricultural sector recovered and generated higher rural incomes, supporting domestic demand. The latter, together with the recovery of the global economy, is forecast to lead to regional GDP growth above 6 per cent per year in 2004 and 2005 (see table A.4).

A strong rebound in agriculture was accompanied by growth in other sectors

The economic recovery in the region in 2003 was broad-based, with the sources of growth differing across countries. Except for Sri Lanka, where services were a major driving force, the agricultural sector provided a major impetus to growth. In the case of Sri Lanka, a lasting truce opened up new chances for domestic services growth, as well as tourism, throughout 2003. Tourism also supported growth in Nepal, although growth in the country continues to lag behind that of its neighbours (see figure IV.7) and is still heavily dependent on private remittances and on foreign assistance to maintain aggregate demand. Services were also important for India's growth. On the other hand, Pakistan's main growth engine was the industrial sector (which also performed strongly in India), with textile exports accounting for a large proportion of the expansion, largely owing to an increase in quotas by the United States.

A continuation of favourable weather conditions will support growth in the agricultural sector in 2004 and possibly 2005, while rising internal as well as external demand will continue to boost manufacturing in the area. The service sector is also likely to perform well, supported by increased domestic demand as well as the strengthening of the international environment (which will have a positive effect on both tourism and serv-

Figure IV.7.
Growth of real GDP in selected South Asian economies, 2002-2004

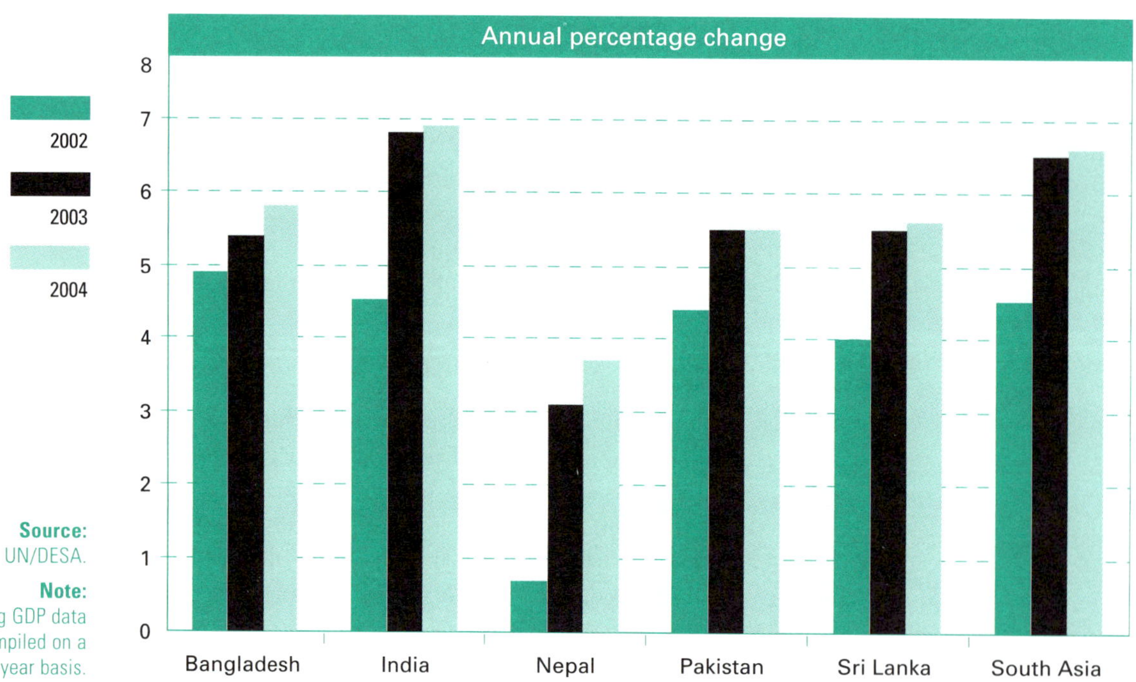

Source: UN/DESA.

Note: Underlying GDP data is compiled on a calendar-year basis.

ice outsourcing). In India, services will become the main growth motor when agriculture slows down after its exceptionally good performance in 2003. Nonetheless, job creation remains a challenge in the region, particularly in view of the massive underemployment and non-productive employment in the agricultural sector.

The external sector mirrors the overall positive growth of the region, with both merchandise exports and imports rising at double-digit rates. Current accounts are not a source of concern in the region, despite growing trade deficits, because of sizeable labour remittances and, in the case of India, the strong performance of information technology (IT) and IT-related service exports. As import demand is anticipated to increase in 2004 and 2005, most economies will suffer a deterioration in their current accounts, which will, however, remain sustainable.

The external sector is thriving

Currencies have remained relatively stable vis-à-vis the United States dollar, with a steady appreciation of the Indian and the Pakistani rupee and small depreciations of other currencies. Bangladesh abandoned its official exchange-rate band against the dollar and adopted a managed float in May 2003, without experiencing disruptive changes in the valuation of its currency. For 2004, further appreciation of the Indian rupee is expected, while the other currencies of the region will experience only a gradual depreciation against the dollar. Beyond 2004, the region will probably witness a return to depreciation, although at a slower rate than in the past.

With the exception of Bangladesh and Nepal, inflation declined in 2003, helped by lower food prices and firm national currencies. In early 2004, however, inflationary pressures picked up owing to the rise in domestic demand, but inflation remains subdued (see table A.10). Monetary policy is therefore expected to remain accommodative. Good harvests in 2004 are expected to keep down the prices of foodstuffs, although Sri Lanka faces stronger inflationary pressures owing to a prolonged drought. The continued weakness of the dollar will help keep import prices in check while higher commodity and utility prices are expected to feed inflation. With inflationary pressure building up throughout the region and the expected tightening of global monetary policies, a moderate turnaround in the region's monetary policies is expected in 2005.

Inflation remains benign but pressures are building up

Budget deficits as a share of GDP declined throughout the region in 2003. Nonetheless, they remain unsustainably high in India and in Sri Lanka, at about 10 per cent in the former and 8 per cent in the latter in 2003. Both countries passed Fiscal Responsibility Acts in 2003, aiming at improving expenditure management and revenue collection. However, tax collection fell short of projections in Sri Lanka and local government deficits in India are still very large, contributing more than 50 per cent of the overall deficit. The steep reduction of Nepal's fiscal deficit in 2003, despite higher security expenses, could be achieved only through cuts in the development budget, thereby hurting medium-term growth. For 2004, continued strong regional growth and improved tax legislation and enforcement, combined with efforts to enhance the efficiency of public spending, are expected to further improve fiscal positions. However, progress in India and Sri Lanka will remain slow. Overall, government spending in the region is not expected to tighten visibly.

Fiscal positions remain fragile despite some improvements

Owing to its reliance on the textile and garment industry for growth, exports and employment generation, the region faces a major challenge with the expiration of the World Trade Organization Agreement on Textiles and Clothing[6] on 1 January 2005 (see chap. II). India is expected to increase market shares in the quota-restricted markets. Meanwhile, Pakistan's exports may prove resilient in the new environment, as they do not

The textile and garment sectors will face increased competition

compete directly with those of China—one of the most efficient producers in the industry. Moreover, Pakistan has been profiting from efficiency gains brought about by large investments in the sector since 2001. Conversely, Sri Lanka's prospects are shakier, while exports of Bangladesh are expected to suffer despite their preferential access to EU, owing to the country's relatively weak competitiveness. Nonetheless, the performance of the textile and garment sectors in the region will be heavily influenced by domestic policies towards investment, infrastructure and efficiency-enhancing structural reforms.

Structural reforms are well under way in a number of countries. While the speed of implementation is generally slow, prospects for further reforms are positive. Privatization is advancing in Pakistan and Sri Lanka and has experienced a major push in India, but is expected to slow under the newly elected Government. Shortcomings in infrastructure and labour regulation still need to be addressed. Political stability and security remain an issue in the region, although the recent improvement in relations between India and Pakistan allows for some cautious optimism. On the other hand, the conflict in Nepal has re-emerged, while the peace process in Sri Lanka still needs to be revived. Finally, instability in Afghanistan and its impact on the border region with Pakistan may negatively affect the latter's prospects.

Western Asia: mixed fortunes brought by the war

GDP growth in Western Asia is projected to decelerate to 2¾ per cent in 2004 from 4.6 per cent in 2003. In the oil-exporting countries, output growth will be constrained by Organization of the Petroleum Exporting Countries (OPEC) production quotas. Even if quotas are not fully honoured, most countries will not be able to expand output as rapidly as in 2003, with the result that growth in the oil-exporting countries is forecast to decelerate to 2½ per cent in 2004 from 5.1 per cent in 2003. Nonetheless, fiscal and external balances will remain favourable in most countries owing to the continued strength of oil prices. Growth in the oil-importing countries of the region will also decelerate from 3.9 per cent in 2003 to 3¼ per cent in 2004 (see table A.4), mostly owing to the slowdown in Turkey; Cyprus, Jordan and Lebanon are expected to have an improved performance. Unemployment has been increasing throughout the region and has reached double-digit levels in most countries. This unfavourable trend is expected to continue in 2004. After several years of decline, inflation is forecast to pick up in 2004, resulting from the pass-through of a weak dollar.

Conflict and violence continue to depress consumer and investor sentiment ...

The conflict between Israel and Palestine continues, with adverse effects on consumer and investment sentiment throughout the region. The economy of Palestine has virtually collapsed, with mass unemployment and widespread poverty, while Israeli GDP registered small positive growth in 2003, after two successive years of contraction. Meanwhile, the situation in Iraq is also having an impact throughout the region. Contrary to expectations, an enabling and supportive environment for the country's reconstruction has not yet emerged. Iraqi oil production and exports have resumed but remain below pre-war levels, while the establishment of economic normalcy in the country is constrained by military and political instability and lack of resources.[7] The non-oil sector was unable to expand in 2003 owing to a deterioration in security, increased instability, insufficient funds and depressed domestic demand. As a result, Iraq's GDP contracted and, owing to supply shortages, inflation accelerated further to an estimated 90 per cent in 2003.

... but oil-exporting countries benefit

The impact of the war in Iraq is not restricted to that country. The war created mixed fortunes in the region: some countries indirectly benefited from it, while others were adversely affected. Oil production in the region increased and oil prices strengthened and remained high during the year (see chap. II). As a result, there was a sharp upturn in growth in most oil-exporting countries of the region and these countries' fiscal and external balances shifted to surplus.

In Saudi Arabia, for example, growth of 6.4 per cent in 2003—the highest since 1991—was basically driven by the oil sector. To compensate for production shortfalls in Iraq, Nigeria and Venezuela, Saudi Arabia, "the world's oil producer of last resort", increased oil production sharply while the non-oil sector (excluding the petrochemicals and fertilizers industries) grew at a slower pace, reflecting the uncertainty resulting from the war in Iraq. To offset the latter, the Government provided incentives to the private sector, including lower interest rates, increased credit supply and greater participation in key sectors of the economy (natural gas, telecommunications, power and water).

Oil revenues improve fiscal and external balances

The country's fiscal and external balances also improved in 2003. Prior to the war, Saudi Arabia had planned for continued fiscal consolidation to contain rising public expenditures and persistent budget deficits. The policy stance was also in line with expected lower oil revenues which, however, did not materialize owing to higher oil prices and the rise in oil production in 2003. The unexpected oil revenue windfall caused the fiscal balance to shift from a deficit of 8 per cent of GDP in 2002 to a surplus of 6 per cent in 2003—the highest surplus in more than 20 years, despite soaring defence spending. Higher oil revenues also benefited the current-account balance, as the growth in export revenue helped to offset the deteriorating income, transfer and service balances and the current-account surplus jumped from 6 per cent of GDP in 2002 to 11 per cent in 2003.

This performance in 2003 has been clouded, however, by severe unemployment. Sluggish economic growth in the past few years, combined with a rapidly growing population, has resulted in unemployment of about 20 per cent, with the youth being the most affected. Like most oil-exporting countries, Saudi Arabia has followed a policy of replacing expatriates with nationals, but with limited success.

Jordan is seriously affected by the invasion of Iraq

The war in Iraq affected the region's oil-importing countries mostly through trade. Jordan was the most affected, as it had been importing all its oil from Iraq, half of it at no cost. The other half was imported at heavily discounted rates and under barter agreements concluded annually with Iraq and subject to the United Nations special dispensation rules on sanctions against Iraq. With the outbreak of the war, Jordan was forced to buy oil in international markets at prevailing prices. The transportation sector suffered a severe setback and output dropped dramatically. Similarly, tourism came to a standstill, while manufacturing output declined owing to the loss of the Iraqi market. As a result, export revenues slowed while import costs increased, reflecting mostly the rising oil import bill, and the trade deficit widened in 2003. Nonetheless, owing to substantial grants from the United States, the current-account surplus reached 7 per cent of GDP in 2003, compared with 5 per cent in 2002. The grants helped to reduce the impact of the Iraq war on the Jordanian economy. Additionally, to support economic growth, the Central Bank of Jordan lowered its discount rate twice during 2003 while the Government introduced an emergency budget for the year. Nevertheless, GDP growth decelerated and the fiscal deficit, which had been on a declining trend, increased to 12 per cent of GDP in 2003. Unemployment jumped to 20 per cent while poverty—estimated at 30 per cent of the population in 2003—also increased.

Except for Jordan and Saudi Arabia, most countries in the region adopted an expansionary fiscal policy in 2003 to cope with the ramifications of the Iraq war. The bulk of the fiscal stimulus, however, was absorbed by current expenditures, especially defence and security-related spending.

Interest rates are reduced during 2003

Monetary easing continued in the region in 2003. The fact that most oil-exporting countries have their currencies pegged to the dollar, implies that their monetary policy follows that of the United States. During the course of 2003, interest rates in many countries declined but maintained a positive differential vis-à-vis those in the United States. Even countries with multiple exchange rates (such as the Syrian Arab Republic) or floating exchange rates (such as Israel, Turkey and Yemen) reduced their interest rates to stimulate their economies. The Syrian Arab Republic, for example, lowered interest rates by 150 basis points to 5.5 per cent in 2003, the first reduction in 22 years. This was also a move to mitigate the loss of oil transit revenues from Iraq due to the war. The loss of such revenues contributed to a widening of the Syrian fiscal deficit to 6 per cent of GDP in 2003 from 1 per cent in 2002.

Currency movements reflect the relationship with the dollar

The currency peg also implied that most currencies depreciated against the euro and the yen in 2003, following the depreciation of the dollar, leading to higher import costs that fed inflationary pressures. Nevertheless, domestic price subsidies on basic goods helped to contain the rise in consumer price inflation in most countries. Countries with non-pegged exchange-rate regimes saw their currencies appreciate against the dollar. With the exception of the Islamic Republic of Iran, Turkey and Yemen, where inflation remains at double-digit levels, inflation was negligible throughout the region in 2003.

Latin America and the Caribbean: an incipient recovery

After two years of crisis-driven stagnation, Latin America registered a modest recovery in 2003 as regional GDP grew by 1.5 per cent. Growth is anticipated to strengthen to about 4 per cent in 2004 (see table A.4), resulting in a positive gain in GDP per capita for the first time since 2000. The incipient growth in 2003 was explained mostly by a recovery of the external sector, particularly in the countries of South America, which were favoured by higher commodity prices and greater external demand while imports remained constrained by weak domestic demand. Investment was stagnant, private consumption was weak and public expenditures were kept in check by limited financing and the pursuit of improved fiscal positions.

Broad-based growth is anticipated in 2004

Economic growth is anticipated to be broad-based across the region in 2004. Domestic absorption is forecast to recover as private consumption and investment are expected to respond to the more favourable policy environment. In addition, external demand is expected to strengthen further as the developed economies and China continue to grow and prices of export commodities remain firm, benefiting the region as a whole. Contrary to previous years, most of the high growth will be concentrated in South America. Argentina's strong growth is expected to continue, but it is Venezuela that will have the fastest growth in the region, mostly a statistical result of the normalization of the level of oil production. Uruguay will finally step out of the recession that began in 1999, with the economy expected to grow at least 5 per cent. In Central America and the Caribbean, Costa Rica and Trinidad and Tobago will continue to lead growth, but growth will accelerate elsewhere in this subregion as well, responding to greater demand from the United States. The

Dominican Republic and Haiti, however, will remain stagnant or contract slightly owing to the aftermath of economic turmoil and political turmoil, respectively.

The region had its third consecutive year of lacklustre growth in 2003; excluding the outliers, Argentina and Venezuela, output increased only 1.2 per cent following 1.4 per cent in 2002. Argentina's strong recovery, especially during the second half of 2003, was due to robust growth of fixed investment (of almost 40 per cent) and private consumption, which compensated for the negative contributions of the external sector and public consumption. Venezuela suffered a second consecutive year of crisis when a general strike interrupted oil production, but some Andean economies—especially Chile, Colombia and Peru, which were favoured by better export prices of metals and minerals and increased external demand—performed well. Conversely, Brazil and, to a lesser extent, Mexico—the two largest economies in the region—performed poorly (see figure IV.8). In the Caribbean subregion, Trinidad and Tobago grew rapidly thanks to its energy sector's benefiting from an expansion of gas production. A financial crisis in the Dominican Republic and continued weak growth in Central America (except for Costa Rica, which enjoyed robust external demand for its high-tech products) also dragged down the region's overall performance.

Another year of unsatisfactory growth for most economies in 2003

The Brazilian economy contracted in 2003 after two years of sluggish performance. Exports performed well but their performance was not sufficient to offset the decline in domestic demand. On the supply side, the contraction was due mostly to a fall in industrial production, especially during the first half of the year, while services stagnated. Agriculture was the only sector that recorded positive growth in 2003. Consumption and investment are anticipated to recover in 2004, supported by a contin-

Figure IV.8.
Growth of real GDP in selected Latin American countries, 2002-2004

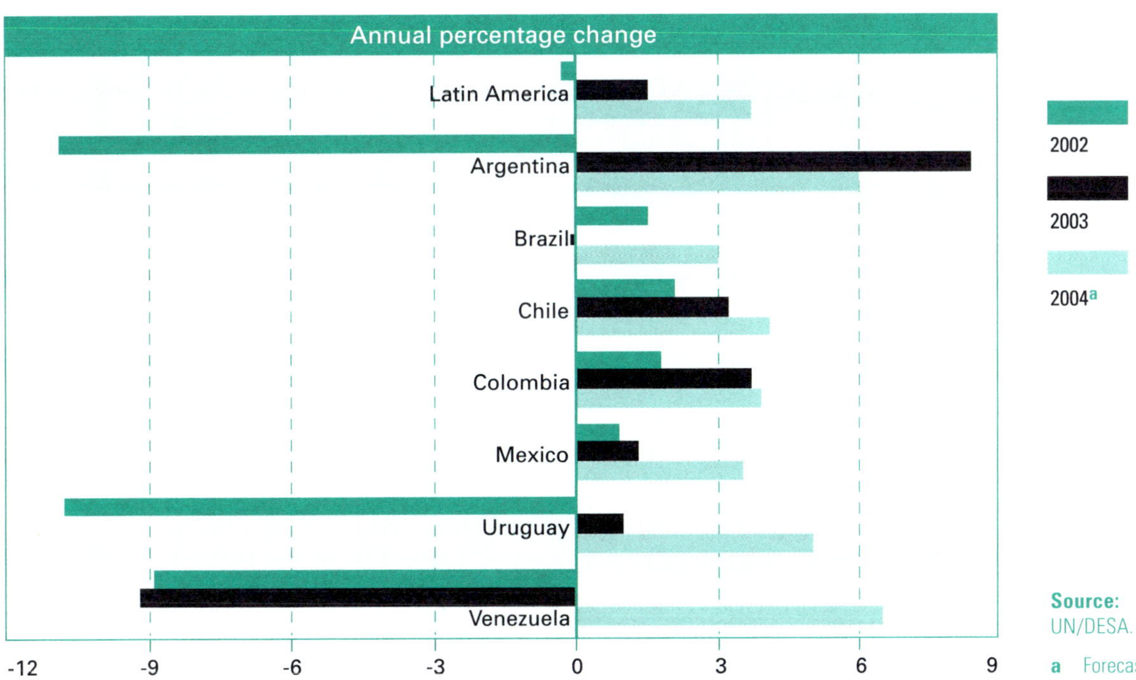

Source: UN/DESA.
a Forecast.

ued—although cautious—lowering of the policy interest rate. Agriculture and industry will lead the recovery.

Mexico continued a three-year period of sluggish growth. Loss of competitiveness resulted in a fall in its exports of manufactured goods, despite some recovery of the United States economy, its major trading partner. In addition, fixed investment suffered from the uncertainty created by the lack of consensus on implementing economic reforms, such as the reduction of the value-added tax, the modernizing of labour laws, the guaranteeing of energy supplies for industry, and the reduction of access to credit. The continuing strengthening of the United States economy will favour Mexican exports and a recovery of non-oil exports should reactivate industrial and manufacturing activities. Consumption was already picking up pace in early 2004, while fiscal policy has remained tight.

Unemployment remains a serious concern

The region's sluggish economic performance has contributed to the high rate of unemployment, which has been about 10 per cent or above since 1998. In 2003, it approached 11 per cent on average for the region while real wages fell. At 18 per cent, Venezuela registered the highest unemployment rate in the region. Argentina was the only country that experienced significant reductions in unemployment in 2003, as the economic recovery helped employment creation. Nonetheless, unemployment in Argentina was still high at the end of the year. The reduction of unemployment will probably be the biggest challenge in the region for 2004, despite the expected improved growth of output.

Inflation resumes its declining trend

After a temporary resurgence of inflation in 2002 due to the devaluation of the currencies of economies in crisis (Argentina, Paraguay, Uruguay and Venezuela), as well as investors' temporary lack of confidence in the Brazilian currency on the eve of elections, inflation declined throughout 2003, closing the year at 8.5 per cent. Average annual inflation rates, however, were higher than in 2002 (see table A.10), reflecting the relatively higher annual inflation in the first half of the year. Declining inflation was brought about by exchange-rate stabilization (and, in some cases, even appreciation), as well as by constraints on domestic demand imposed by austere monetary policies in several countries. The continued strength of national currencies and cautious monetary policy will continue to lower inflation in 2004.

Economic stimuli from macroeconomic policies continue to be limited

Although macroeconomic policy in general is anticipated to be slightly more accommodative in 2004, the need to continue improving fiscal balances and the wariness of inflationary pressures may limit the scope for economic stimuli. For example, after cutting the basic interest rate by 1,000 basis points, Brazil's Central Bank has been very cautious in lowering rates further. Similarly, the Bank of Mexico's zeal to achieve an inflation target of 3 per cent in 2004 has kept monetary policy tighter than originally envisaged.

Meanwhile, fiscal policy will remain restrictive in several countries. Brazil followed an austere fiscal policy in 2003 and will likely maintain its primary surplus target of 4.25 per cent of GDP in 2004. In Argentina, government finances were favoured by greater tax revenues generated by the increase in economic activity, especially from income and value-added taxes. Although the short-term fiscal position of Argentina is improving, longer-term prospects are not clear as negotiations on how to restructure its large external debt are stalled. Thus, downside risks will remain until concrete solutions are found.

Although most countries reduced their fiscal deficits in 2003, they remain at 4 per cent of GDP and above in such countries as Bolivia, Colombia, Haiti and Honduras. In the case of Bolivia and Haiti, political and economic turmoil prevented any further containment of the deficit, while the other two countries are working towards fiscal reforms to improve their position.

Concerned about the procyclical nature of their fiscal policies, several Latin American Governments have requested IMF to reconsider the methodology applied to the estimation of fiscal targets imposed in Fund-supported programmes. The aim is to better accommodate these countries' needs to invest in the infrastructure required to address supply bottlenecks and to allow for faster growth, without sacrificing social spending, particularly when it is most required. There has been some move towards using the government primary balance (in other words, excluding interest payments) as a target, but the call is for consideration to be given to the use of alternative fiscal targets. One possibility is a move towards balance-sheet accounting whereby capital expenditures would be excluded from fixed targets because the resulting accumulation of assets would offset the increased liabilities. Such expenditures could then be used counter-cyclically during slowdowns and crises. In addition, it is argued that the financial results of public sector enterprises should be considered in the same way as those in the private sector; this may imply excluding them from fiscal targets, as is the case in EU. It is argued that common standards should be applied in these areas, not only among developing countries but also between developed and developing countries. In response, IMF has indicated a willingness to consider the exclusion of the cost of public productive infrastructure projects from the primary surplus targets for several South American countries and is rethinking the effects of adjustment within their programmes.[8]

Greater flexibility is sought in fiscal targeting

Notes

1 The labour force participation rate for people between ages 16 and 24 has been declining steadily since 2001, dropping from 66 to about 61 per cent at present. It is estimated that if the participation rate were at its level of 2001, the unemployment rate would be 1 percentage point higher.

2 Flow-of-funds data recorded a negative saving rate for the household sector in 2003, while national accounts data indicated a significant decline in the household saving rate, although it remained positive.

3 Inflationary pressure during the slowdown magnified the effect of slowing nominal income. In addition, survey evidence indicates that consumers have persistently overestimated inflation since the introduction of the euro. This has been one explanation for the depressed state of private consumption in many EU member countries.

4 The European Central Bank (ECB) has defined price stability as being an upper bound of 2 per cent for inflation.

5 The cyclically adjusted primary balance for the euro zone had declined by almost 1 percentage point between 2000 and 2002, indicating a significant discretionary stimulus. The fiscal stance in 2003, similarly measured, was broadly neutral: further tax cuts in some countries were balanced by controls on the expenditure side and increases in indirect taxes and social security contributions rates (see *European Economy*, No. 2/2004 (Luxembourg, European Commission, 2004), pp. 37-38).

6 The text of the Agreement is available from http://www.wto.org/english/tratop_e/texti_e/texti_e.htm (accessed 12 August 2004).

7 See *World Economic Situation and Prospects, 2004* (United Nations publication, Sales No. E.04.II.C.2), p. 56.

8 See Independent Evaluation Office, IMF, *Evaluation Report: Fiscal Adjustment in IMF-Supported Programs* (Washington, D.C., 2003) and IMF, "Follow Up on the Recommendations of the Independent Evaluation Office Report on Fiscal Adjustment in IMF-Supported Programs", prepared by the Policy Development and Review and Fiscal Affairs Departments (in consultation with other Departments), 9 February 2004, Washington, D.C.

Annex
Statistical Tables

Annex
Statistical tables

The present annex contains the main sets of data on which the analysis provided in the *World Economic and Social Survey, 2004* is based. The data are presented in greater detail than in the text and for longer time periods, and incorporate information available as of 15 May 2004.

The annex was prepared by the Economic Monitoring and Assessment Unit of the Department of Economic and Social Affairs of the United Nations Secretariat. It is based on information obtained from the United Nations Statistics Division and the Population Division of the Department of Economic and Social Affairs of the United Nations Secretariat, as well as from the United Nations regional commissions, the International Monetary Fund (IMF), the World Bank, the Organization for Economic Cooperation and Development (OECD), the United Nations Conference on Trade and Development (UNCTAD) and national and private sources. Estimates for the most recent years were made by the Economic Monitoring and Assessment Unit in consultation with the regional commissions and participants in Project LINK (see directly below). Data presented in this *Survey* may differ, however, from those published by these other organizations for a series of reasons, including differences in timing, sample composition, and aggregation methods (see also section on "Data quality" below for additional sources of data discrepancies). Historical data may differ from those in previous editions of the *Survey* because of updating and changes in the availability of data for individual countries.

Forecasts are based on the results of the April 2004 forecasting exercise of the above-mentioned Project LINK, an international collaborative research group for econometric modelling, which is coordinated jointly by the Economic Monitoring and Assessment Unit and the University of Toronto. LINK itself is a global model that links together the trade and financial relations of 79 country and regional economic models, which are managed by over 60 national institutions and by the Unit. The primary linkages are merchandise trade and prices, as well as the interest and currency exchange rates of major countries. The models assume that the existing or officially announced macroeconomic policies as of 1 April 2004 are in effect. The iterative process by the LINK system used to generate a consistent forecast for the world economy is such that international trade flows and prices, among other variables, are determined endogenously and simultaneously. The one exception is the international price of crude oil, which is derived using a satellite model of the oil sector.[a] The average price of the basket of seven crude oils of the Organization of the Petroleum Exporting Countries (OPEC) is estimated to increase by 4.5 per cent in 2004 and to decline by some 3.5 per cent in 2005.

Country classification

For analytical purposes, the *World Economic and Social Survey* classifies all countries of the world into one of three categories: developed economies, economies in transition and developing countries. The composition of these groupings is specified in the tables presented below. The groupings are intended to reflect basic economic conditions in countries. Several countries (in particular economies in transition) have characteristics that could place them in more than one category but, for purposes of analysis, the groupings were made mutually exclusive. Alternative groupings of countries may be appropriate at different times and for different analytical purposes.

The nature of each of the three categories may be given in broad strokes. The **developed economies** (see table A) on average have the highest material standards of living. Their production is heavily and increasingly oriented towards the provision of a wide range of services; agriculture is typically a very small share of output and the share of manufacturing is generally declining. On average, workers in developed countries are the world's most productive, frequently using the most advanced production techniques and equipment. The developed economies are often centres for research in science and technology. Governments of developed countries are likely to offer assistance to other countries and they do not generally seek foreign assistance.

The **economies in transition** are characterized by the transformation that they began at the end of the 1980s, when they turned away from centralized administration of resource allocation as the main organizing principle of their societies towards the establishment or re-establishment of market economies. Some of these economies began this transformation while having many of the characteristics of developed economies and others had several characteristics of developing economies. However, for the purposes of the analysis in the *Survey,* their most distinguishing characteristic is their transitional nature.

Table A.
Developed economies[a]

Europe			
European Union	Other Europe	Other countries	Major industrialized economies
Euro zone Austria Belgium Finland France Germany Greece Ireland Italy Luxembourg Netherlands Portugal Spain *Other EU* Denmark Sweden United Kingdom of Great Britain and Northern Ireland	Iceland Malta Norway Switzerland	Australia Canada Japan New Zealand United States of America	Canada France Germany Italy Japan United Kingdom of Great Britain and Northern Ireland United States of America

a Countries systematically monitored by the Economic Monitoring and Assessment Unit of the United Nations Secretariat.

Table B.
Economies in transition[a]

Baltic States	Central and Eastern Europe	Commonwealth of Independent States
	Central Europe	
Estonia	Czech Republic	Armenia
Latvia	Hungary	Azerbaijan
Lithuania	Poland	Belarus
	Slovakia	Georgia
	Slovenia	Kazakhstan
		Kyrgyzstan
	South-Eastern Europe	Republic of Moldova
	Albania	Russian Federation
	Bulgaria	Tajikistan
	Croatia	Turkmenistan
	Romania	Ukraine
	Serbia and Montenegro	Uzbekistan
	The former Yugoslav Republic of Macedonia	

a Economies systematically monitored by the Economic Monitoring and Assessment Unit of the United Nations Secretariat.

The rest of the world is grouped together as the **developing economies**. This is a heterogeneous grouping, although one with certain common characteristics. Average material standards of living in developing countries are lower than in developed countries and many of these countries have deep and extensive poverty. Developing countries are usually importers rather than developers of innovations in science and technology and their application in new products and production processes. They also tend to be relatively more vulnerable to economic shocks.

Beginning with this current issue of the *World Economic and Social Survey*, estimates of the growth of output in developing countries have been based on the data of 95 economies, accounting for 98-99 per cent of the 2000 gross domestic product (GDP) and population of all developing countries and territories. The countries in the sample account for more than 95 per cent of GDP and 93 per cent of population of each of the geographical regions into which the developing countries are divided, with the exception of sub-Saharan Africa for which the countries included in the sample account for at least 90 per cent of GDP.

The *Survey* uses the following designations of geographical regions for developing countries: Africa, Latin America and the Caribbean, and Asia and the Pacific (comprising Western Asia, China, East Asia and South Asia, including the Pacific islands).[b] Country classification by geographical region is specified in table C below.

The *Survey* also uses a geographical subgrouping of sub-Saharan Africa, which contains African countries south of the Sahara Desert, excluding Nigeria and South Africa. The intent of this grouping is to give a picture of the situation in the large number of smaller sub-Saharan economies by avoiding any distortion that may be introduced by including the two large countries that dominate the region in terms of GDP, population and international trade.

For analytical purposes, developing countries are classified as **fuel exporters** or **fuel importers** because the ability to export fuel or the need to import fuel has a large effect on a country's capacity to import other goods and services—and therefore on the growth

Table C.

Developing economies by region[a]

	Latin America and the Caribbean	Africa	Asia and the Pacific		
			East Asia	South Asia	Western Asia
Net fuel exporters	Bolivia Colombia Ecuador Mexico Trinidad and Tobago Venezuela	Algeria Angola Cameroon Congo Egypt Gabon Libyan Arab Jamahiriya[b] Nigeria	Brunei Darussalam[b] Indonesia Viet Nam		Bahrain Iran (Islamic Republic of) Iraq Kuwait[b] Oman[b] Qatar[b] Saudi Arabia[b] Syrian Arab Republic United Arab Emirates[b]
Net fuel importers	Argentina Barbados Brazil Chile Costa Rica Cuba Dominican Republic El Salvador Guatemala Guyana Haiti Honduras Jamaica Nicaragua Panama Paraguay Peru Uruguay	Benin Botswana Burkina Faso Burundi Central African Republic Chad Côte d'Ivoire Democratic Republic of the Congo Ethiopia Ghana Guinea Kenya Madagascar Malawi Mali Mauritius Morocco Mozambique Namibia Niger Rwanda Senegal South Africa Sudan Togo Tunisia Uganda United Republic of Tanzania Zambia Zimbabwe	Hong Kong SAR[c] Malaysia Papua New Guinea Philippines Republic of Korea Singapore[b] Taiwan Province of China[b] Thailand China	Bangladesh India Myanmar Nepal Pakistan Sri Lanka	Cyprus Israel Jordan Lebanon Turkey Yemen

a Countries systematically monitored by the Economic Monitoring and Assessment Unit of the United Nations Secretariat

b Net-creditor economy.

c Special Administrative Region of China

of output, as growth in developing countries is often constrained by the availability of foreign exchange. Fuels, rather than energy sources more broadly, are considered because fuel prices are more directly linked to oil prices, and oil prices are particularly volatile and often have a considerable impact on countries' incomes and capacity to import.

A country is defined as a **fuel exporter** if, simultaneously: (a) its domestic production of primary commercial fuel (including oil, natural gas, coal and lignite, but excluding hydro- and nuclear electricity) exceeds domestic consumption by at least 20 per cent; (b) the value of its fuel exports amounts to at least 20 per cent of its total exports; and (c) it is not classified as a least developed country.

A subgroup of the fuel-importing developing countries identified in some tables is the **least developed countries**. The list of least developed countries is decided by the Economic and Social Council and, ultimately, by the General Assembly, on the basis of the recommendations of the Committee for Development Policy. The Committee proposes criteria for identifying the least developed countries and makes recommendations regarding the eligibility of individual countries. The basic criteria for inclusion require meeting certain thresholds with regard to per capita gross national income, an economic vulnerability index and a human assets index.[c] As of May 2004, the following 50 countries were on the list:

Afghanistan, Angola, Bangladesh, Benin, Bhutan, Burkina Faso, Burundi, Cambodia, Cape Verde, Central African Republic, Chad, Comoros, Democratic Republic of the Congo, Djibouti, Equatorial Guinea, Eritrea, Ethiopia, Gambia, Guinea, Guinea-Bissau, Haiti, Kiribati, Lao People's Democratic Republic, Lesotho, Liberia, Madagascar, Malawi, Maldives, Mali, Mauritania, Mozambique, Myanmar, Nepal, Niger, Rwanda, Samoa, Sao Tome and Principe, Senegal, Sierra Leone, Solomon Islands, Somalia, Sudan, Timor-Leste, Togo, Tuvalu, Uganda, United Republic of Tanzania, Vanuatu, Yemen, Zambia.

A classification of **net-creditor** and **net-debtor** countries is used in some tables. This is based on the net foreign asset position of each country at the end of 1995, as assessed by IMF in its *World Economic Outlook,* October 1996.[d] The **net-creditor** countries are signalized by footnote indicator [b] in table C.

Another group used in this *Survey* comprises the **heavily indebted poor countries** (HIPC), which are considered by the World Bank and IMF for their debt-relief initiative (the Enhanced HIPC Initiative). In May 2004, the heavily indebted poor countries were: Angola, Benin, Bolivia, Burkina Faso, Burundi, Cameroon, Central African Republic, Chad, Comoros, Congo, Côte d'Ivoire, Democratic Republic of the Congo (formerly Zaire), Ethiopia, Gambia, Ghana, Guinea, Guinea-Bissau, Guyana, Honduras, Kenya, Lao People's Democratic Republic, Liberia, Madagascar, Malawi, Mali, Mauritania, Mozambique, Myanmar, Nicaragua, Niger, Rwanda, Sao Tome and Principe, Senegal, Sierra Leone, Somalia, Sudan, Togo, Uganda, United Republic of Tanzania, Viet Nam and Zambia.

Data quality

Statistical information that is consistent and comparable over time and across countries is of vital importance for monitoring economic developments, discussing social issues and poverty, or assessing environmental change. The multifaceted nature of these and other related issues calls for an integrated approach to national and international economic, environmental and social data.

The 1993 revision of the System of National Accounts (SNA)[e] and the 1993 *Balance of Payments Manual*[f] (the IMF Manual) constitute a major step forward in efforts to develop an integrated and harmonized system of statistics that reflect economic and social change. The SNA embodies concepts, definitions and classifications that are interrelated at both the macro- and microlevels. Concepts in the IMF Manual have been harmonized, as closely as possible, with those of the SNA and with IMF methodologies pertaining to banking, government finance and money statistics. In addition, through a system of satellite accounts, which are semi-integrated with the central framework of the SNA, it is possible to establish linkages between national accounts data and other statistical data, such as social statistics, health statistics, social protection statistics and tourism statistics.

Governments are increasingly reporting their data on the basis of these standards and, where available, such data are used in the statistics in this annex. However, inconsistency of coverage, definitions and data-collection methods among reporting countries mars some of the national and international statistics that are perforce used in this *Survey* and other international publications. Another perennial problem is late, incomplete or unreported data. In such cases, adjustments and estimations are possible, and are made in selected cases. In some areas, many developed countries report not only on an annual basis, but also quarterly or even more frequently. Considerable progress has been made by some developing countries and economies in transition in publishing annual and quarterly data on a timely and regular basis, but major lacunae have developed in other cases, particularly for economies in conflict.

One widespread source of inaccuracy is the use of out-of-date benchmark surveys and censuses or obsolete models and assumptions about behaviour and conditions. On the other hand, when statistical administrations seek to improve their estimates by using new sources of data and updated surveys, there can be discontinuities in the series. National income estimates are especially affected, sometimes being subject to revisions on the order of 10-30 per cent.

National accounts and related indicators mainly record market transactions conducted through monetary exchange. Barter, production by households, subsistence output and informal sector activities are not always recorded; together, the omitted items can constitute a large share of total activity and their omission can lead to a considerable underestimation of national output. As the degree of underestimation varies across countries, comparisons may give faulty results. In addition, as the non-market sector is absorbed over time into the mainstream of production through increasing monetization, output growth will be overstated.

Weaknesses at the national level become major analytical handicaps when comparisons are made between countries or groupings of countries at a given time or over time. Missing, unreliable or incompatible country data necessitate estimation and substitution by international organizations if they are to retain consistent country composition of aggregated data over time. In particular, the absence of reliable GDP estimates for many developing countries and economies in transition requires the use of estimates in preparing country aggregations for many data series, as GDP weights often underlie such aggregations.

The veracity of estimates of output and of other statistical data of developing countries is related to the stage of development of their statistical systems. In Africa in particular, there are wide divergences in the values of the economic aggregates provided by different national and international sources for many countries. In addition, data for countries in which there is civil strife or war often provide only rough orders of magnitude.

Finally, in countries experiencing high rates of inflation and disequilibrium exchange rates, substantial distortions can invade national accounts data.

The extent of economic activity not captured by national statistics and its evolution over time have become a concern in some countries, particularly economies in transition. In addition, the proliferation of new modes of production, transactions and entities has rendered the previous institutional and methodological framework for statistics inadequate. A comprehensive reform of national statistical systems has thus been under way in many economies in transition. As a result, important revisions to several data series have been released and further revisions of measures of past and current performance are expected.[g]

There are also problems with other types of statistics such as those on unemployment, consumer price inflation, and the volume of exports and imports. Cross-country comparisons of unemployment must be made with caution, owing to differences in definition among countries. For this reason in particular, table A.7 employs the standardized definitions of unemployment rates, where data are available (developed economies only). In a number of cases, then, data differ substantially from national definitions.

Consumer price indices are among the oldest of the economic data series collected by Governments, but they are still surrounded by controversy, even in countries with the most advanced statistical systems. This is attributable particularly to the introduction of new goods and changes in the quality of goods and consumer behaviour that are often not captured because of, inter alia, infrequent consumer-spending surveys and infrequent revisions to the sample baskets of commodities.

There are no clear-cut solutions to many of the problems noted above. Even when there are, inadequate resources allocated to the improvement of statistical systems and reporting can perpetuate statistical shortcomings. In this light, some of the economic and social indicators presented in this *Survey* should be recognized as approximations and estimations.

Data definitions and conventions

Aggregate data are either sums or weighted averages of individual country data. Unless otherwise indicated, multi-year averages of growth rates are expressed as compound annual percentage rates of change. The convention followed is to omit the base year in a multi-year growth rate, for example, the 10-year average growth rate of a variable in the 1980s would be identified as the average annual growth rate in 1981-1990.

Output

National practices are followed in defining real GDP for each country and these national data are aggregated to create regional and global output figures. The growth of output in each group of countries is calculated from the sum of GDP of individual countries measured at 2000 prices and exchange rates. Data for GDP in 2000 in national currencies were converted into dollars (with adjustments in selected cases[h]) and extended forward and backwards in time using changes in real GDP for each country. This method supplies a reasonable set of aggregate growth rates for a period of about 15 years, centred on 2000.

Alternative aggregation methodologies for calculating world output

The *World Economic and Social Survey* utilizes a weighting scheme derived from exchange-rate conversions of national data in order to aggregate rates of growth of output of individual countries into regional and global totals, as noted above. This is similar to the approach followed in some other international reports, such as those of the World Bank. However, the aggregations used by IMF in its *World Economic Outlook* and by OECD in its *Economic Outlook* rely on country weights derived from national GDP in "international dollars", as converted from local currency using purchasing power parities (PPPs). The different weights arising from these two approaches are given in table D. The question which approach to use is controversial.

The reason advanced for using PPP weights is that, when aggregating production in two countries, a common set of prices should be used to value the same activities in both countries. This is frequently not the case when market exchange rates are used to convert local currency values of GDP. The PPP approach revalues gross expenditure in different countries using a single set of prices, in most cases some average of the prices in the countries being compared. By construction, these revalued GDP magnitudes are then related to a numeraire country, usually the United States of America, by assuming that GDP at PPP values for that country is identical with its GDP at the market exchange rate. The PPP conversion factor is then, in principle, the number of units of national currency needed to buy the goods and services that can be bought with one unit of the currency of the numeraire country.[i]

In principle as well as in practice, however, PPPs are difficult to calculate because goods and services are not always directly comparable across countries, making direct comparisons of their prices correspondingly difficult. It is particularly difficult to measure the output and prices of many services, such as health care and education.

One problem in employing PPP estimates for calculating the relative sizes of economies is that even the most recently completed set of PPP prices covers only a comparatively small group of countries. Initially, in 1985, there were PPP data for only 64 countries. Subsequent work under the auspices of the International Comparison Programme (ICP) has increased this number, but it remains far lower than the number of countries for which this *Survey* needs data.

However, certain regularities have been observed, on the one hand, between GDP and its major expenditure components when measured in market prices and, on the other, between GDP and its components measured in "international" prices as derived in the ICP exercises. On that basis (and using other partial data on consumer prices), a technique was devised to approximate PPP levels of GDP and its major expenditure components for countries that had not participated in ICP. The results are known as the Penn World Tables.[j]

Neither the PPP approach nor the exchange-rate approach to weighting country GDP data can be applied in a theoretically pure or fully consistent way. The data requirements for a global ICP are enormous, although coverage has grown in each round. Similarly, since a system of weights based on exchange rates presumes that those rates are determined solely by external transactions and services and that domestic economies operate under competitive and liberal conditions, its application has been constrained by exchange controls and price distortions in many countries. Moreover, there are a large number of non-traded goods and services in each country to which the "law of one price"

Table C.
Output and per capita output in the base year

	GDP (billions of dollars)		GDP per capita (dollars)	
	Exchange-rate basis 2000	PPP basis 2000	Exchange-rate basis 2000	PPP basis 2000
World	31 279	45 499	5 243	7 627
Developed economies	24 040	24 226	28 189	28 408
of which:				
United States	9 817	9 817	34 661	34 661
European Union	7 893	7 822	20 965	20 776
Japan	4 764	3 418	37 482	26 894
Economies in transition	766	2 796	1861	6 788
Developing countries	6 473	18 477	1 377	3 930
By region:				
Latin America and the Caribbean	1 858	3 827	3 630	7 476
Africa	567	1 715	744	2 250
Western Asia	828	1 677	3 474	7 035
Eastern and Southern Asia	2 139	6 023	1 118	3 148
China	1 080	5 235	847	4 105
By analytical grouping:				
Net-creditor countries	756	1 067	12 625	17 818
Net-debtor countries	5 717	17 410	1 232	3 751
Net fuel exporters	1 693	4 081	1 956	4 715
Net fuel importers	4 780	14 395	1 265	3 810
Memorandum items:				
Sub-Saharan Africa	145	593	314	1 283
Least developed countries	194	736	302	1 145

Source: UN/DESA.

does not apply. However, the global trend towards liberalization may make possible a more consistent application over time of the exchange-rate method. Even so, the methods are conceptually different and thus yield different measures of world output growth.

The differences for the periods 1981-1990 and 1991-2003 are shown in table A.1. The estimates employ the same countries and the same data for the growth rates of GDP of the individual countries in the two computations. The differences in the aggregate growth rates are purely the result of using the two different sets of weights shown in table D.

Table A.1 indicates that the world economy as a whole has grown faster when country GDPs are valued at PPP conversion factors. This is because the developing countries, in the aggregate, grew more rapidly than the rest of the world in the 1990s and in the early years of the new millennium and the share of GDP of these countries is larger under PPP measurements than under market exchange rates. The influence of China is particularly important, given its high growth rate for nearly two decades.

International trade and finance

Trade values in table A.13 are based largely on customs data for merchandise trade converted into dollars using average annual exchange rates and are mainly drawn from IMF, *International Financial Statistics*. These data are supplemented by balance-of-payments data in certain cases. Estimates of the dollar values of trade include estimates by the regional commissions and the Economic Monitoring and Assessment Unit, while forecasts for both volume and value of imports and exports largely rely on Project LINK.

The main source of data for table A.14 is the IMF Direction of Trade Statistics database, while tables A.15 and A.16 are drawn from the more detailed trade data in the United Nations External Trade Statistics Database (COMTRADE).

Total imports and exports comprise all 10 sections (0 to 9) of the Standard International Trade Classification.[k] The following aggregations were used:

Total primary commodities refer to SITC sections 0 to 4:

- *Foods* comprise SITC sections 0 and 1, namely, food and live animals chiefly for food; and beverages and tobacco.
- *Agricultural raw materials* include SITC section 2 (crude materials, inedible, except fuels), except for divisions 27 and 28 (crude fertilizers and crude minerals, and metalliferous ores and metal scrap, respectively), and section 4 (animal and vegetable oils, fats and waxes).
- *Fuels* refer to SITC section 3 (mineral fuels, lubricants and related materials).

Total manufactures comprise sections 5 to 8:

- *Textiles* include divisions 65 (textile yarn, fabrics, made-up articles, not elsewhere specified or included, and related products) and 84 (articles of apparel and clothing accessories).
- *Chemicals* are SITC section 5.
- *Machinery and transport equipment* refer to SITC division 7.
- *Metals* include divisions 67 (iron and steel) and 68 (non-ferrous metals).

Table A.18 is, with the exception of data for OPEC in 2004, based on the International Energy Agency (IEA) *Monthly Oil Market Report*. The estimate of supply from OPEC in 2004 is based on production data for the first quarter of 2004 and information about OPEC production quotas. The country groups and regions used in this *Survey* differ from those used by IEA, and adjustments were made to take account of these differences.

The IMF *Balance of Payments Statistics* is the main source of data for tables A.19 to A.22. The tables are based, therefore, on the definitions and methodologies as specified by the IMF *Balance of Payments Manual* mentioned earlier. Data from the regional commissions, and official and private sources, as well as estimates by the Economic Monitoring and Assessment Unit, were used to complement the IMF data. Whenever necessary, data reported in national currency were converted into United States dollars at the average market exchange rate in the period. Current-account transactions estimates are presented for the three country groupings specified in tables A, B and C above. Regional and subregional aggregates are sums of individual economy data. Accordingly, the current-account balance for the euro zone countries reflects the aggregation of individual country positions; it therefore does not exclude intra euro-zone transactions.

Notes

a Additional information on Project LINK is available from: http://www.un.org/analysis/link/index.htm.

b Names and composition of geographical areas follow those of "Standard country or area codes for statistical use" (ST/ESA/STAT/SER.M/49/Rev.3), with the exception of Western Asia, in which the *Survey* includes the Islamic Republic of Iran (owing to the large role of the petroleum sector in its economy). Also, "Eastern Europe", as used in this *Survey*, is a contraction of "Central and Eastern Europe"; thus, the composition of the region designated by the term differs from that of strictly geographical groupings.

c See *Local Development and Global Issues: Report of the Committee for Development Policy on its fifth session, 7-11 April 2003* (United Nations publication, Sales No. E.03.II.A.3).

d Washington, D.C., IMF, 1996.

e Commission of the European Communities, IMF, OECD, United Nations and World Bank, *System of National Accounts, 1993* (United Nations publication, Sales No. E.94.XVII.4).

f IMF, *Balance of Payments Manual*, 5th ed. (Washington, D.C., IMF, 1993).

g See *World Economic and Social Survey, 1995* (United Nations publication, Sales No. E.95.II.C.1), statistical annex, sect. entitled "Data caveats and conventions".

h When individual exchange rates seemed unrealistic, alternative exchange rates were substituted, using averages of the exchange rates in relevant years or the exchange rate of a more normal year, adjusted using relative inflation rates since that time.

i Since a common set of international prices is used, the translation of purchasing power values relative to any numeraire country is defined, given the built-in transitivity property.

j See Robert Summers and Alan Heston, *The Penn World Table (Mark 5): An Expanded Set of International Comparisons, 1950-1988*, National Bureau of Economic Research (NBER) Working Paper, No. R1562 (Cambridge, Massachusetts, May 1991).

k See *Standard International Trade Classification, Revision 3*, Statistical Papers, No. 34/Rev.3 (United Nations publication, Sales No. E.86.XVII.12 and Corr.1 and 2).

List of tables

I. Global output and macroeconomic indicators

II. International trade

III. International finance and financial markets

I. Global output and macroeconomic indicators

Table A.1.
World population, output and per capita GDP, 1980-2003

	Growth of GDP (annual percentage change) Exchange-rate basis (2000 dollars)		Growth of GDP (annual percentage change) Purchasing power parity (PPP) basis		Growth rate of population (annual percentage change)		Population (millions)		GDP per capita Exchange-rate basis (2000 dollars)	
	1981-1990	1991-2003	1981-1990	1991-2003	1981-1990	1991-2003	1980	2003	1980	2003
World	3.0	2.6	3.0	3.1	1.7	1.3	4 367	6 165	4 084	5 378
Developed economies	3.1	2.2	3.0	2.3	0.6	0.6	756	864	18 448	29 085
of which:										
United States	3.3	3.0	3.3	3.0	1.0	1.0	230	291	22 392	35 716
European Union[a]	2.4	1.9	2.4	1.9	0.3	0.3	355	378	14 301	21 642
Japan	3.9	1.3	3.9	1.3	0.6	0.3	117	128	23 951	38 309
Economies in transition[b]	1.7	-0.6	1.9	-0.9	0.7	0.0	378	409	2 236	2 151
Developing countries	3.0	4.4	3.4	5.0	2.1	1.6	3 233	4 893	942	1 461
by region:										
Latin America and the Caribbean	1.2	2.6	1.3	2.5	2.0	1.6	356	535	3 382	3 529
Africa	2.0	2.6	1.9	2.5	2.9	2.5	446	817	818	761
Western Asia	-0.2	2.9	-1.3	2.9	3.3	2.3	137	254	4 554	3 507
Eastern and Southern Asia	7.0	6.4	6.9	6.8	1.8	1.4	2 295	3 288	373	1 141
Region excluding China	6.4	5.0	5.8	4.8	2.1	1.7	1 296	1 984	527	1 203
East Asia	6.9	5.0	6.3	4.7	1.9	1.2	411	584	1 120	2 892
South Asia	5.2	5.0	5.2	5.0	2.2	1.9	885	1 400	251	498
China	9.1	9.6	9.1	9.6	1.5	0.9	999	1 303	174	1 048
by analytical grouping:										
Net-creditor countries	0.7	3.6	0.9	3.6	3.1	-1.5	37	41	12 781	19 680
Net-debtor countries	3.4	4.5	3.6	5.1	2.1	1.7	3 197	4 852	806	1 308
Net fuel exporters	0.8	2.8	0.8	2.9	2.6	1.9	552	913	2 093	1 976
Net fuel importers	4.2	5.0	4.6	5.7	2.0	1.5	2 682	3 980	705	1 343
Memo items:										
Sub-Saharan Africa	1.7	2.6	0.9	2.5	3.1	2.7	261	498	367	319
Least developed countries	2.1	3.7	1.3	3.4	2.7	2.6	381	682	293	324

Source:
UN/DESA.

a Including the eastern Länder (States) of Germany from 1991.
b Including the former German Democratic Republic until 1990.

Table A.2.
Developed economies: rates of growth of real GDP, 1995-2005

Annual percentage change[a]												
	1995-2003	1995	1996	1997	1998	1999	2000	2001	2002	2003	2004[b]	2005[b]
Developed economies	2.5	2.4	2.9	3.3	2.6	3.1	3.5	1.0	1.3	2.1	3¼	2¾
United States	3.2	2.5	3.7	4.5	4.2	4.5	3.7	0.5	2.2	3.1	4½	3½
Canada	3.4	2.8	1.6	4.2	4.1	5.5	5.3	1.9	3.3	1.7	2¾	3¾
Japan	1.3	1.9	3.4	1.9	-1.1	0.1	2.8	0.4	-0.4	2.5	3	1¾
Australia	3.6	4.1	3.9	4.5	5.7	3.6	1.6	2.7	3.5	2.6	4	2½
New Zealand	3.1	3.7	3.2	2.9	0.1	5.2	2.2	3.5	3.9	3.4	2½	2¼
EU-15	2.2	2.4	1.7	2.5	2.8	3.0	3.5	1.6	1.1	0.8	2	2¼
Euro zone	2.0	2.3	1.4	2.3	2.7	3.0	3.5	1.6	0.9	0.5	1¾	2¼
Austria	2.0	1.7	2.0	1.3	3.3	3.6	3.4	0.8	1.4	0.9	2	2½
Belgium	2.0	2.3	1.2	3.5	2.0	3.2	3.8	0.6	0.7	0.8	1½	2
Finland	3.4	3.8	4.0	6.3	5.3	3.2	5.1	0.7	1.4	1.3	2½	2½
France	2.0	1.8	1.1	1.9	3.1	3.2	3.6	2.1	1.2	0.2	1¾	2½
Germany	1.3	1.7	0.8	1.4	2.0	2.0	2.9	0.6	0.2	-0.1	1½	1¾
Greece	3.5	1.9	2.4	3.6	3.4	3.6	4.1	4.2	3.8	4.7	4¼	3
Ireland	8.2	9.7	8.0	10.8	8.6	11.8	10.1	6.2	6.9	1.6	3¾	4½
Italy	1.7	2.9	1.1	2.0	1.8	1.6	3.0	1.8	0.4	0.3	1	2¼
Luxembourg	5.3	1.4	3.3	8.3	6.9	7.8	9.0	1.3	1.7	2.1	2	3
Netherlands	2.6	3.0	3.0	3.8	4.3	4.0	3.5	1.2	0.2	0.0	1¼	1½
Portugal	2.8	2.9	3.2	3.5	3.5	8.5	3.7	1.6	0.4	-1.4	1¼	2¼
Spain	3.2	2.7	2.4	3.5	3.8	4.9	4.2	2.8	2.0	2.3	3	3¼
Other EU	2.7	3.0	2.5	3.2	3.1	3.0	3.8	1.9	1.7	1.9	3	2½
Denmark	2.1	2.8	2.5	3.0	2.5	2.6	2.8	1.6	1.0	0.0	2	2¼
Sweden	2.8	4.1	1.3	2.4	3.6	4.6	4.3	0.9	2.1	1.6	2½	2½
United Kingdom	2.7	2.8	2.7	3.3	3.1	2.8	3.8	2.1	1.7	2.2	3¼	2¾
Other Europe	1.9	2.0	2.4	3.2	2.5	1.8	3.1	1.6	0.7	0.0	1¾	2½
Iceland	3.5	0.1	5.2	4.7	5.6	4.2	5.6	2.7	-0.5	4.0	4½	4½
Malta	3.4	9.3	4.0	4.8	3.4	4.1	6.3	-1.1	2.3	-1.7	½	1½
Norway	3.0	4.4	5.3	5.2	2.6	2.1	2.8	2.7	1.4	0.3	2¾	2¼
Switzerland	1.2	0.5	0.3	1.7	2.4	1.5	3.2	0.9	0.2	-0.3	1	2½
Memo item:												
Major developed economies	2.4	2.3	2.9	3.2	2.5	3.0	3.4	0.8	1.3	2.3	3½	2¾

Source:
UN/DESA, based on IMF, *International Financial Statistics.*

a Calculated as a weighted average of individual country growth rates of gross domestic product (GDP), where weights are based on GDP in 2000 prices and exchange rates. For methodology, see *World Economic and Social Survey, 1992* and corrigenda (United Nations publication, Sales No. E.92.II.C.1 and Corr.1 and 2), annex, introductory text.

b Forecast, partly based on Project LINK.

Table A.3.
Economies in transition: rates of growth of real GDP, 1995-2005

Annual percentage change[a]

	1995-2003[b]	1995	1996	1997	1998	1999	2000	2001	2002	2003[c]	2004[d]	2005[d]
Economies in transition	2.9	-0.2	0.2	2.5	-0.5	3.6	6.5	4.4	4.0	5.7	5¾	5½
Central and Eastern Europe and Baltic States	3.6	5.9	4.3	3.6	3.0	2.0	4.0	2.8	2.8	3.8	4¼	4½
Central and Eastern Europe	3.5	6.1	4.4	3.4	2.9	2.1	3.9	2.7	2.7	3.6	4	4¼
Albania	6.1	13.3	9.0	-10.3	12.7	7.3	7.7	6.5	4.7	6.0	6	6
Bosnia and Herzegovina	15.6	..	54.2	36.6	15.4	9.5	5.4	4.5	5.5	3.2	4	4
Bulgaria	1.3	2.9	-9.4	-5.6	4.0	2.3	5.4	4.1	4.9	4.3	4¼	4
Croatia	4.2	6.8	5.9	6.8	2.5	-0.9	2.9	4.4	5.2	4.3	4	4
Czech Republic	2.2	5.9	4.3	-0.8	-1.0	0.5	3.3	3.1	2.0	2.9	3½	4
Hungary	3.5	1.4	1.4	4.6	4.9	4.2	5.2	3.8	3.5	2.9	3¼	3¾
Poland	4.3	7.1	6.0	6.8	4.8	4.1	4.0	1.0	1.4	3.7	4½	4½
Romania	1.8	7.1	4.0	-6.1	-4.8	-1.2	2.1	5.7	5.0	4.9	4¾	4¾
Serbia and Montenegro	2.1	6.1	5.9	7.4	2.5	-17.7	6.4	5.5	3.8	2.0	3	4
Slovakia	4.1	5.8	6.1	4.6	4.2	1.5	2.0	3.8	4.4	4.2	4¼	4¾
Slovenia	3.8	4.1	3.6	4.8	3.6	5.6	3.9	2.7	3.4	2.3	3	3½
The former Yugoslav Republic of Macedonia	1.4	-1.1	1.2	1.4	3.4	4.3	4.5	-4.5	0.9	3.0	3½	4
Baltic States	5.2	2.9	4.2	8.1	5.8	0.0	5.6	6.9	6.3	7.5	6½	7
Estonia	5.1	4.3	3.9	9.8	4.6	-0.6	7.3	6.5	6.0	4.7	5¼	5½
Latvia	5.2	-0.9	3.7	8.4	4.8	2.8	6.8	7.9	6.1	7.4	6¾	7
Lithuania	5.3	5.2	4.7	7.0	7.3	-1.7	3.9	6.4	6.8	9.0	7	7½
Commonwealth of Independent States	2.3	-5.2	-3.7	1.4	-4.0	5.4	9.3	5.9	5.1	7.6	7¼	6½
Armenia	7.6	6.9	5.9	3.3	7.3	3.3	5.9	9.6	12.9	13.9	8	7
Azerbaijan	5.9	-11.8	1.3	5.8	10.0	7.4	11.1	9.9	10.6	11.2	9½	8½
Belarus	4.0	-10.4	2.8	11.4	8.4	3.4	5.8	4.7	5.0	6.8	6½	5½
Georgia	5.6	2.6	11.2	10.5	3.1	2.9	1.8	4.8	5.5	8.6	5	4½
Kazakhstan	3.9	-8.2	0.5	1.7	-1.9	2.7	9.8	13.5	9.8	9.2	8½	8
Kyrgyzstan	3.7	-5.4	7.1	9.9	2.1	3.7	5.4	5.3	-0.5	6.7	5	4½
Republic of Moldova	0.6	-1.4	-5.9	1.6	-6.5	-3.4	2.1	6.1	7.8	6.3	5½	4¾
Russian Federation	2.3	-4.1	-3.6	1.4	-5.3	6.4	10.0	5.1	4.7	7.3	7	6½
Tajikistan	1.7	-12.4	-16.7	1.7	5.3	3.7	8.3	10.2	9.5	10.2	8	7½
Turkmenistan[e]	5.0	-7.2	6.7	-11.4	7.1	16.5	10.0	8.0	9.0	9.0	8	7½
Ukraine	0.0	-12.2	-10.0	-3.0	-1.9	-0.2	5.9	9.2	5.2	9.4	8½	7
Uzbekistan	3.5	-0.9	1.7	5.2	4.4	4.4	4.0	4.5	4.2	4.4	6	4½

Source:
UN/DESA, based on data of Economic Commission for Europe (ECE).

a Calculated as a weighted average of individual country growth rates of gross domestic product (GDP), where weights are based on GDP in 2000 prices and exchange rates.

b For Bosnia and Herzegovina, 1996-2003 is calculated.

c Partly estimated.

d Forecast, based in part on Project LINK.

e Reliability of figures for Turkmenistan is questionable owing to not well documented deflation procedures.

Table A.4.

Developing economies: rates of growth of real GDP, 1995-2005

	Annual percentage change[a]											
	1995-2003	1995	1996	1997	1998	1999	2000	2001	2002	2003[b]	2004[c]	2005[c]
Developing economies[d]	4.2	4.7	5.8	5.4	2.0	3.6	5.8	2.3	3.4	4.4	5¼	5¼
Africa	3.4	3.1	5.3	3.4	3.0	3.0	3.3	3.1	2.9	3.3	4	4¾
Net fuel exporters	3.6	3.8	4.6	4.0	3.0	3.4	3.9	2.7	3.3	3.9	4	5
Net fuel importers	3.1	2.5	5.8	2.8	3.0	2.7	2.7	3.4	2.6	2.8	4	4½
Eastern and Southern Asia	5.8	8.2	7.4	6.2	1.3	6.3	7.2	4.0	5.7	6.1	7	6¼
of which:												
East Asia	4.2	8.6	7.7	6.5	0.4	6.4	7.7	3.8	5.9	6.0	7	6¼
South Asia	5.5	6.3	6.1	4.9	5.3	6.0	5.1	4.6	4.5	6.5	6½	6¼
Western Asia	3.1	4.1	4.9	3.9	2.6	-0.2	5.6	-0.5	3.1	4.6	2¾	3
Net fuel exporters	3.1	1.7	4.2	3.2	2.2	1.1	5.1	2.6	2.4	5.1	2½	3
Net fuel importers	3.2	7.5	5.8	4.8	3.2	-2.0	6.2	-4.4	4.1	3.9	3¼	3
Latin America and the Caribbean	2.1	0.5	3.9	5.3	2.4	1.1	4.4	0.4	-0.3	1.5	4	4½
Net fuel exporters	2.2	-3.4	4.1	6.0	3.6	2.5	5.9	0.4	0.1	0.7	4	4½
Net fuel importers	2.1	3.2	3.8	4.9	1.6	0.2	3.4	0.4	-0.7	2.0	3¾	4½
Memo items:												
Sub-Saharan Africa (excluding Nigeria and South Africa)	3.8	4.9	5.8	4.4	4.0	3.1	2.5	3.2	3.1	2.8	5	5½
Least developed countries	4.8	5.5	5.7	5.0	4.5	4.5	4.7	5.1	4.1	3.9	5½	5½
East Asia (excluding China)	4.5	7.5	6.6	5.2	-4.1	5.9	7.4	1.3	4.4	3.6	5½	4½
Major developing economies												
Argentina	0.2	-2.8	5.5	8.1	3.9	-3.4	-0.5	-4.4	-10.9	8.4	6	4½
Brazil	2.1	4.2	2.9	3.5	0.2	0.8	4.5	1.5	1.5	-0.1	3½	5
Chile	4.5	9.9	7.0	7.6	3.9	-1.1	5.4	3.1	2.1	3.2	4	4½
China	8.5	10.5	9.6	8.8	7.8	7.1	8.0	7.3	8.0	9.1	9	8
Colombia	1.8	5.4	2.1	2.8	0.5	-4.3	2.7	1.6	1.8	3.7	4	3¾
Egypt	4.3	4.7	5.0	5.5	4.5	6.3	5.1	2.9	3.0	1.8	2¾	3½
Hong Kong SAR[e]	3.3	4.7	4.8	5.2	-5.1	3.0	12.1	0.6	2.3	3.3	5¼	4¾
India	5.8	6.7	6.4	5.3	5.6	6.4	5.1	5.1	4.5	6.8	7	6½
Indonesia	2.4	8.1	8.0	4.7	13.1	0.1	4.8	3.3	3.7	4.1	4½	4½
Iran (Islamic Republic of)	4.6	4.2	5.0	2.5	2.2	2.5	6.1	5.0	7.6	6.2	4¼	4
Israel	2.6	7.1	4.5	2.1	2.2	2.2	6.0	-0.9	-1.2	1.3	2¾	3¾
Korea, Republic of	5.2	8.9	7.1	5.5	-5.8	10.7	8.8	3.0	6.3	3.1	5½	4¾

Table A.4 (continued)

	1995-2003	1995	1996	1997	1998	1999	2000	2001	2002	2003[b]	2004[c]	2005[c]
Major developing economies (continued)												
Malaysia	4.5	9.5	8.2	7.7	-7.5	5.6	8.3	0.4	4.1	5.2	6	5¼
Mexico	2.7	-6.2	5.5	6.8	4.8	5.2	6.9	-0.2	0.9	1.3	3½	4½
Nigeria	3.0	2.5	4.3	2.7	1.9	1.1	3.8	3.9	3.3	4.0	4	3½
Pakistan	4.0	4.9	5.2	1.3	3.7	4.1	3.9	3.1	4.4	5.5	5½	5½
Peru	3.5	8.6	2.5	6.7	-0.4	1.4	3.6	0.6	5.2	3.9	4	4½
Philippines	3.8	4.8	5.5	5.2	-0.5	3.4	4.0	3.3	4.4	4.5	4¼	4
Saudi Arabia	2.4	-0.2	4.0	3.0	1.6	0.5	4.5	1.2	1.0	6.4	¼	1½
Singapore	4.5	8.9	7.0	7.8	0.3	5.9	10.3	-2.0	2.2	1.1	6	4¼
South Africa	2.7	3.1	4.3	2.6	0.8	2.1	3.4	2.8	3.0	1.9	3	3½
Taiwan Province of China	4.3	6.1	5.6	6.8	4.6	5.4	5.9	-1.9	3.6	3.2	5¼	4¼
Thailand	2.7	8.6	6.7	-1.3	10.2	4.2	4.4	1.6	5.3	6.7	7	5½
Turkey	3.5	8.0	7.0	6.8	3.8	-5.1	7.1	-8.0	7.8	5.8	3½	2½
Venezuela	-1.4	3.1	-1.3	5.1	0.2	-6.1	3.2	2.8	-8.9	-9.2	6½	3¾

Source:
United Nations.

a Calculated as a weighted average of individual country growth rates of gross domestic product (GDP), where weights are based on GDP in 2000 prices and exchange rates.

b Partly estimated.

c Forecast, based in part on Project LINK.

d Covering countries that account for 98 per cent of the population of all developing countries.

e Special Administrative Region of China.

Table A.5.
Developed economies: investment, saving and net transfer, 1990-2002

		Percentage of GDP		
		Gross domestic investment	Gross domestic saving	Net financial transfer
Total[a]	1990	23.0	22.5	0.5
	1995	21.5	22.2	-0.7
	2000	21.9	21.2	0.7
	2002	19.6	19.0	0.6
Major developed economies[a]	1990	22.7	22.1	0.6
	1995	21.5	22.0	-0.4
	2000	21.8	20.6	1.2
	2002	19.3	18.1	1.2
European Union (EU-15)	1990	16.8	16.3	0.5
	1995	14.7	15.9	-1.2
	2000	15.1	15.6	-0.4
	2002	13.8	15.1	-1.3
Germany[b]	1990	23.8	23.8	0.1
	1995	22.6	23.3	-0.6
	2000	21.7	22.1	-0.4
	2002	17.9	22.2	-4.3
Japan	1990	32.7	33.7	-0.9
	1995	28.1	29.5	-1.4
	2000	26.2	27.6	-1.4
	2002	23.6	24.9	-1.3
United States of America	1990	17.6	16.4	1.2
	1995	18.1	17.0	1.1
	2000	20.7	17.0	3.7
	2002	18.2	14.1	4.1

Source:
OECD, *National Accounts.*

a National data converted to dollars for aggregation at annual average exchange rates.
b Prior to 1991, data referring to Western Germany only.

Table A.6.
Developed economies: unemployment rates,[a] 1995-2005

Percentage of labour force											
	1995	1996	1997	1998	1999	2000	2001	2002	2003	2004[b]	2005[b]
Developed economies	7.3	7.3	7.0	6.7	6.3	5.9	6.1	6.8	7.0	6¾	6¾
United States	5.6	5.4	4.9	4.5	4.2	4.0	4.7	5.8	6.0	5½	5½
Canada	9.4	9.6	9.1	8.3	7.6	6.8	7.2	7.7	7.6	7½	7½
Japan	3.2	3.4	3.4	4.1	4.7	4.7	5.0	5.4	5.3	5	4¾
Australia	8.2	8.2	8.2	7.7	6.9	6.3	6.8	6.4	6.0	6	5¾
New Zealand	6.3	6.1	6.6	7.5	6.8	6.0	5.3	5.2	4.7	5	5
EU-15	10.2	10.3	10.1	9.5	8.7	7.8	7.4	7.7	8.0	8	8
Euro zone	10.6	10.8	10.9	10.3	9.4	8.5	8.0	8.4	8.8	9	8¾
Austria	3.9	4.4	4.4	4.5	4.0	3.6	3.6	4.3	4.4	4¼	4
Belgium	9.7	9.5	9.2	9.3	8.6	6.9	6.7	7.3	8.1	8¼	8¼
Finland	15.2	14.6	12.7	11.3	10.2	9.8	9.1	9.1	9.0	9	8¾
France	11.4	11.9	11.8	11.4	10.7	9.3	8.5	8.8	9.4	9½	9½
Germany	8.2	8.9	9.9	9.3	8.4	7.8	7.8	8.6	9.3	9¼	9
Greece	9.1	9.7	9.6	11.0	11.8	11.0	10.4	10.0	9.3	8½	8¼
Ireland	12.3	11.7	9.9	7.5	5.6	4.3	3.9	4.4	4.6	5	5
Italy	11.5	11.5	11.6	11.7	11.3	10.4	9.4	9.0	8.6	8¼	8
Luxembourg	2.9	2.9	2.7	2.7	2.4	2.3	2.1	2.8	3.7	4	4¼
Netherlands	6.6	6.0	4.9	3.8	3.2	2.9	2.5	2.7	3.8	5¼	5¾
Portugal	7.3	7.2	6.8	5.2	4.5	4.1	4.1	5.1	6.4	6½	6
Spain	18.8	18.1	17.0	15.2	12.8	11.3	10.6	11.3	11.3	11¼	10¾
Other EU	8.4	8.1	7.1	6.3	5.9	5.3	4.9	5.0	5.1	5	5
Denmark	6.8	6.3	5.2	4.9	4.8	4.4	4.4	4.6	5.6	5¾	5¼
Sweden	8.8	9.6	9.9	8.2	6.7	5.6	4.9	4.9	5.6	6¼	6
United Kingdom	8.5	8.0	6.9	6.2	5.9	5.4	5.0	5.1	5.0	4¾	4¾
Other Europe	4.2	4.2	4.2	3.5	3.1	3.0	3.0	3.5	4.3	4½	4½
Iceland[c]	4.9	3.7	3.9	2.7	2.0	2.3	2.3	3.3	4.1	4	3½
Malta[c]	3.7	4.4	5.5	5.6	5.8	5.0	5.1	5.2	5.7	6¾	6¼
Norway	5.5	4.8	4.0	3.2	3.2	3.4	3.6	3.9	4.5	4½	4
Switzerland	3.5	3.9	4.2	3.6	3.0	2.7	2.6	3.2	4.1	4½	4¾
Memo item:											
Major developed economies	6.7	6.8	6.5	6.3	6.1	5.7	6.1	6.8	7.0	6¾	6½

Source:
UN/DESA, based on data of OECD.

a Unemployment data are standardized by OECD for comparability among countries and over time, in conformity with the definitions of the International Labour Organization (see OECD, *Standardized Unemployment Rates: Sources and Methods* (Paris, 1985).

b Forecast.

c Not standardized.

Table A.7.
Economies in transition: unemployment rates,[a] 1995-2005

Percentage of labour force, end of period											
	1995	1996	1997	1998	1999	2000	2001	2002	2003[b]	2004[c]	2005[d]
Central and Eastern Europe											
Albania	12.9	12.3	14.9	17.6	18.2	16.9	14.6	15.8	14.0	15	15
Bosnia and Herzegovina	..	..	39.0	38.7	39.0	39.4	39.9	42.7	42.0	42	40
Bulgaria	11.1	12.5	13.7	12.2	16.0	17.9	17.9	16.3	14.3	12¾	12
Croatia	17.6	15.9	17.6	18.6	20.8	22.6	23.1	21.3	19.5	19	17
Czech Republic	2.9	3.5	5.2	7.5	9.4	8.8	8.9	9.8	9.3	11	9½
Hungary	10.4	10.5	10.4	9.1	9.6	8.9	8.0	8.0	8.4	8¼	8
Poland	14.9	13.2	10.3	10.4	13.1	15.1	17.5	20.0	20.0	19½	19
Romania	9.5	6.6	8.8	10.3	11.5	10.5	8.8	8.4	7.2	8	7¾
Serbia and Montenegro	24.7	26.1	25.6	27.2	27.4	26.6	22.5	25.0	28.0	28	25
Slovakia	13.1	12.8	12.5	15.6	19.2	17.9	18.6	17.8	15.6	15¼	14
Slovenia	14.5	14.4	14.8	14.6	13.0	12.0	11.8	11.6	11.6	10¾	10½
The former Yugoslav Republic of Macedonia	36.6	38.8	41.7	32.3	44.0	45.1	41.8	45.3	45.3	43	42
Baltic States											
Estonia[d]	5.0	5.6	4.6	5.1	6.7	7.7	7.7	6.8	6.1	5¾	5½
Latvia	6.6	7.2	7.0	9.2	9.1	7.8	7.7	8.5	8.0	7¼	7
Lithuania	7.3	6.2	6.7	6.9	10.0	12.6	12.9	10.9	9.2	8½	8
Commonwealth of Independent States											
Armenia	8.1	9.7	11.0	8.9	11.5	10.9	9.8	9.1	9.8	9½	9
Azerbaijan	1.1	1.1	1.3	1.4	1.2	1.2	1.3	1.3	1.4	1¼	1¼
Belarus	2.7	4.0	2.8	2.3	2.0	2.1	2.3	3.0	3.1	3½	3
Georgia	3.4	3.2	8.0	4.2	5.6	..	..	..	..	..	..
Kazakhstan	2.1	4.1	3.9	3.7	3.9	3.7	2.8	2.6	1.8	1½	1¼
Kyrgyzstan	3.0	4.5	3.1	3.1	3.0	3.1	3.1	3.1	3.0	2¾	2¾
Republic of Moldova	1.4	1.5	1.7	1.9	2.1	1.8	1.7	1.5	1.2	1	1¼
Russian Federation[e]	9.0	10.0	11.2	13.3	12.2	9.8	8.7	8.8	8.1	8	7¾
Tajikistan	1.8	2.4	2.8	2.9	3.1	3.0	2.6	2.7	2.4	2¼	2¼
Turkmenistan	..	..	..	..	..	..	..	..	..	..	..
Ukraine	0.6	1.5	2.8	4.3	4.3	4.2	3.7	3.8	3.6	3½	3½
Uzbekistan	0.3	0.3	0.3	0.4	0.5	0.6	..	..	..	..	..

Source:
UN/DESA, based on data of Economic Commission for Europe (ECE).

a End-of-period registered unemployment data.
b Partly estimated.
c Forecast.
d Job seekers till October 2000; thereafter, registered unemployed as percentage of labour force.
e Based on Russian Goskomstat estimates according to ILO definition, which includes all persons not having employment but actively seeking work.

Table A.8.
Developed economies: consumer price inflation,[a] 1995-2005

	Average annual percentage change										
	1995	1996	1997	1998	1999	2000	2001	2002	2003	2004[b]	2005[b]
Developed economies	2.2	2.1	2.0	1.4	1.3	2.2	2.0	1.3	1.7	1½	1½
United States	2.8	2.9	2.3	1.6	2.2	3.4	2.8	1.6	2.3	2	1¾
Canada	2.2	1.6	1.6	1.0	1.7	2.7	2.5	2.2	2.8	1½	1¾
Japan	-0.1	0.1	1.7	0.7	-0.3	-0.7	-0.7	-0.9	-0.3	-¼	¾
Australia	4.6	2.6	0.3	0.9	1.5	4.5	4.4	3.0	2.8	2	2
New Zealand	3.8	2.6	0.9	1.3	1.4	2.7	2.7	2.3	1.8	2½	2
EU-15	2.9	2.4	2.0	1.7	1.2	2.4	2.4	2.0	2.2	2	1¾
Euro zone	2.8	2.4	1.8	1.3	1.1	2.3	2.6	2.1	2.0	1¾	1½
Austria	2.3	1.8	1.3	0.9	0.6	2.4	2.7	1.8	1.4	1½	1½
Belgium	1.5	2.1	1.6	1.0	1.1	2.5	2.5	1.6	1.6	1¼	1¼
Finland	1.0	0.6	1.2	1.4	1.2	3.4	1.7	1.7	0.6	½	1¼
France	1.8	2.0	1.2	0.7	0.5	1.7	1.7	1.9	2.1	1½	1½
Germany	1.7	1.4	1.9	0.9	0.6	1.9	2.5	1.3	1.0	1¼	1¼
Greece	8.9	8.2	5.5	4.8	2.6	3.1	3.4	3.6	3.6	3½	3
Ireland	2.5	1.7	1.4	2.4	1.6	5.6	4.9	4.7	3.5	2½	2¾
Italy	5.2	4.0	2.0	2.0	1.7	2.5	2.8	2.5	2.7	2½	2¼
Luxembourg	1.9	1.4	1.4	1.0	1.0	3.1	2.7	2.1	2.1	2¼	2
Netherlands	1.9	2.0	2.2	2.0	2.2	2.5	4.5	3.5	2.1	1	½
Portugal	4.1	3.1	2.2	2.7	2.3	2.8	4.4	3.5	3.3	2	2¼
Spain	4.7	3.6	2.0	1.8	2.3	3.4	2.8	3.1	3.0	1¾	1½
Other EU	3.2	2.2	2.7	2.8	1.5	2.7	1.9	1.8	2.7	2½	2½
Denmark	2.1	2.1	2.2	1.9	2.5	2.9	2.3	2.4	2.1	2	2
Sweden	2.5	0.5	0.7	-0.3	0.5	0.9	2.4	2.2	1.9	1	1¼
United Kingdom	3.4	2.4	3.1	3.4	1.6	2.9	1.8	1.6	2.9	2¾	2½
Other Europe	2.1	1.0	1.4	1.0	1.5	2.2	1.9	1.0	1.4	½	1
Iceland	1.7	2.3	1.7	1.7	3.2	5.2	6.4	5.2	2.1	2¼	2¾
Malta	4.4	2.1	3.1	2.4	2.1	2.4	2.9	2.2	1.3	3½	2¼
Norway	2.5	1.3	2.6	2.3	2.3	3.1	3.0	1.3	2.5	1	2
Switzerland	1.8	0.8	0.5	0.0	0.8	1.5	1.0	0.6	0.6	¼	¼
Memo item:											
Major developed economies	2.1	2.0	2.1	1.4	1.3	2.1	1.8	1.1	1.7	1½	1½

Source:
UN/DESA, based on data of IMF, *International Financial Statistics*.

a Data for country groups are weighted averages, where weights for each year are 2000 GDP in United States dollars.

b Forecast, partly based on Project LINK.

Table A.9.
Economies in transition: consumer price inflation, 1995-2005

Average annual percentage change											
	1995	1996	1997	1998	1999	2000	2001	2002	2003	2004[a]	2005[a]
Economies in transition	127.7	38.0	38.4	20.5	44.0	17.8	13.4	9.3	7.3	7	6
Central and Eastern Europe and Baltic States	25.4	23.7	58.9	15.5	10.3	11.5	8.3	4.6	3.0	4	3½
Central and Eastern Europe	25.1	23.7	61.2	15.9	10.7	12.0	8.6	4.7	3.1	4	3½
Albania	8.0	12.7	33.2	20.3	0.4	0.0	3.1	5.5	3.0	2½	3
Bosnia and Herzegovina	-12.1	-21.2	11.8	4.9	-0.6	1.7	1.8	0.9	0.2	½	1
Bulgaria	62.1	121.6	1 058.4	18.7	2.6	10.3	7.4	5.8	2.3	5	4
Croatia	4.0	3.6	3.7	5.2	3.5	6.5	5.4	4.7	1.5	2½	2¾
Czech Republic	9.1	8.8	8.5	10.7	2.1	3.9	4.7	1.8	0.1	3¼	2½
Hungary	28.2	23.6	18.3	14.3	10.0	9.8	9.2	5.3	4.7	7	4½
Poland	27.8	19.9	14.9	11.8	7.3	10.1	5.5	1.9	0.8	2	2½
Romania	32.3	38.8	154.9	59.1	45.8	45.7	34.5	22.5	15.0	12	9
Serbia and Montenegro	71.8	90.5	23.2	30.4	44.1	77.5	90.4	19.2	9.6	8	7
Slovakia	10.0	5.8	6.1	6.7	10.6	12.0	7.1	3.3	8.6	7¾	5
Slovenia	13.5	9.9	8.4	7.9	6.1	8.9	8.4	7.5	5.6	3½	3
The former Yugoslav Republic of Macedonia	15.9	2.5	0.9	-1.4	-1.3	6.6	5.2	2.3	1.2	2½	2½
Baltics States	32.3	22.0	9.2	6.3	1.9	2.3	2.8	1.6	0.7	2¼	1¼
Estonia	28.9	23.1	11.1	10.6	3.5	3.9	5.8	3.5	1.3	2¾	1¼
Latvia	25.0	17.6	8.4	4.7	2.4	2.8	2.5	1.9	2.9	3	1¾
Lithuania	39.5	24.7	8.8	5.1	0.8	1.0	1.3	0.3	-1.2	1½	1
Commonwealth of Independent States	231.9	52.6	17.6	25.6	78.2	24.1	18.5	14.1	11.7	9¾	8½
Armenia	175.5	18.7	13.8	8.7	0.7	-0.8	3.2	1.0	4.7	3½	3½
Azerbaijan	411.5	19.8	3.6	-0.8	-8.6	1.8	1.5	2.8	2.2	3½	4
Belarus	709.3	52.7	63.9	73.2	293.7	168.9	61.1	42.8	28.5	25	20
Georgia	261.4	39.4	7.1	3.5	19.3	4.2	4.6	5.7	4.8	5	5½
Kazakhstan	176.3	39.2	17.5	7.3	8.4	13.4	8.5	6.0	6.4	6½	5
Kyrgyzstan	43.5	32.0	23.4	10.5	35.9	18.7	6.9	2.1	3.1	4	4½
Republic of Moldova	29.9	23.5	11.8	7.7	39.3	31.3	9.6	5.3	11.7	8	7
Russian Federation	197.4	47.8	14.7	27.8	85.7	20.2	18.6	15.1	12.0	10	8½
Tajikistan	682.1	422.4	85.4	43.1	27.5	32.9	38.6	12.2	17.1	15	13
Turkmenistan	1 105.3	714.0	83.7	16.8	23.5	7.0	8.2	15.0	11.0	12	12
Ukraine	376.7	80.2	15.9	10.6	22.7	28.2	12.0	0.8	5.2	3½	6½
Uzbekistan	304.6	54.0	58.8	17.7	29.0	24.9	26.6	24.2	22.0	19	15

Source:
UN/DESA, based on data of Economic Commission for Europe (ECE).

a Forecast.

Table A.10.

Developing economies: consumer price inflation,[a] 1995-2005

Average annual percentage change											
	1995	1996	1997	1998	1999	2000	2001	2002	2003[b]	2004[c]	2005[c]
Developing economies	22.5	14.9	10.1	10.3	6.5	5.4	5.5	6.2	6.7	5½	5¼
by region:											
Africa[d]	21.9	14.3	7.8	6.6	5.2	6.0	5.9	7.8	11.3	14¼	12½
Eastern and Southern Asia	10.4	7.0	4.6	7.4	1.8	1.3	2.5	2.1	2.5	3¼	3
of which:											
East Asia	10.5	6.5	3.9	6.4	1.1	0.6	2.2	1.6	2.2	3	3
South Asia	10.2	8.9	7.5	12.0	4.8	4.0	3.8	4.3	3.9	4¼	4
Western Asia	35.4	29.6	28.0	26.9	21.4	17.2	16.9	15.8	9.9	7	10½
Latin America and the Caribbean	38.7	23.0	13.3	9.8	9.3	7.9	6.1	9.2	11.3	6¾	5
Memo items:											
Sub-Saharan Africa (excluding Democratic Republic of the Congo, Nigeria and South Africa)	23.5	23.9	12.8	8.9	9.8	10.0	10.1	13.9	29.2	41¾	37½
Least developed countries[d]	22.6	20.9	15.3	19.2	11.5	4.8	7.6	11.1	13.2	11½	11½
East Asia excluding China	5.9	5.3	4.7	11.6	2.9	0.9	3.5	3.2	2.9	3	3
Major developing economies											
Argentina	3.4	0.2	0.5	0.9	-1.2	-0.9	-1.1	25.9	15.7	5	4½
Brazil	66.0	15.8	6.9	3.2	4.9	7.0	6.8	8.4	15.9	7	4½
Chile	8.2	7.4	6.1	5.1	3.3	3.8	3.6	2.5	3.2	2	3
China	16.9	8.3	2.8	-0.8	-1.4	0.3	0.5	-0.7	1.2	3	2½
Colombia	21.0	20.2	18.5	18.7	10.9	9.2	8.0	6.3	7.3	6	5½
Egypt	15.7	7.2	4.6	4.2	3.1	2.7	2.3	2.7	4.2	5¼	3½
Hong Kong SAR[e]	9.1	6.3	5.8	2.9	-4.0	-3.7	-1.6	-3.0	-2.6	1	1¾
India	10.2	9.0	7.2	13.2	4.7	4.0	3.7	4.4	3.8	4¼	4
Indonesia	9.4	8.0	6.7	57.6	20.3	4.5	12.0	11.5	6.6	5	5
Iran (Islamic Republic of)	49.7	28.9	17.3	17.9	20.1	14.5	11.3	14.3	16.5	15½	14
Israel	10.0	11.3	9.0	5.4	5.2	1.1	1.1	5.6	0.7	2½	2¾
Korea, Republic of	4.4	5.0	4.4	7.5	0.8	2.2	4.1	2.7	3.5	3¼	3¼
Malaysia	3.5	3.5	2.7	5.3	2.7	1.5	1.4	1.8	1.1	1¾	2¼
Mexico	35.0	34.4	20.6	15.9	16.6	9.5	6.4	5.0	4.7	4½	4
Nigeria	72.8	29.3	8.2	10.3	4.8	14.5	13.0	12.9	14.0	12¾	9¾
Pakistan	12.3	10.4	11.4	6.2	4.1	4.4	3.1	3.3	2.9	4	4
Peru	11.1	11.5	8.6	7.2	3.5	3.8	2.0	0.2	2.3	2½	2½
Philippines	8.0	9.0	5.9	9.7	6.7	4.4	6.1	3.1	3.0	3¾	4
Saudi Arabia	4.9	1.2	0.1	-0.4	-1.3	-1.1	-1.1	0.3	0.5	¾	½
Singapore	1.7	1.4	2.0	-0.3	0.0	1.4	1.0	-0.4	0.5	1	1¼
South Africa	8.6	7.4	8.6	7.0	5.2	5.3	4.8	8.9	6.0	5	4½
Taiwan Province of China	3.7	3.1	1.8	2.6	0.2	-1.9	0.6	-0.2	-0.3	½	¾
Thailand	5.8	5.9	5.6	8.1	0.3	1.6	1.7	0.6	1.8	2	2¼
Turkey	88.1	80.3	85.7	84.6	64.9	54.9	54.4	45.0	25.3	14	26½
Venezuela	59.9	99.9	50.0	35.8	23.6	16.2	12.5	22.4	32.9	29	20

Source:
UN/DESA, based on IMF, *International Financial Statistics.*

a Weights used are GDP in 2000 US dollars.
b Partly estimated.
c Forecast, based in part on Project LINK.
d Excluding Democratic Republic of the Congo.
e Special Administrative Region of China.

Table A.11.
Major developed economies: financial indicators, 1995-2003

Percentage									
	1995	1996	1997	1998	1999	2000	2001	2002	2003
Short-term interest rates[a]									
Canada[a]	6.9	4.3	3.3	4.9	4.7	5.5	4.1	2.5	2.9
France[b]	6.4	3.7	3.2	3.4	3.0	4.4	4.3	3.3	2.3
Germany[b]	4.5	3.3	3.2	3.4	3.0	4.4	4.3	3.3	2.3
Italy[b]	10.5	8.8	6.9	5.0	3.0	4.4	4.3	3.3	2.3
Japan	1.2	0.5	0.5	0.4	0.1	0.1	0.1	0.0	0.0
United Kingdom	6.1	6.0	6.6	7.2	5.2	5.8	5.1	3.9	3.6
United States	5.8	5.3	5.5	5.4	5.0	6.2	3.9	1.7	1.1
Long-term interest rates[c]									
Canada	8.3	7.5	6.4	5.5	5.7	5.9	5.8	5.7	5.3
France	7.6	6.4	5.6	4.7	4.7	5.5	5.0	4.9	4.2
Germany	6.5	5.6	5.1	4.4	4.3	5.2	4.7	4.6	3.8
Italy	12.2	9.4	6.9	4.9	4.7	5.6	5.2	5.0	4.2
Japan	2.5	2.2	1.7	1.1	1.8	1.7	1.3	1.3	1.0
United Kingdom	8.3	8.1	7.1	5.4	4.7	4.7	4.8	4.8	4.6
United States	6.6	6.4	6.4	5.3	5.6	6.0	5.0	4.6	4.0
General government financial balances[d]									
Canada	-5.3	-2.8	0.2	0.1	1.7	3.1	1.4	0.8	1.2
France	-5.6	-4.1	-3.0	-2.7	-1.6	-1.4	-0.2	-3.2	-4.1
Germany	-3.2	-3.4	-2.7	-2.1	-1.4	1.3	-2.8	-3.5	-3.9
Italy	-7.6	-6.5	-2.7	-2.8	-1.9	-0.6	-2.6	-2.3	-2.4
Japan[e]	-4.7	-5.0	-3.8	-5.5	-7.2	-7.4	-6.1	-7.9	-8.2
United Kingdom	-5.8	-4.4	-2.0	0.4	1.3	3.8	0.7	-1.6	-3.2
United States	-3.1	-2.2	-0.9	0.3	0.7	1.4	-0.2	-3.3	-4.9

Source:
UN/DESA, based on IMF, *International Financial Statistics;* OECD, *Economic Outlook;* and EUROPA (EU on line), *European Economy.*

a Money market rates.
b From January 1999 onward, representing the three-month Euro Interbank Offered Rate (EURIBOR), which is an Interbank deposit bid rate.
c Yield on long-term government bonds.
d Surplus (+) or deficit (-) as a percentage of nominal GNP or GDP.
e The 1998 deficit does not take account of the assumption by the central Government of the debt of the Japan National Railway Settlement Corporation and the National Forest Special Account, which amounts to 5.2 percentage points of GDP. Deferred tax payments on postal savings accounts are included in 2000 and 2001.

Table A.12.

Selected economies: real effective exchange rates, broad measurement,[a] 1995-2003

2000 = 100									
	1995	1996	1997	1998	1999	2000	2001	2002	2003
Developed economies									
Australia	98.3	106.9	108.5	99.9	101.3	100.0	94.9	98.3	109.8
Canada	104.4	106.1	107.2	102.5	101.4	100.0	96.4	94.7	102.3
Denmark	104.9	104.1	101.2	104.9	106.5	100.0	102.6	106.6	113.7
Euro zone	120.2	119.3	109.1	112.2	109.3	100.0	101.4	105.2	117.3
Japan	109.7	93.1	88.1	88.4	96.9	100.0	89.7	83.8	83.0
New Zealand	117.8	128.2	131.3	116.6	111.9	100.0	99.3	111.3	130.5
Norway	101.6	99.2	98.6	98.9	100.4	100.0	102.6	108.6	108.7
Sweden	110.1	114.0	108.0	109.2	105.1	100.0	91.6	93.8	97.7
Switzerland	114.9	111.2	102.5	107.2	107.5	100.0	103.3	109.4	111.2
United Kingdom	85.3	87.1	99.4	103.8	102.2	100.0	97.2	98.3	95.6
United States	85.2	86.9	90.9	99.0	98.9	100.0	106.2	106.2	98.1
Developing economies									
Argentina	86.6	89.4	93.8	96.5	102.1	100.0	104.9	57.1	62.5
Brazil	110.6	107.4	112.8	112.7	84.4	100.0	90.2	90.0	98.3
Chile	94.4	97.4	101.8	98.1	95.5	100.0	94.5	92.9	91.7
China	86.2	91.5	97.8	103.2	97.7	100.0	105.0	102.6	97.7
Colombia	114.5	117.7	125.0	119.5	107.4	100.0	100.5	99.0	87.9
Ecuador	80.7	81.0	84.5	83.6	79.7	100.0	100.9	110.0	112.8
Egypt	73.1	80.0	89.5	95.5	98.4	100.0	91.1	81.9	66.2
Hong Kong SAR[b]	91.6	97.1	105.2	113.6	105.5	100.0	101.8	101.3	95.1
India	104.2	98.5	102.8	98.4	98.7	100.0	102.3	98.9	98.1
Indonesia	140.4	145.0	134.8	68.0	103.8	100.0	96.3	116.1	122.8
Israel	90.1	91.7	95.5	94.8	94.1	100.0	99.7	89.9	86.9
Korea, Republic of	111.7	112.9	105.0	83.9	93.9	100.0	90.3	93.3	92.9
Kuwait	83.9	90.4	94.5	99.9	97.4	100.0	107.3	109.2	102.7
Malaysia	121.7	126.1	122.1	100.7	99.8	100.0	105.2	105.0	100.3
Mexico	63.9	72.4	82.2	82.8	90.7	100.0	105.7	106.5	99.1
Morocco	90.2	92.0	92.6	97.6	99.8	100.0	97.9	98.6	97.3
Nigeria	58.1	77.9	88.9	100.8	102.8	100.0	110.8	116.4	105.6
Pakistan	104.4	103.0	106.2	109.1	105.5	100.0	94.1	99.0	100.3
Panama	91.0	92.6	95.7	99.2	99.6	100.0	102.4	103.8	100.9
Peru	104.2	105.9	107.3	109.0	100.0	100.0	104.0	103.9	99.9
Philippines	117.0	129.4	121.6	96.6	103.1	100.0	107.5	111.8	107.2
Saudi Arabia	87.4	90.4	96.1	102.3	99.5	100.0	103.6	102.2	94.4
Singapore	101.7	101.7	99.1	94.0	92.4	100.0	99.6	97.9	97.3
South Africa	118.0	109.5	115.8	105.1	100.9	100.0	90.7	81.1	107.4
Taiwan Province of China	108.5	106.0	107.0	100.0	96.3	100.0	95.5	93.1	89.1
Thailand	115.4	118.0	109.0	98.6	102.5	100.0	96.4	100.5	99.9
Turkey	100.4	92.4	93.4	93.8	92.9	100.0	89.0	101.0	108.0
Venezuela	80.7	68.1	78.0	89.1	96.4	100.0	109.4	93.2	94.3

Source:
J.P. Morgan Chase.

a Indices based on a "broad" measure currency basket of 18 OECD currencies (including the euro) and 30 developing-economy currencies (mostly Asian and Latin American). The real effective exchange rate, which adjusts the nominal index for relative price changes, gauges the effect on international price competitiveness of the country's manufactures due to currency changes and inflation differentials. A rise in the index implies a fall in competitiveness and vice versa. The relative price changes are based on indices most closely measuring the prices of domestically produced finished manufactured goods, excluding food and energy, at the first stage of manufacturing. The weights for currency indices are derived from 2000 bilateral trade patterns of the corresponding countries.

b Special Administrative Region of China.

II. International trade

Table A.13.
World trade: changes in value and volume of exports and imports, by major country group, 1995-2004

Annual percentage change										
	1995	1996	1997	1998	1999	2000	2001	2002[a]	2003[b]	2004
Dollar value of exports										
World	19.4	4.3	3.5	-2.3	3.9	14.9	-3.6	5.3	14.9	14
Developed economies	18.9	2.6	2.3	0.3	2.2	11.3	-3.9	3.3	13.1	14½
North America	14.6	6.4	9.3	-0.7	5.0	13.3	-6.4	-3.0	5.7	10
Western Europe	22.5	3.0	-1.5	1.8	-0.3	10.6	-0.3	5.9	17.2	17
Japan	11.6	-7.3	2.5	-7.9	8.6	10.0	-17.3	3.9	8.0	10¼
Economies in transition	29.1	8.0	2.2	-2.1	-1.0	16.3	6.2	7.4	26.4	22¼
Central and Eastern Europe and Baltic States	30.1	5.7	6.5	13.5	-1.2	20.5	12.5	8.8	28.4	25½
Commonwealth of Independent States	27.9	10.9	-1.8	-17.0	-1.0	10.0	-3.8	5.1	24.9	19½
Developing countries	19.5	7.6	6.4	-6.5	7.7	22.8	-4.1	9.2	16.7	11½
Latin America and the Caribbean	20.9	10.2	10.4	-2.4	5.6	19.4	-3.6	1.9	7.5	7½
Africa	12.5	19.7	2.5	-15.0	10.3	7.3	-6.7	3.7	19.0	7½
Western Asia	12.3	13.6	-5.7	-24.1	25.1	40.1	-3.3	6.6	12.0	¼
Eastern and Southern Asia	21.3	5.0	4.0	-6.9	6.5	22.2	-4.2	12.3	19.9	15
China	22.9	1.6	20.8	0.5	6.1	27.8	6.8	22.3	34.6	18
Dollar value of imports										
World	19.4	4.8	2.8	-2.3	5.4	13.7	-3.6	2.9	14.7	14½
Developed economies	18.0	3.6	2.6	1.9	5.2	11.7	-3.6	2.1	13.8	13½
North America	11.3	6.2	10.3	4.6	10.9	18.1	-6.2	1.9	7.2	8½
Western Europe	20.7	2.3	0.0	3.8	1.4	7.6	-1.6	3.5	17.9	17½
Japan	22.0	4.0	-3.0	-17.2	11.2	21.4	-7.4	-7.3	5.0	3½
Economies in transition	33.4	13.9	9.0	0.5	-8.0	15.2	11.1	6.8	25.3	22
Central and Eastern Europe and Baltic States	37.0	16.5	6.7	13.0	-2.5	15.2	9.3	7.3	27.1	25
Commonwealth of Independent States	24.4	6.7	15.9	-19.0	-24.0	15.0	21.7	6.4	21.4	16¾
Developing economies	21.0	6.3	4.3	-10.2	4.4	19.0	-5.9	4.5	14.9	14¾
Latin America and the Caribbean	11.6	9.7	16.2	5.2	-3.7	15.7	-3.5	-6.1	5.3	9¾
Africa	21.2	2.0	6.0	-1.0	1.0	7.5	-0.1	6.4	16.0	8¼
Western Asia	23.1	9.3	0.6	-6.4	-0.3	2.7	4.0	8.6	16.8	19½
Eastern and Southern Asia	24.8	5.3	2.0	-20.0	7.6	25.4	-9.2	7.6	17.7	16
China	11.6	7.6	2.5	-1.5	18.2	35.8	8.2	21.2	39.9	23

Table A.13 (continued)

	1995	1996	1997	1998	1999	2000	2001	2002[a]	2003[b]	2004
Volume of exports										
World	9.4	4.8	9.3	3.6	5.1	10.8	-0.9	3.0	6.3	7½
Developed economies	7.3	4.2	9.2	4.0	4.4	10.1	-1.3	-0.1	1.9	6½
North America	9.1	6.2	10.9	3.7	6.4	11.1	-5.3	-4.8	2.0	10½
Western Europe	7.6	3.8	7.7	5.4	3.9	10.6	2.4	0.7	0.5	4¾
Japan	3.3	0.6	9.6	-3.7	2.7	5.1	-11.8	7.0	10.0	10
Economies in transition	13.7	6.0	-0.9	6.9	4.0	15.9	8.4	6.7	8.9	8½
Central and Eastern Europe and Baltic States	16.7	4.5	0.8	15.0	7.0	20.5	11.1	5.3	8.3	9¼
Commonwealth of Independent States	10.0	7.9	-2.9	0.2	2.0	9.6	5.0	9.5	11.4	8¼
Developing countries	13.7	6.5	9.9	1.9	7.2	11.7	-1.3	9.2	14.7	8¾
Latin America and the Caribbean	9.9	9.3	12.8	7.8	6.6	7.6	1.9	0.8	5.0	4
Africa	7.3	8.2	5.2	-0.9	2.1	8.0	1.0	2.3	10.9	5½
Western Asia	6.0	9.0	-0.7	-1.5	0.6	-19.9	4.7	2.9	6.5	4
Eastern and Southern Asia	16.6	5.8	9.3	0.1	10.0	19.2	-3.1	13.2	18.6	10½
China	18.9	2.4	26.3	4.1	7.4	25.5	7.9	23.6	32.6	13
Volume of imports										
World	7.8	6.1	9.0	3.0	5.3	11.6	-1.0	1.0	5.4	6¾
Developed economies	7.0	4.9	8.7	5.9	6.1	9.1	-1.2	-0.3	3.4	5¾
North America	7.2	5.6	13.3	10.3	10.4	13.8	-3.5	0.4	4.0	7½
Western Europe	5.9	4.4	7.6	6.1	3.4	7.6	0.6	0.4	2.5	5¼
Japan	12.5	3.5	2.7	-10.0	9.5	0.3	-4.7	-8.3	4.3	5
Economies in transition	9.9	13.8	9.0	2.0	-6.0	17.6	11.5	7.6	9.7	9½
Central and Eastern Europe and Baltic States	11.4	17.9	7.6	10.0	5.0	15.2	10.4	5.2	8.1	8¼
Commonwealth of Independent States	6.0	2.4	13.6	-15.0	-28.0	29.2	18.1	14.2	15.8	14½
Developing countries	9.7	8.5	10.2	-4.7	4.0	17.5	-2.5	3.9	9.7	8¾
Latin America and the Caribbean	4.2	8.4	23.1	7.2	-6.9	3.9	2.2	-8.2	2.0	6
Africa	10.8	3.8	6.3	2.0	1.5	15.0	0.3	3.0	5.7	2½
Western Asia	11.3	11.8	6.4	-2.6	2.3	15.4	5.2	4.8	5.7	7
Eastern and Southern Asia	12.5	8.2	8.4	-12.7	6.9	23.7	-6.0	6.6	13.4	10½
China	0.1	11.4	9.4	6.0	18.6	52.8	10.9	17.8	31.8	12¼

Source:
United Nations, based on data of United Nations Statistics Division, ECE, ECLAC and IMF.

a Partly estimated.

b Forecast.

Table A.14.
Direction of trade: exports (f.o.b.), 1990-2003

		Destination[a]											
		World[b] bn. $	Devd.	EU	US	Japan	EIT	Devg.	LAC	Africa	SSA	WA	ESA
			Percentage										
World[b]	1990	3 381.6	72.1	43.7	14.5	6.1	..	22.8	3.8	2.8	1.1	3.5	12.8
	1995	5 078.0	65.1	37.5	14.7	5.8	4.3	29.0	5.0	2.3	0.8	3.2	18.5
	2000	6 383.3	66.7	35.7	18.7	5.4	4.1	28.4	5.6	2.0	0.7	3.2	17.6
	2003	7 412.7	64.6	36.9	16.2	4.7	5.2	29.2	4.6	2.1	0.7	3.6	18.9
Developed economies (Devd.)	1990	2 444.4	76.4	50.4	12.4	4.2	..	19.9	3.9	2.8	1.0	3.3	9.9
	1995	3 427.8	70.6	45.4	12.4	3.9	3.5	24.9	5.1	2.4	0.7	3.1	14.3
	2000	4 027.9	71.9	44.1	15.4	3.2	3.9	23.8	6.2	2.0	0.5	3.2	12.4
	2003	4 537.6	71.0	46.3	13.4	2.7	5.3	23.1	5.0	2.1	0.6	3.5	12.5
European Union (EU)	1990	1 488.4	81.8	65.9	7.0	2.1	..	13.2	1.8	3.5	1.2	3.4	4.4
	1995	2 018.3	77.4	62.4	6.7	2.1	5.3	15.7	2.5	3.0	0.9	3.5	6.8
	2000	2 284.2	78.9	62.1	9.3	1.8	6.2	14.2	2.4	2.6	0.7	3.7	5.5
	2003	2 834.9	77.3	61.5	8.7	1.6	7.8	14.1	1.9	2.7	0.7	3.8	5.7
United States (US)	1990	393.1	63.9	26.3	-	12.4	..	34.6	13.7	2.0	0.5	3.4	15.5
	1995	583.5	57.3	21.2	-	11.0	1.1	41.5	16.5	1.7	0.3	3.5	19.8
	2000	772.0	55.6	21.3	-	8.4	0.9	43.4	21.7	1.4	0.3	3.1	17.3
	2003	723.2	55.0	20.9	-	7.2	1.0	43.9	20.6	1.5	0.4	3.1	18.7
Japan	1990	287.7	58.6	20.4	31.7	-	..	40.1	3.4	1.9	0.9	3.5	31.3
	1995	443.0	47.7	15.9	27.5	-	0.5	51.7	4.2	1.7	0.7	2.2	43.7
	2000	478.2	50.9	16.4	30.1	-	0.6	48.5	3.9	1.0	0.3	2.3	41.3
	2003	464.2	44.6	15.4	24.4	-	0.9	54.5	3.4	1.2	0.4	3.2	46.7
Economies in transition (EIT)	1995	205.7	50.6	41.6	3.9	1.8	35.6	13.0	1.6	1.3	0.2	3.9	6.2
	2000	284.8	58.1	49.0	4.9	1.2	28.0	13.1	1.7	1.2	0.3	4.9	5.2
	2003	394.9	59.0	50.6	3.7	0.9	26.2	14.5	1.3	1.1	0.2	5.8	6.3
Developing economies (Devg.)	1990	831.2	61.3	23.4	22.2	12.2	..	32.5	4.0	2.5	1.4	4.0	21.9
	1995	1 442.1	54.1	18.1	21.9	10.9	1.6	41.2	5.2	2.4	1.2	3.4	30.2
	2000	2 068.1	57.7	17.5	26.8	10.0	1.1	39.3	5.1	2.1	1.0	3.0	29.2
	2003	2 477.2	53.7	17.6	23.3	9.1	1.8	42.7	4.4	2.3	1.1	3.4	32.5
Latin America and the Caribbean (LAC)	1990	127.9	71.9	24.5	39.0	5.6	..	24.7	16.5	1.5	0.4	2.1	4.6
	1995	228.5	68.0	16.7	44.4	3.9	0.9	29.1	20.7	1.3	0.4	1.3	5.9
	2000	366.0	74.0	11.3	57.8	2.2	0.7	22.7	17.6	0.8	0.2	1.0	3.4
	2003	395.7	69.9	13.1	51.0	2.0	1.1	26.1	16.6	1.2	0.3	1.4	6.9
Africa	1990	98.7	71.0	50.6	14.8	3.1	..	14.2	1.1	7.1	5.2	2.3	3.7
	1995	102.3	65.9	47.1	13.2	3.0	1.4	23.9	1.9	10.5	7.8	3.0	8.5
	2000	138.0	70.9	47.9	17.5	2.1	1.0	25.4	3.6	9.3	6.9	2.7	9.9
	2003	174.4	71.0	46.7	17.3	3.4	1.5	25.4	2.4	8.8	6.4	3.3	10.9

Table A.14 (continued)

		Destination[a]											
		World[b]	Devd.	EU	US	Japan	EIT	Devg.	LAC	Africa	SSA	WA	ESA
		bn. $	Percentage										
Sub-Saharan Africa (SSA)	1990	28.1	74.9	49.8	16.7	3.6	..	21.2	1.7	11.8	9.2	1.3	6.4
	1995	29.8	69.6	46.6	17.6	3.7	1.7	26.8	1.2	13.5	9.5	2.2	9.9
	2000	41.5	59.1	35.8	18.4	2.2	1.6	34.0	1.9	11.8	8.5	1.4	18.9
	2003	51.7	60.2	36.1	18.6	2.6	2.8	32.9	1.6	11.5	8.4	2.2	17.6
Western Asia (WA)	1990	149.3	59.7	25.4	13.7	17.7	..	31.0	3.0	2.9	0.9	10.6	14.6
	1995	169.6	50.3	22.8	10.3	15.1	3.4	34.4	1.6	3.0	0.8	9.9	19.8
	2000	272.2	53.9	20.9	14.3	16.4	1.9	37.5	1.1	2.8	0.9	6.6	27.0
	2003	311.7	52.2	20.9	14.0	15.1	2.5	37.6	1.0	3.1	0.8	7.6	25.8
Eastern and Southern Asia (including China) (ESA)	1990	455.2	56.8	16.5	21.9	14.3	..	39.1	1.5	1.7	1.0	2.8	33.1
	1995	941.7	50.2	14.5	19.5	12.7	1.4	47.2	2.4	1.7	0.8	2.7	40.4
	2000	1 291.9	52.5	15.3	21.6	11.8	1.1	45.9	2.5	1.5	0.6	2.8	39.1
	2003	1 595.5	48.1	15.0	19.0	10.3	1.8	49.6	2.3	1.7	0.7	3.2	42.5

Source:
UN/DESA, based on IMF, *Direction of Trade Statistics*.

a Owing to incomplete specification of destinations in underlying data, shares of trade to destinations do not add up to 100 per cent.

b Including data for economies in transition; before 1994, data for economies in transition are highly incomplete.

Table A.15.
Composition of world merchandise trade: exports, 1990-2002

Billions of dollars and percentage

Exporting country group	Total exports (billions of dollars)			Primary commodities: Total			of which: Food			of which: Agricultural raw materials			of which: Fuels		
	1990	1995	2002	1990	1995	2002	1990	1995	2002	1990	1995	2002	1990	1995	2002
World (billions of dollars)	2 848.5	4 906.4	6 071.3	797.5	990.1	1 180.7	268.8	413.9	419.0	119.2	176.0	150.8	372.7	331.4	544.5
World (percentage share)	-	-	-	100.0	100.0	100.0	100.0	100.0	100.0	100.0	100.0	100.0	100.0	100.0	100.0
Developed economies	1 865.1	3 338.6	3 803.4	45.1	51.6	48.1	63.0	65.8	65.4	62.2	60.3	60.6	23.0	31.3	31.4
Economies in transition[a]	124.6	194.7	300.6	6.1	6.5	8.2	3.5	3.7	3.6	5.3	6.8	6.4	8.2	9.1	12.4
Developing countries	858.9	1 973.0	1 967.2	48.8	41.9	43.6	33.5	30.5	30.9	32.5	32.9	33.0	68.8	59.6	56.3
Africa	92.5	111.4	104.9	8.5	7.1	6.9	4.1	4.0	3.2	5.1	4.1	3.0	13.7	12.1	11.1
Latin America and the Caribbean	154.3	237.6	357.5	11.0	10.7	11.7	14.5	12.6	13.6	7.3	8.5	11.2	9.3	8.5	9.6
Eastern and Southern Asia	459.1	862.6	1 273.0	13.4	13.1	12.1	13.1	12.2	12.3	19.0	19.1	17.7	12.3	11.1	10.2
Western Asia	153.0	163.9	231.9	16.0	11.1	12.9	1.9	1.8	1.9	1.1	1.1	1.1	33.6	27.9	25.4
Memo items:															
Sub-Saharan Africa	29.7	33.5	39.4	2.6	2.4	2.7	2.6	2.6	2.4	3.1	2.7	2.5	2.3	2.1	3.0
Least developed countries	58.4	24.2	34.6	2.9	1.5	1.7	2.0	1.3	1.0	3.0	1.7	1.4	3.9	1.5	2.3

Table A.15 (continued)

Exporting country group	Manufactures			of which:												
	Total			Textiles			Chemicals			Machinery and transport			Metals		
	1990	1995	2002	1990	1995	2002	1990	1995	2002	1990	1995	2002	1990	1995	2002
World (billions of dollars)	1 992.0	3 797.8	4 808.1	178.2	325.9	366.9	236.4	455.4	624.9	953.1	1 890.6	2 514.8	152.7	267.0	236.4
World (percentage share)	100.0	100.0	100.0	100.0	100.0	100.0	100.0	100.0	100.0	100.0	100.0	100.0	100.0	100.0	100.0
Developed economies	73.3	72.0	65.7	42.1	42.2	36.4	81.0	80.2	80.5	79.7	77.7	67.8	65.2	63.0	64.1
Economies in transition[a]	3.7	3.3	4.1	2.1	4.1	4.5	3.6	4.3	3.0	3.7	1.4	3.4	8.5	14.4	12.2
Developing countries	23.0	24.7	30.2	55.7	53.7	59.1	15.4	15.5	16.5	16.5	20.9	28.8	26.3	22.5	23.7
Africa	1.1	0.9	0.5	2.5	2.5	2.5	1.4	1.0	0.5	0.3	0.2	0.1	6.2	3.2	1.0
Latin America and the Caribbean	3.3	3.3	4.5	3.4	4.3	6.5	2.9	2.8	2.7	2.6	2.8	4.5	9.4	7.9	8.1
Eastern and Southern Asia	17.3	19.2	23.6	47.3	43.4	45.5	8.2	9.5	11.1	13.2	17.3	23.3	8.7	9.6	12.3
Western Asia	1.3	1.3	1.6	2.5	3.4	4.6	2.9	2.2	2.3	0.4	0.5	0.8	2.0	1.9	2.2
Memo items:															
Sub-Saharan Africa	0.5	0.2	0.2	0.5	0.5	0.4	0.3	0.1	0.1	0.2	0.0	0.0	2.2	0.8	0.6
Least developed countries	1.6	0.2	0.3	1.6	1.3	2.5	1.6	0.1	0.1	1.6	0.0	0.0	2.6	0.2	0.5

Source:
UN/DESA, based on COMTRADE.

a Data for 1995 onward, including trade flows between the States of the former Union of Soviet Socialist Republics (USSR). Prior to 1992, these flows were considered internal.

Table A.16.
Composition of world merchandise trade: imports, 1990-2002

Billions of dollars and percentage

Exporting country group	Total imports (billions of dollars)			Primary commodities: Total			of which: Food			Agricultural raw materials			Fuels		
	1990	1995	2002	1990	1995	2002	1990	1995	2002	1990	1995	2002	1990	1995	2002
World (billions of dollars)	2 848.5	4 906.4	6 071.3	797.5	990.1	1 180.7	268.8	413.9	419.0	119.2	176.0	150.8	372.7	331.4	544.5
World (percentage share)	-	-	-	100.0	100.0	100.0	100.0	100.0	100.0	100.0	100.0	100.0	100.0	100.0	100.0
Developed economies	1 941.6	3 381.7	4 222.8	68.6	72.3	71.7	66.2	71.3	72.8	66.0	67.9	63.1	69.0	75.3	72.5
Economies in transition[a]	128.9	193.4	290.6	5.5	5.3	5.8	8.2	6.0	5.5	3.9	2.6	4.5	4.2	6.2	6.3
Developing countries	778.0	1 331.3	1 557.9	25.9	22.4	23.2	25.6	22.7	21.7	30.1	29.5	32.4	26.8	18.5	21.2
Africa	98.8	112.7	99.3	3.0	2.6	2.1	4.9	3.6	3.3	3.7	3.1	2.4	1.4	1.4	1.2
Latin America and the Caribbean	110.7	233.9	295.0	4.4	4.5	4.5	4.7	4.6	5.2	3.9	4.5	5.2	4.5	4.8	3.9
Eastern and Southern Asia	467.3	834.7	967.3	15.2	12.4	13.8	10.9	10.5	9.3	19.8	19.4	21.2	18.3	10.8	14.5
Western Asia	101.2	150	196.3	3.3	2.8	2.8	5.2	4.0	3.9	2.8	2.6	3.5	2.7	1.5	1.7
Memo items:															
Sub-Saharan Africa	29.6	39.6	35.3	1.0	1.0	0.7	1.5	1.3	1.3	0.8	1.0	0.8	0.7	0.7	1.4
Least developed countries	27.4	35.7	38.4	1.0	1.0	0.8	1.6	1.4	1.3	1.7	1.0	1.1	2.7	0.5	0.4

Table A.16 (continued)

Exporting country group	Manufactures: Total 1990	Total 1995	Total 2002	*of which:* Textiles 1990	Textiles 1995	Textiles 2002	Chemicals 1990	Chemicals 1995	Chemicals 2002	Machinery and transport 1990	Machinery and transport 1995	Machinery and transport 2002	Metals 1990	Metals 1995	Metals 2002
World (billions of dollars)	1 992.0	3 773.2	4 708.4	178.2	321.3	360.4	236.4	468.0	640.8	953.1	1 881.2	2 421.8	152.7	258.7	245.2
World (percentage share)	100.0	100.0	100.0	100.0	100.0	100.0	100.0	100.0	100.0	100.0	100.0	100.0	100.0	100.0	100.0
Developed economies	68.0	68.1	69.2	69.5	68.1	69.5	61.6	67.3	69.7	66.8	66.5	67.9	63.9	66.8	62.6
Economies in transition[a]	4.2	3.6	4.7	2.6	4.9	4.6	4.4	4.1	5.2	5.1	3.1	4.3	4.4	3.2	5.6
Developing countries	27.9	28.4	26.1	27.9	27.0	25.9	34.0	28.6	25.1	28.1	30.4	27.8	31.7	30.0	31.7
Africa	3.6	2.2	1.5	2.5	2.4	2.3	4.5	2.5	1.5	4.0	2.3	1.5	3.2	2.0	1.9
Latin America and the Caribbean	3.8	4.9	4.9	2.1	4.0	5.1	5.9	5.7	5.8	4.0	5.4	5.0	3.4	3.2	3.9
Eastern and Southern Asia	16.9	18.2	16.3	19.8	16.9	14.8	19.4	17.5	14.9	16.9	19.9	18.0	20.0	21.4	21.6
Western Asia	3.6	3.1	3.3	3.5	3.6	3.7	4.1	3.0	2.9	3.2	2.8	3.3	5.0	3.4	4.4
Memo items:															
Sub-Saharan Africa	1.1	0.8	0.5	0.8	0.7	0.7	1.1	0.8	0.5	1.3	0.8	0.6	0.7	0.6	0.5
Least developed countries	1.0	0.7	0.6	1.2	3.7	3.7	0.9	3.1	3.1	1.1	0.7	0.6	2.2	0.5	0.6

Source: UN/DESA, based on COMTRADE.

a Data for 1995 onward, including trade flows between the States of the former Union of Soviet Socialist Republics (USSR). Prior to 1992, these flows were considered internal.

Table A.17.
Indices of prices of primary commodities, 1995-2004

	Non-fuel commodities[a]									*Memo item:*
	Food	Tropical beverages	Vegetable oilseeds and oils	Agricultural raw materials	Minerals and metals	Combined index		Manufactured export prices	Real prices of non-fuel commodities[b]	Crude petroleum[c]
						Dollar	SDR			
1995	133	156	166	152	123	138	120	122	113	61.1
1996	142	132	159	137	108	132	120	118	112	73.5
1997	135	176	158	123	108	131	125	110	119	67.7
1998	117	146	169	109	91	113	111	110	103	44.5
1999	95	115	130	98	89	98	95	105	93	63.3
2000	100	100	100	100	100	100	100	100	100	100.0
2001	105	78	92	98	90	97	100	98	99	83.8
2002	101	85	115	92	88	95	98	99	96	88.3
2003	101	90	135	108	99	103	96	108	95	101.8
2000										
I	95	112	111	95	102	99	96	103	96	94.6
II	98	103	107	99	99	99	99	101	98	95.6
III	101	96	94	104	101	101	102	99	102	105.7
IV	106	89	88	102	98	101	103	97	104	104.1
2001										
I	110	86	85	103	98	102	105	100	102	88.3
II	105	82	84	100	94	98	103	97	101	92.9
III	106	75	102	99	87	96	100	97	99	87.4
IV	99	72	98	89	84	90	94	96	94	66.7
2002										
I	99	80	100	87	88	92	98	95	97	71.9
II	100	82	110	91	90	94	98	97	97	88.8
III	100	86	121	94	87	95	95	100	95	94.5
IV	104	93	130	93	89	98	98	101	97	97.2
2003										
I	107	95	131	100	94	102	99	104	99	110.7
II	98	89	129	103	94	99	93	108	91	93.7
III	95	88	126	105	99	99	94	108	92	99.2
IV	104	88	154	119	110	109	100	111	98	104.6
2004										
I	110	96	171	124	132	120	107	..	..	111.4

Source:
UNCTAD, *Monthly Commodity Price Bulletin*; United Nations, *Monthly Bulletin of Statistics*; and Middle East Economic Survey, available from http://www.mees.com/Energy_Tables/basket.htm (accessed 10 August 2004).

a UNCTAD data has been re-based to year 2000=100.

b Combined index of non-fuel commodity prices in dollars deflated by manufactured export price index.

c Composite price of the OPEC basket of seven crudes.

Table A.18.
World oil supply and demand, 1995-2004

	1995	1996	1997	1998	1999	2000	2001	2002	2003	2004
World oil supply[a,b] (millions of barrels per day)	70.1	72.0	74.3	75.5	74.1	76.9	77.0	76.6	79.4	81.1
Developed economies	18.0	18.4	18.6	18.4	18.1	18.5	18.3	18.3	17.9	17.8
Economies in transition	7.3	7.3	7.4	7.5	7.7	8.1	8.7	9.6	10.5	11.2
Developing countries	43.3	44.8	46.7	48.0	46.7	48.6	48.2	47.0	49.2	50.3
OPEC	27.7	28.4	29.9	30.8	29.4	30.7	30.2	28.6	30.5	31.0
Non-OPEC[c]	15.7	16.4	16.8	17.1	17.3	17.9	18.0	18.4	18.8	19.3
Processing gains[d]	1.5	1.5	1.6	1.6	1.7	1.7	1.7	1.8	1.8	1.8
World total demand[e]	69.9	71.6	73.1	73.5	75.3	76.2	76.8	77.0	78.7	80.6
Oil prices (dollars per barrel)										
OPEC basket	16.86	20.29	18.68	12.28	17.47	27.60	23.12	24.36	28.10	29.38
Brent oil	17.06	20.45	19.12	12.72	17.81	28.27	24.42	25.00	28.80	30.00

Source:
United Nations, based on International Energy Agency and OPEC, *Monthly Oil Market Report*, various issues, and Middle East Economic Survey, available from http://www.mees.com/Energy_Tables/basket.htm (accessed 21 April 2004).

a Including crude oil, condensates, natural gas liquids (NGLs), oil from non-conventional sources and other sources of supply.
b Totals may not add up owing to rounding.
c Including Ecuador starting in 1993; including neutral zone and excluding Gabon starting in 1995.
d Net volume gains and losses in refining process (excluding net gain/loss in the economies in transition and China) and marine transportation losses.
e Including deliveries from refineries/primary stocks and marine bunkers, and refinery fuel and non-conventional oils.

III. International finance and financial markets

Table A.19:

World balance of payments on current account, by country group, 1995-2003

Billions of dollars

	1995	1996	1997	1998	1999	2000	2001	2002	2003[a]
Developed countries	46.7	34.2	80.6	-35.5	-171.7	-281.3	-246.0	-255.6	-305.2
Euro area	48.3	74.6	94.5	57.7	14.3	-31.5	8.9	65.2	30.0
Japan	111.0	65.8	96.8	118.7	114.6	119.7	87.8	112.4	135.9
United States	-105.2	-117.2	-127.7	-204.7	-290.9	-411.5	-393.7	-480.9	-541.8
Developing countries[b]	-97.2	-68.7	-46.6	-14.2	63.1	116.9	84.5	152.4	206.6
Net fuel exporters	-16.3	18.9	1.9	-52.7	15.2	97.7	41.3	38.7	71.9
Net fuel importers	-80.9	-87.6	-48.5	38.5	47.9	19.2	43.2	113.7	134.6
Net-creditor countries	20.1	39.2	35.4	7.4	36.5	82.2	72.6	74.7	109.3
Net-debtor countries	-117.3	-107.9	-82.0	-21.7	26.7	34.7	11.9	77.7	97.3
Economies in transition	-3.5	-12.4	-27.3	-29.0	-2.5	25.8	12.8	7.0	7.9
Central and Eastern Europe	-6.4	-16.2	-19.0	-19.3	-24.0	-21.1	-18.6	-22.1	-25.2
Commonwealth of Independent States	3.8	5.2	-6.5	-7.3	23.7	48.3	33.0	31.3	36.4
World residual[c]	54.0	47.0	-6.6	78.8	111.0	138.6	148.7	96.2	90.8
Trade residual	-118.0	-106.4	-120.4	-77.5	-54.5	-21.1	-3.0	-45.4	-49.7

Source:
United Nations, based on data of IMF and other national and international sources.

Note:
Aggregates for major country groupings may not add up due to rounding.

a Partially estimated.
b Ninety-five economies.
c Unreported trade, services, income and transfers, as well as errors and timing asymmetries in reported data.

Table A.20.

Current-account transations: developed economies, 1995-2003

Billions of dollars

	1995	1996	1997	1998	1999	2000	2001	2002	2003[a]
All developed economies[b]									
Goods: exports (f.o.b.)	3 434.8	3 528.8	3 616.5	3 644.6	3 712.9	3 975.9	3 834.6	3 921.0	4 460.4
Goods: imports (f.o.b.)	-3 313.4	-3 436.2	-3 520.7	-3 617.8	-3 821.4	-4 213.9	-4 033.1	-4 118.8	-4 712.3
Trade balance	121.5	92.6	95.9	26.7	-108.5	-238.0	-198.5	-197.8	-251.9
Net services, income and current transfers	-74.8	-58.4	-15.3	-62.3	-63.1	-43.4	-47.5	-57.8	-53.3
Net investment income	9.0	15.2	35.4	19.0	22.7	47.8	38.0	22.3	..
Current-account balance	46.7	34.2	80.6	-35.5	-171.7	-281.3	-246.0	-255.6	-305.2
Major industrialized countries									
Goods: exports (f.o.b.)	2 477.7	2 537.5	2 626.7	2 626.9	2 686.0	2 896.4	2 761.5	2 798.7	3 161.4
Goods: imports (f.o.b.)	-2 397.7	-2 494.7	-2 586.0	-2 632.0	-2 810.9	-3 166.5	-3 010.2	-3 052.7	-3 462.6
Trade balance	79.9	42.8	40.7	-5.1	-124.9	-270.1	-248.7	-254.1	-301.3
Net services, income and current transfers	-83.8	-57.4	-21.6	-51.2	-65.1	-42.8	-34.3	-48.3	-45.0
Net investment income	30.2	45.1	55.9	48.5	43.6	72.6	74.3	66.0	..
Current-account balance	-3.8	-14.7	19.1	-56.2	-190.1	-312.9	-282.9	-302.3	-346.3
Euro area									
Goods: exports (f.o.b.)	1 653.1	1 688.3	1 668.0	1 766.2	1 757.2	1 793.0	1 819.4	1 914.9	2 258.5
Goods: imports (f.o.b.)	-1 528.5	-1 540.2	-1 515.7	-1 616.0	-1 651.9	-1 742.2	-1 713.5	-1 760.3	-2 106.4
Trade balance	124.6	148.1	152.3	150.2	105.3	50.8	105.8	154.6	152.1
Net services, income and current transfers	-76.3	-73.3	-57.8	-92.5	-91.0	-82.3	-97.0	-89.4	-122.1
Net investment income	-32.6	-30.8	-23.8	-45.5	-41.2	-34.5	-46.9	-57.5	..
Current-account balance	48.3	74.8	94.5	57.7	14.3	-31.5	8.9	65.2	30.0
Japan									
Goods: exports (f.o.b.)	428.7	400.3	409.2	374.0	403.7	459.5	383.6	395.6	449.0
Goods: imports (f.o.b.)	-296.9	-316.7	-307.6	-251.7	-280.4	-342.8	-313.4	-301.8	-343.0
Trade balance	131.8	83.6	101.6	122.4	123.3	116.7	70.2	93.8	106.0
Net services, income and current transfers	-20.7	-17.8	-4.8	-3.6	-8.7	2.9	17.6	18.6	29.9
Net investment income	45.0	53.5	58.2	54.6	57.5	60.4	69.3	65.9	..
Current-account balance	111.0	65.8	96.8	118.7	114.6	119.7	87.8	112.4	135.9
United States									
Goods: exports (f.o.b.)	577.0	614.0	680.3	672.4	686.3	774.6	721.8	685.4	717.4
Goods: imports (f.o.b.)	-749.4	-803.1	-876.5	-917.1	-1 030.0	-1 224.4	-1 146.0	-1 164.8	-1 263.2
Trade balance	-172.3	-189.1	-196.2	-244.7	-343.7	-449.8	-424.1	-479.4	-545.7
Net services, income and current transfers	67.1	71.9	68.5	40.1	52.8	38.3	30.4	-1.5	3.9
Net investment income	29.2	28.7	25.1	11.5	22.3	24.2	15.7	-1.3	..
Current-account balance	-105.2	-117.2	-127.7	-204.7	-290.9	-411.5	-393.7	-480.9	-541.8

Source: United Nations, based on data of IMF and national sources.

a Partially estimated.

b Figures may not add up owing to rounding.

Table A.21.
Current-account transactions: economies in transition, 1995-2003

Billions of dollars									
	1995	1996	1997	1998	1999	2000	2001	2002	2003[a]
Economies in transition[b]									
Goods: exports (f.o.b.)	220.1	236.4	244.8	239.5	236.7	294.6	309.7	341.7	435.4
Goods: imports (f.o.b.)	-221.3	-253.2	-271.8	-268.7	-238.7	-267.4	-295.6	-329.4	-409.2
Trade balance	-1.2	-16.8	-27.0	-29.3	-2.0	27.3	14.1	12.3	26.2
Net services, income and current transfers	-2.3	4.4	-0.3	0.3	-0.4	-1.5	-1.3	-5.3	-18.3
Net investment income	-7.8	-9.8	-13.8	-18.4	-15.1	-15.8	-13.4	-18.4	..
Current-account balance	-3.5	-12.4	-27.3	-29.0	-2.5	25.8	12.8	7.0	7.9
CIS									
Goods: exports (f.o.b.)	115.6	126.0	124.3	106.7	107.6	146.4	145.3	155.2	196.4
Goods: imports (f.o.b.)	-99.8	-112.6	-117.9	-98.5	-73.3	-83.9	-96.2	-106.3	-133.1
Trade balance	15.8	13.4	6.4	8.1	34.3	62.5	49.1	48.8	63.3
Net services, income and current transfers	-12.0	-8.2	-12.9	-15.4	-10.6	-14.2	-16.1	-17.6	-26.9
Net investment income	-3.3	-5.9	-9.4	-13.0	-9.4	-9.6	-6.4	-8.5	..
Current-account balance	3.8	5.2	-6.5	-7.3	23.7	48.3	33.0	31.3	36.4
Russian Federation									
Goods: exports (f.o.b.)	82.4	89.7	86.9	74.4	75.5	105.0	101.9	107.6	135.9
Goods: imports (f.o.b.)	-62.6	-68.1	-72.0	-58.0	-39.5	-44.9	-53.8	-61.0	-75.4
Trade balance	19.8	21.6	14.9	16.4	36.0	60.2	48.1	46.6	60.5
Net services, income and current transfers	-12.9	-10.7	-15.0	-16.2	-11.4	-13.3	-14.5	-16.7	-24.6
Net investment income	-3.1	-5.0	-8.4	-11.6	-7.9	-7.0	-4.1	-6.3	..
Current-account balance	7.0	10.8	-0.1	0.2	24.6	46.8	33.6	29.9	35.9
Baltic States									
Goods: exports (f.o.b.)	5.8	6.7	8.3	8.7	7.5	9.4	10.5	12.1	15.4
Goods: imports (f.o.b.)	-7.7	-9.4	-11.4	-12.4	-10.8	-12.3	-13.7	-16.0	-20.6
Trade balance	-1.9	-2.7	-3.1	-3.8	-3.3	-2.9	-3.2	-3.9	-5.2
Net services, income and current transfers	1.2	1.3	1.2	1.3	1.2	1.5	1.6	1.7	1.9
Net investment income -	-	-0.1	-0.3	-0.3	-0.4	-0.5	-0.6	-0.7	..
Current-account balance	-0.8	-1.4	-1.9	-2.4	-2.1	-1.5	-1.6	-2.2	-3.3

Table A.21 (continued)	1995	1996	1997	1998	1999	2000	2001	2002	2003[a]
Central and Eastern Europe									
Goods: exports (f.o.b.)	98.8	103.7	112.2	124.1	121.6	138.8	154.0	174.4	223.6
Goods: imports (f.o.b.)	-113.8	-131.2	-142.5	-157.8	-154.7	-171.1	-185.7	-207.1	-255.5
Trade balance	-15.1	-27.4	-30.3	-33.6	-33.0	-32.3	-31.7	-32.7	-32.0
Net services, income and current transfers	8.6	11.3	11.3	14.4	9.0	11.2	13.2	10.6	6.8
Net investment income	-4.5	-3.8	-4.0	-5.1	-5.3	-5.8	-6.4	-9.2	..
Current-account balance	-6.4	-16.2	-19.0	-19.3	-24.0	-21.1	-18.6	-22.1	-25.2
Central Europe									
Goods: exports (f.o.b.)	78.1	82.6	90.4	101.9	100.8	114.4	128.1	144.9	186.9
Goods: imports (f.o.b.)	-86.1	-100.4	-109.3	-122.4	-122.2	-134.7	-143.9	-158.8	-199.6
Trade balance	-8.0	-17.8	-18.9	-20.5	-21.5	-20.3	-15.7	-14.0	-12.7
Net services, income and current transfers	6.2	7.2	7.0	7.8	3.2	3.5	3.6	0.3	-1.4
Net investment income	-3.8	-3.0	-3.2	-4.0	-4.1	-4.6	-5.0	-6.4	..
Current-account balance	-1.8	-10.6	-12.0	-12.7	-18.3	-16.8	-12.1	-13.7	-14.1
Southern and Eastern Europe									
Goods: exports (f.o.b.)	20.7	21.1	21.8	22.3	20.9	24.4	25.9	29.5	36.7
Goods: imports (f.o.b.)	-27.8	-30.8	-33.1	-35.4	-32.4	-36.4	-41.8	-48.2	-56.0
Trade balance	-7.1	-9.7	-11.3	-13.1	-11.5	-12.0	-16.0	-18.7	-19.3
Net services, income and current-transfers	2.5	4.1	4.3	6.5	5.8	7.7	9.6	10.3	8.2
Net investment income	-0.7	-0.9	-0.8	-1.1	-1.2	-1.2	-1.4	-1.6	..
Current-account balance	-4.6	-5.6	-7.0	-6.6	-5.8	-4.3	-6.4	-8.4	-11.1

Source:
UN/DESA, based on data of IMF.

a Partially estimated.
b Figures may not add up owing to rounding.

Table A.22.

Current-account transactions: developing economies, 1995-2003

Billions of dollars	1995	1996	1997	1998	1999	2000	2001	2002	2003[a]
Developing countries[b]									
Goods: exports (f.o.b.)	1 435.0	1 580.1	1 688.7	1 556.3	1 689.9	2 090.3	1 947.2	2 081.3	2 425.4
Goods: imports (f.o.b.)	-1 437.3	-1 549.5	-1 637.2	-1 476.3	-1 524.9	-1 858.6	-1 759.9	-1 850.4	-2 150.0
Trade balance	-2.3	30.6	51.6	80.0	165.0	231.8	187.3	230.9	275.4
Net services, income and current transfers	-95.0	-99.4	-98.2	-94.2	-101.9	-114.8	-102.8	-78.5	-68.9
Net investment income	-83.1	-89.9	-88.7	-98.4	-109.0	-103.9	-103.7	-111.9	
Current-account balance	-97.2	-68.7	-46.6	-14.2	63.1	116.9	84.5	152.4	206.6
Net fuel exporters									
Goods: exports (f.o.b.)	345.9	413.5	438.1	373.4	448.0	618.1	556.5	568.1	631.7
Goods: imports (f.o.b.)	-284.4	-309.0	-348.8	-351.4	-354.4	-420.5	-423.4	-435.0	-454.8
Trade balance	61.5	104.5	89.3	22.0	93.6	197.6	133.0	133.2	176.9
Net services, income and current transfers	-77.8	-85.6	-87.4	-74.7	-78.4	-99.9	-91.7	-94.5	-105.0
Net investment income	-24.3	-26.2	-23.2	-24.7	-26.1	-30.4	-30.9	-31.8	
Current-account balance	-16.3	18.9	1.9	-52.7	15.2	97.7	41.3	38.7	71.9
Net fuel importers									
Goods: exports (f.o.b.)	1 089.1	1 166.6	1 250.7	1 182.9	1 241.9	1 472.2	1 390.8	1 513.1	1 793.7
Goods: imports (f.o.b.)	-1 152.8	-1 240.5	-1 288.4	-1 124.9	-1 170.5	-1 438.1	-1 336.5	-1 415.4	-1 695.1
Trade balance	-63.7	-73.9	-37.7	58.0	71.5	34.1	54.3	97.7	98.6
Net services, income and current transfers	-17.1	-13.7	-10.8	-19.5	-23.5	-15.0	-11.1	16.0	36.1
Net investment income	-58.8	-63.8	-65.5	-73.6	-72.9	-73.5	-72.8	-80.0	
Current-account balance	-80.9	-87.6	-48.5	38.5	47.9	19.2	43.2	113.7	134.6
Net creditor countries									
Goods: exports (f.o.b.)	346.6	383.8	390.6	320.6	361.4	474.9	414.8	428.5	492.5
Goods: imports (f.o.b.)	-289.4	-298.2	-314.5	-275.9	-283.8	-340.1	-295.5	-305.7	-333.8
Trade balance	57.2	85.6	76.1	44.6	77.6	134.8	119.3	122.8	158.6
Net services, income and current transfers	-37.0	-46.4	-40.7	-37.2	-41.1	-52.6	-46.7	-48.1	-49.4
Net investment income	-14.2	-12.8	-18.5	-15.6	-17.0	-17.2	-15.3	-10.7	
Current-account balance	20.1	39.2	35.4	7.4	36.5	82.2	72.6	74.7	109.3
Net debtor countries									
Goods: exports (f.o.b.)	1 088.4	1 196.3	1 298.1	1 235.7	1 328.5	1 615.4	1 532.4	1 652.8	1 932.9
Goods: imports (f.o.b.)	-1 147.8	-1 251.3	-1 322.7	-1 200.4	-1 241.1	-1 518.5	-1 464.4	-1 544.7	-1 816.1
Trade balance	-59.4	-55.0	-24.6	35.3	87.4	96.9	68.0	108.1	116.8
Net services, income and current transfers	-57.9	-53.0	-57.5	-57.0	-60.8	-62.2	-56.1	-30.4	-19.5
Net investment income	-97.3	-102.7	-107.1	-114.0	-116.0	-121.1	-118.0	-112.6	
Current-account balance	-117.3	-107.9	-82.0	-21.7	26.7	34.7	11.9	77.7	97.3

Table A.22 (continued)

	1995	1996	1997	1998	1999	2000	2001	2002	2003[a]
Totals by region:									
Latin America and the Caribbean									
Goods: exports (f.o.b.)	235.9	264.0	293.4	289.4	305.6	366.9	350.9	354.2	387.2
Goods: imports (f.o.b.)	-234.9	-261.8	-311.0	-329.9	-317.6	-368.3	-359.6	-336.1	-357.0
Trade balance	0.9	2.3	-17.6	-40.4	-11.9	-1.4	-8.7	18.1	30.2
Net services, income and current transfers	-39.4	-41.2	-48.4	-49.7	-44.5	-45.9	-45.5	-33.9	-25.8
Net investment income	-42.6	-44.6	-49.5	-53.4	-52.8	-54.5	-56.5	-52.8	
Current-account balance	-38.5	-39.0	-66.0	-90.1	-56.4	-47.3	-54.2	-15.8	4.4
Africa									
Goods: exports (f.o.b.)	110.7	122.8	124.6	105.2	116.7	151.3	139.7	143.8	170.5
Goods: imports (f.o.b.)	-111.6	-111.7	-118.3	-118.4	-115.9	-121.0	-123.5	-129.1	-144.6
Trade balance	-1.0	11.1	6.3	-13.2	0.8	30.3	16.1	14.7	25.8
Net services, income and current transfers	-11.8	-8.4	-10.8	-7.9	-8.9	-12.9	-10.2	-9.9	-16.3
Net investment income	-12.7	-13.6	-10.8	-10.1	-11.6	-13.3	-13.3	-13.1	
Current-account balance	-12.8	2.7	-4.4	-21.1	-8.1	17.4	5.9	4.8	9.5
Western Asia									
Goods: exports (f.o.b.)	177.0	216.2	219.8	178.7	216.5	299.3	273.4	284.7	328.9
Goods: imports (f.o.b.)	-165.8	-179.9	-188.4	-184.6	-178.7	-210.7	-202.0	-219.5	-249.0
Trade balance	11.1	36.3	31.4	-5.9	37.8	88.6	71.4	65.2	79.8
Net services, income and current transfers	-20.8	-30.6	-26.3	-13.7	-23.3	-32.7	-33.2	-36.7	-38.3
Net investment income	0.5	0.7	1.9	2.0	0.0	-3.6	-5.2	-4.5	
Current-account balance	-9.6	5.7	5.2	-19.6	14.5	55.9	38.2	28.5	41.5
Eastern and Southern Asia									
Goods: exports (f.o.b.)	911.5	977.1	1 050.9	983.0	1 051.1	1 272.8	1 183.3	1 298.6	1 538.9
Goods: imports (f.o.b.)	-924.9	-996.1	-1 019.6	-843.4	-912.7	-1 158.5	-1 074.8	-1 165.7	-1 399.3
Trade balance	-13.4	-19.1	31.4	139.6	138.4	114.3	108.5	132.9	139.6
Net services, income and current transfers	-23.0	-19.1	-12.8	-22.9	-25.2	-23.3	-13.9	2.1	11.6
Net investment income	-28.4	-32.4	-29.3	-36.8	-34.5	-32.5	-28.8	-41.5	
Current-account balance	-36.4	-38.2	18.6	116.7	113.2	90.9	94.5	135.0	151.1

Source: UN/DESA, based on data of IMF and official national and other sources.

a Partially estimated.

b Ninety-five economies. Figures may not add up owing to rounding.

Table A.23.

Net IMF lending to developing countries, by facility, 1994-2003

	1994	1995	1996	1997	1998	1999	2000	2001	2002	2003
	Billions of dollars									
Regular facilities	-0.8	12.5	-2.6	13.0	14.1	-9.8	-6.5	17.6	15.3	4.4
Repayment terms:										
3¼-5 years (credit tranche)[a]	0.1	12.4	-1.4	13.6	11.2	-9.6	-5.8	18.5	15.2	4.4
3½-7 years (SFF/EAP)[b]	-1.4	-1.6	-1.3	-0.7	-0.1	0.0	0.0	0.0	-0.1	-0.0
4½-10 years (Extended Fund Facility (EFF))	0.5	1.8	0.1	0.2	3.1	-0.2	-0.7	-0.9	0.2	0.0
Concessional facilities	0.9	1.5	0.2	-0.1	0.2	0.1	-0.2	0.0	-0.1	0.6
Trust Fund[c]	0.0	0.0	0.0	0.0	0.0	0.0	0.0	0.0	0.0	0.0
SAF[d]	-0.2	-0.1	-0.4	-0.3	-0.2	-0.2	-0.1	-0.1	-0.3	-0.1
ESAF/PRGF[d]	1.1	1.6	0.5	0.2	0.4	0.2	-0.1	0.1	0.2	0.7
Additional facilities[e]	-0.9	-1.6	-0.7	-0.9	-0.7	0.7	0.0	0.0	-0.3	-0.4
Compensatory financing[f]	-0.9	-1.6	-0.7	-0.9	-0.7	0.7	0.0	0.0	-0.3	-0.4
STF[f]	0.0	0.0	0.0	0.0	0.0	0.0	0.0	0.0	0.0	-0.0
Total	-0.7	12.5	-3.1	12.0	13.7	-9.0	-6.7	17.6	15.0	4.6
Memo items:										
Selected characteristics of lending agreements										
Number initiated during year	26	18	20	14	15	16	18	12	15	18
Average length (months)	25	23	29	33	29	32	28	22	29	29
Total amount committed ($bn)	6.6	23.2	5.2	38.4	29.5	13.0	22.1	24.2	50.8	17.6

Source:
IMF, *International Financial Statistics and IMF Survey.*

a Primarily stand-by arrangements, including Supplemental Reserve Facility (SRF) (created December 1997) for use when a sudden and disruptive loss of market confidence causes pressure on the capital account and on reserves, creating a large short-term financing need (higher-cost and shorter-term than regular drawings), and adding to commitments under stand-by or extended arrangements for up to one year, with drawings in two or more tranches. Also includes emergency assistance for natural disasters and, since 1995, for post-conflict situations.

b Supplementary Financing Facility (SFF) (1979-1981) and Enhanced Access Policy (EAP) (1981-1992) provided resources from funds borrowed by IMF from member States on which the Fund paid a higher interest rate than the remuneration paid to countries that had a net-creditor position with the Fund. Thus, users of SFF and EAP resources paid a higher interest rate than on drawings from ordinary resources, which are at below-market interest rates. (However, interest payments under SFF were partly subsidized for countries eligible to borrow from the World Bank's International Development Association (IDA); there was no subsidy on EAP drawings.)

c Mainly using resources from IMF gold sales, the Trust Fund lent during 1977-1981 under 1-year adjustment programmes; eligibility was based on maximum per capita income criteria; loans had 10-year maturities, with repayments beginning in the sixth year; the interest rate was 0.5 per cent per year.

d Structural Adjustment Facility (SAF) and Enhanced Structural Adjustment Facility (ESAF) (the first financed mainly from Trust Fund reflows and the second from loans and grants) made loans to IDA-eligible countries with protracted balance-of-payments problems; funds were disbursed over 3 years (under Policy Framework Paper arrangements), with repayments beginning in 5.5 years and ending in 10 years; the interest rate was 0.5 per cent. On 22 November 1999, these facilities were renamed the Poverty Reduction and Growth Facility (PRGF) and now support policy reforms contained in Poverty Reduction Strategy Papers (PRSPs).

e Compensatory Financing Facility (CFF) from 1963 to 1988; Compensatory and Contingency Financing Facility (CCFF) from August 1988; CFF again from February 2000 (same terms as credit tranche).

f See description in table A.24 below.

Table A.24.
Net IMF lending to economies in transition, by facility, 1994-2003

	Billions of dollars									
	1994	1995	1996	1997	1998	1999	2000	2001	2002	2003
Regular facilities	0.2	4.4	3.7	2.1	3.0	-3.0	-3.1	-0.7	-0.9	-0.8
Repayment terms:										
3¼-5 years (credit tranche)	0.5	4.9	1.2	0.0	-0.8	-3.1	-3.2	-0.6	-0.1	-0.1
3½-7 years (SFF/EAP)	-0.3	0.0	0.0	0.0	0.0	0.0	0.0	0.0	0.0	0.2
4½-10 years (Extended Fund Facility (EFF))	0.0	-0.5	2.6	2.2	3.9	0.1	0.2	0.0	-0.8	-0.9
Concessional facilities (ESAF)	0.0	0.1	0.2	0.2	0.2	0.1	0.1	0.1	0.0	-0.0
Additional facilities										
Compensatory financing	-0.7	-0.6	-0.2	0.1	2.9	0.1	0.0	-2.8	-0.1	-0.0
STF[a]	2.8	0.9	0.0	0.0	-0.5	-0.8	-1.1	-0.8	-1.0	-0.7
Total	2.3	4.8	3.7	2.4	5.6	-3.6	-4.1	-4.1	-1.8	-1.5
Memo items:										
Selected characteristics of lending agreements										
Number initiated during year	8	12	12	7	6	4	5	9	5	2
Average length (months)	18	13	28	21	32	19	28	25	27	14
Total amount committed ($bn)	2.1	9.2	13.2	2.1	3.4	5.6	0.3	1.5	1.4	0.2

Source:
IMF, *International Financial Statistics.*

a The Systemic Transformation Facility (STF), created in April 1993 and closed to new drawings in December 1995, assisted economies in transition with severe balance-of-payments problems arising from discontinuance of former trade arrangements. For members that had not yet had a stand-by arrangement, drawings could be made in two tranches in support of a written statement of policy reform intentions, the second 6-18 months after the first, assuming satisfactory progress towards an upper credit tranche arrangement (repayment terms were the same as for the Extended Fund Facility (EFF)). See table A.23 above for description of other facilities.

Table A.25.

Net ODA from major sources, by type, 1983-2002

Donor group or country	Growth rate of ODA[a] (2001 prices and exchange rates) 1983-1982	Growth rate of ODA[a] (2001 prices and exchange rates) 1993-2002	ODA as % of GNI 2002	Total ODA (millions of dollars) 2002	Percentage distribution of ODA, by type, 2002: Bilateral: Grants[b]	Bilateral: Technical cooperation	Bilateral: Loans	Multilateral: United Nations	Multilateral: IDA	Multilateral: Other
Total DAC countries	2.63	-0.26	0.23	56 109	68.3	26.5	1.6	8.3	5.8	31.3
Total EU	2.85	-0.07	0.35	27 821	70.2	20.6	-2.4	8.0	3.7	38.7
Austria	-5.30	-8.87	0.26	486	70.6	17.1	-0.4	4.0	5.3	32.0
Belgium	-1.30	2.25	0.43	996	68.7	27.1	-2.3	4.2	5.2	36.0
Denmark	-4.72	3.15	0.96	1 540	62.0	25.7	-1.2	15.1	3.3	39.3
Finland	11.61	-3.90	0.35	1 434	53.7	20.1	0.9	15.4	7.1	40.6
France[c]	3.85	-3.46	0.38	5 125	70.6	27.8	-4.7	2.9	4.8	36.5
Germany	1.93	-2.14	0.27	4 980	73.8	33.5	-10.8	8.6	0.3	40.1
Greece			0.21	253	38.8	8.0	0.0	8.3	1.6	66.8
Ireland	0.89	16.36	0.4	360	67.1	3.3	0.0	11.4	2.2	36.4
Italy	7.93	-4.19	0.2	2 157	46.4	4.4	-3.3	9.4	5.8	61.5
Luxembourg	18.74	13.55	0.77	139	78.9	2.0	-0.0	6.5	2.9	22.3
Netherlands	10.61	2.50	0.81	3 068	77.4	15.3	-4.0	13.0	0.2	29.0
Portugal	35.89	1.67	0.27	283	56.7	39.3	-0.9	3.8	2.4	46.8
Spain	10.22	4.24	0.26	1 559	44.9	14.0	13.4	3.9	3.7	45.8
Sweden	2.42	1.31	0.83	1 848	62.4	3.4	10.4	12.2	19.4	40.1
United Kingdom	-0.15	3.14	0.31	4 581	68.7	17.7	2.5	6.9	-0.9	31.0
Australia	0.38	0.72	0.26	916	78.3	42.9	0.0	6.2	7.8	23.5
Canada	3.50	-2.34	0.28	2 011	76.1	16.4	-0.2	8.5	6.4	25.1
Japan	5.21	-1.46	0.23	9 731	47.1	18.5	25.0	8.3	8.1	26.6
New Zealand	0.23	-2.28	0.22	110	75.4	29.5	0.0	10.0	4.5	27.3
Norway	4.73	1.67	0.89	1 517	67.4	10.5	0.0	20.0	4.8	36.3
Switzerland	7.46	-0.48	0.32	863	79.9	16.4	0.6	10.8	0.6	20.2
United States	1.57	-1.19	0.13	13 140	84.7	50.3	-5.1	7.5	8.8	20.7
Arab countries[d]										
Saudi Arabia	..	..	..	2 478	—	86.6	—	—	13.4	—
Kuwait	..	..	..	20	—	100.0	—	—	0.0	—
Other developing economies[d]										
Korea, Republic of	..	..	..	279	—	74.2	—	—	25.8	—
Taiwan Province of China			..	..	—		—	—	100.0	—

Source: UN/DESA, based on OECD, *Development Co-operation: 2003 Report* (Paris, 2003).

a Average annual rates of growth, calculated from average levels in 1981-1982,1991-1992 and 2001-2002.

b Including technical cooperation.

c Excluding flows from France to the Overseas Departments, namely, Guadeloupe, French Guiana, Martinique and Réunion.

d Bilateral ODA includes all grants and loans; multilateral ODA includes United Nations, IDA and "other", including technical cooperation.

Table A.26.
Regional distribution of ODA from major sources, 1991-2002

Donor group or country	All developing countries 1991-1992	All developing countries 2001-2002	Latin America 1991-1992	Latin America 2001-2002	Africa 1991-1992	Africa 2001-2002	Western Asia 1991-1992	Western Asia 2001-2002	Eastern and Southern Asia[a] 1991-1992	Eastern and Southern Asia[a] 2001-2002
	Millions of dollars, two-year average		of which:							
Total ODA[b] (net)	61 299.3	57 003.0	5 709.6	5 554.9	24 925.9	19 394.5	4 877.4	2 201.3	16 593.2	16 555.2
DAC countries										
Bilateral	42 882.0	37 904.2	4 575.2	4 171.5	16 371.5	11 700.9	3 696.7	868.4	10 889.5	10 814.1
Australia	731.8	717.0	10.6	40.4	62.3	129.3	41.3	20.2	613.8	559.8
Austria	124.4	352.9	59.9	44.9	287.7	119.0	49.1	20.1	39.5	46.9
Belgium	1 521.8	1 607.4	153.1	149.0	288.5	303.6	29.1	7.5	360.7	239.0
Canada	1 739.3	1 351.0	185.4	140.7	523.7	303.6	21.4	5.4	367.0	208.7
Denmark	721.6	1 036.4	38.9	82.7	343.5	422.1	18.8	4.6	135.0	216.0
Finland	503.4	237.8	35.2	18.5	248.0	83.7	44.9	4.3	106.2	53.3
France[c]	6 037.7	3 105.4	253.7	143.2	3 978.1	2 066.0	147.7	69.2	1 215.8	275.8
Germany	4 976.9	3 093.5	524.5	344.8	1 912.8	917.9	663.3	271.3	1 029.5	659.6
Greece	0.0	94.8	0.0	0.3	0.0	2.2	0.0	3.3	0.0	10.2
Ireland	28.8	225.8	0.3	7.8	19.3	158.2	0.6	0.4	1.1	18.4
Italy	2 337.8	724.4	407.0	62.6	1 065.7	502.3	73.0	22.0	179.0	21.7
Japan	8 624.4	7 075.0	809.5	665.3	1 335.7	895.5	689.6	135.9	4 889.1	4 282.3
Luxembourg	23.0	111.5	3.3	15.3	11.7	47.4	0.9	0.6	5.4	24.3
Netherlands	1 879.6	2 358.8	337.8	244.2	576.4	904.1	67.1	59.8	372.0	572.2
New Zealand	77.7	88.2	0.4	2.5	1.0	5.8	0.0	1.2	53.4	73.1
Norway	772.4	1 042.8	63.2	73.6	431.2	388.4	5.1	30.4	162.9	241.2
Portugal	195.8	184.7	0.1	2.2	195.6	105.4	0.0	0.0	0.1	68.9
Spain	930.3	1 074.0	375.5	553.8	313.9	187.4	3.6	30.5	161.8	97.6
Sweden	1 608.9	1 227.4	163.2	132.6	752.8	380.2	33.8	9.5	273.5	223.2
Switzerland	702.0	704.5	87.7	71.6	272.2	171.1	28.9	9.8	159.9	155.0
United Kingdom	1 758.8	3 063.7	112.6	229.0	760.3	1 525.9	59.0	29.0	421.8	737.0
United States	8 635.5	9 427.1	1 093.5	1 340.5	3 536.5	2 581.9	2 011.5	395.8	508.5	2 049.9
Multilateral	16 571.9	17 288.8	1 095.3	1 329.0	7 715.0	7 204.8	696.0	774.9	5 507.8	4 999.8
Total DAC	59 453.9	55 192.9	5 670.5	5 500.5	24 086.5	18 905.7	4 392.7	1 643.2	16 397.3	15 813.9
Arab countries										
Bilateral[d]	1 902.5	1 458.2	..	..	..	..	..	..	..	..
Multilateral	218.2	142.3	..	..	..	..	..	..	..	..

Source: UN/DESA, calculations based on OECD, *Geographical Distribution of Financial Flows to Aid Recipients*.

a Including Central Asian transition economies.
b Excluding assistance provided by centrally planned and transition economies, owing to measurement difficulties. Donor total includes amounts to certain European countries and unallocated amounts and hence is larger than the sum of the amounts per region.
c Excluding flows from France to the Overseas Departments, namely, Guadeloupe, French Guiana, Martinique and Réunion.
d Approximately 35-40 per cent of Arab bilateral aid is geographically unallocated, depending on the year.

Table A.27.
Resource commitments of multilateral development institutions,[a] 1995-2003

Millions of dollars									
	1995	1996	1997	1998	1999	2000	2001	2002	2003
Financial institutions	43 516	44 701	45 760	57 928	42 770	36 882	41 787	38 523	43 053
African Development Bank	802	823	1 880	1 742	1 765	1 984	2 373	2 039	2 600
Asian Development Bank	5 759	5 878	9 648	6 208	5 158	5 830	5 513	5 700	6 317
Caribbean Development Bank	110	99	54	122	153	184	120	129	198
European Bank for Reconstruction and Development	2 616	2 774	2 625	2 658	2 784	2 901	3 276	4 130	4 200
Inter-American Development Bank	7 454	6 951	6 224	10 403	9 577	5 336	8 067	4 753	7 078
Inter-American Investment Corporation	36	72	67	223	190	143	128	123	194
International Fund for Agricultural Development	414	447	430	443	434	409	434	390	430
World Bank Group	26 361	27 729	24 899	36 352	22 899	20 238	22 004	21 382	22 230
International Bank for Reconstruction and Development	15 950	15 325	15 098	24 687	13 789	10 699	11 709	10 176	10 572
International Development Association	5 973	6 490	5 345	7 325	5 691	5 861	6 859	8 040	7 550
International Finance Corporation	4 438	5 914	4 456	4 340	3 419	3 678	3 436	3 166	4 108
Operational agencies of the United Nations	3 931	3 726	3 453	4 290	4 198	3 803	4 690	4 569	6 545
United Nations Development Programme[b]	1 014	1 231	1 529	1 764	1 632	1 458	1 526	1 493	1 737
United Nations Population Fund	340	285	322	326	245	171	236	296	248
United Nations Children's Fund	1 481	1 133	521	962	891	1 016	1 152	1 188	1 285
World Food Programme	1 096	1 077	1 081	1 238	1 430	1 158	1 776	1 592	3 275
Total commitments	47 447	48 427	49 213	62 218	46 968	40 685	46 477	43 092	49 598
Memo item:									
Commitments in units of 2000 purchasing power[c]	37 656	39 694	43 169	57 081	44 731	40 685	47 426	43 527	45 924

Source:
Annual reports and information supplied by individual institutions.

a Loans, grants, technical assistance and equity participation, as appropriate; all data are on a calendar-year basis.

b Including United Nations Development Programme (UNDP)-administered funds.

c Total commitments deflated by the United Nations index of manufactured export prices in dollars of developed economies: 2000=100.

كيفيـة الحصـول على منشـورات الأمـم المتحـدة

يمكن الحصول على منشورات الأمم المتحدة من المكتبات ودور التوزيع في جميع أنحاء العالم . استعلم عنها من المكتبة التي تتعامل معها أو اكتب إلى : الأمم المتحدة ، قسم البيع في نيويورك أو في جنيف .

如何购取联合国出版物

联合国出版物在全世界各地的书店和经售处均有发售。请向书店询问或写信到纽约或日内瓦的联合国销售组。

HOW TO OBTAIN UNITED NATIONS PUBLICATIONS

United Nations publications may be obtained from bookstores and distributors throughout the world. Consult your bookstore or write to: United Nations, Sales Section, New York or Geneva.

COMMENT SE PROCURER LES PUBLICATIONS DES NATIONS UNIES

Les publications des Nations Unies sont en vente dans les librairies et les agences dépositaires du monde entier. Informez-vous auprès de votre libraire ou adressez-vous à : Nations Unies, Section des ventes, New York ou Genève.

КАК ПОЛУЧИТЬ ИЗДАНИЯ ОРГАНИЗАЦИИ ОБЪЕДИНЕННЫХ НАЦИЙ

Издания Организации Объединенных Наций можно купить в книжных магазинах и агентствах во всех районах мира. Наводите справки об изданиях в вашем книжном магазине или пишите по адресу: Организация Объединенных Наций, Секция по продаже изданий, Нью-Йорк или Женева.

COMO CONSEGUIR PUBLICACIONES DE LAS NACIONES UNIDAS

Las publicaciones de las Naciones Unidas están en venta en librerías y casas distribuidoras en todas partes del mundo. Consulte a su librero o diríjase a: Naciones Unidas, Sección de Ventas, Nueva York o Ginebra.

Litho in United Nations, New York
52709—November 2004—4,670
ISBN 92-1-109145-4

United Nations publication
Sales No. E.04.II.C.1
E/2004/75/Rev.1
ST/ESA/291